Every Family Has a Story
Tales from the Pages of AVOTAYNU

Edited by Gary Mokotoff

Avotaynu

Bergenfield, NJ
2008

Requests for permission to make copies of any part of this publication should be addressed to:

Avotaynu, Inc.
155 N. Washington Ave.
Bergenfield, NJ 07621

Printed in the United States of America

Title page photo: Auerbach family reunion, 1938. Courtesy of Ruth Auerbach Mokotoff. All other photos courtesy of authors.

Library of Congress Cataloging-in-Publication Data

Every family has a story: tales from the pages of Avotaynu / edited by Gary Mokotoff.
    p. cm.
 ISBN 978-1-886223-35-6 (alk. paper)
 1. Jews—Genealogy. I. Mokotoff, Gary.

CS36.J4E94 2008
929'.1072—dc22
                          2008003410

To Sallyann Amdur Sack
Editor of AVOTAYNU

She has provided the Jewish genealogical community with more than 20 years of articles that have expanded our knowledge of how to research the histories of our families.

Contents

Preface: Reflections
by Harry D. Boonin
Winter 1988

This past October [1988] marked 11 years since I became involved in genealogy. During these years I often asked myself if it is a proper thing to devote so much time to the study of one's family and one's family origins. Alternatively, I answered myself in the positive and in the negative. The few years we are allotted are precious gifts, given to us to use and to do with as we see fit. We know a freedom that no other generation or no other people have known. Are our forefathers more important than our children? Is it proper to take time away from a newborn grandson to devote to a long-dead third cousin? Who answers these questions? Where do we turn?

We are sought out at family gatherings. Praise is heaped on us for what we are doing. Our relatives revel in our retelling of old family tales, glory in our finds and delight in the discoveries concerning our immigrant ancestors and *shtetl* life in the Old Country. They marvel at our energy and perseverance. We would be less than human if we did not feel some pride in ourselves for being able to bring joy to our families who mean so much to us. But do we tell them that family gatherings are few, and a great deal of our time is spent alone, in front of a computer or a typewriter, among outdated forms, unanswered letters and old family photographs? To do something by oneself may be self-gratifying, but does it justify the joy that it ultimately may bring? How many hours alone equal how much joy? Where do we find the correct formula for this equation?

Who do we do this genealogy for? For ourselves? For future generations? For those who perished in the Holocaust? Can the bones scattered outside Auschwitz be brought together to be covered with skin and flesh to love again and to be loved? Can those bones be taught to listen to what we have learned? Have we merely learned to teach ourselves? Our grandchildren understand little of what we do. Are they smarter and wiser than we—or are we smarter and wiser than our grandchildren?

But the aspect of genealogy that brings me the most joy and the most pain is the intensity we bring to the effort. The ultimate question is why are we so intense? While not ignoring our families and our jobs, our top priority in life sometimes becomes blurred. When we travel, we scurry for telephone books to make awkward calls to persons we have never met. At home, our mind wanders to a new theory for locating the maiden name of our great-grandmother's youngest sister. We listen poorly and half hear stories at cocktail parties, stories that hold the attention of all but us. We sometimes wish to be home filling out some new form to send to a recently discovered obscure repository to request a scrap of paper that could lead to the ultimate discovery of another scrap of paper. Our mind whirls while we shower. Ideas rush into our heads as a mountain river crashes to the valley below. The ideas and the theories never stop. They race onward, onward. And pain. Sometimes our well-meaning friends misconstrue our intensity. Then how precise do we have to be in our explanations? Should we never be rude?

At the Seventh Summer Seminar on Jewish Genealogy in Washington, DC, this past summer [1988], we gathered again—and in larger numbers—with more enthusiasm and with greater pride in our accomplishments. There we were not alone as we are during the year, but we were together. Hundreds of Jewish genealogists, removed from their natural habitat of dim lights, unanswered correspondence and scattered books, joined together once again. The friendships that began tentatively seven years ago have long since been established and were again renewed. Returning home from Washington, I again asked myself the meaning of what we are doing. But as I question, the years fly by. It is already fall and the leaves are changing. Cool breezes turn cold (I am told this summer was hot), and the letters downstairs must still be answered.

Harry D. Boonin is the founding president of the Jewish Genealogical Society of Philadelphia, author of The Jewish Quarter of Philadelphia and the recently published The Life and Times of Congregation Kesher Israel, a book about the immigrant synagogue in Philadelphia and the surrounding neighborhood.

Introduction

Since 1985, AVOTAYNU has published more than 2,500 articles of interest to persons who are tracing their Jewish family history. Most are designed to assist the reader in advancing his/her knowledge of genealogical research. Editor Sallyann Amdur Sack and I recognized there is another side to family history research, what we have called the human side of genealogy. These are the research discoveries that have affected the researcher and those that have impacted the people found. Starting in 1987, we invited AVOTAYNU readers to write articles on these subjects. They were invariably published in the Winter issue of the year. This book contains some of the more interesting stories published. Some describe triumph over tragedy, others just tragedy. Some are meant to amuse the reader; others will make the reader cry.

Typical is the first article in this book, which was also the first human interest article in the winter 1987 issue. It describes how a woman, adopted shortly after birth, was not motivated to find her birth family until she became involved in genealogical research. She discovered she had seven natural siblings—three older than she and four younger—and she was the only one adopted out! How she found her birth family, why she was adopted out and an epilogue to the story that appeared in 1987 make the article one of the top stories in this book.

The book is divided into six sections. *Potpourri* consists of articles on a variety of topics, each having an unusual aspect that makes it one of the more remarkable stories in the book. *People* describes persons discovered by genealogists that have a tale worth retelling. *Family* consists of stories about finding family, discovering ancestors and other family-oriented accounts. *Back to the Old Country* describes visits to ancestral lands. Those published in the Soviet Union era demonstrate how different and difficult travel was in those days. *Crypto-Jews* relates articles about a fascinating group of Jews—those who converted to Judaism during the Spanish/Portuguese Inquisition era, but continued to practice Judaism in secret. It is amazing that an ethnic group could maintain their heritage in secret for more than 500 years. *Luck* consists of three brief essays about an aspect that every researcher—genealogist or other—experiences. Different views are presented. *Genealogy* consists of articles only a genealogist could love. Related are unusual stories in family history research. Non-genealogists are given insight into how genealogical research is accomplished. Finally, *Holocaust* contains those stories that demonstrate why the Holocaust is an integral part of every Jewish family historian's research. This section actually ends in an upbeat manner. The last two stories in the book describe how Jewish genealogists and local townspeople in Eastern Europe have worked together to memorialize the Jewish citizens of the town who were murdered during the Holocaust.

There are some considerations regarding formatting of the articles. Following the title and author of the article is the issue of AVOTAYNU in which the original article appeared. Some of the articles have "Epilogues" which describe events that unfolded after the article was written. Additions by the editor are shown in brackets. They are primarily notations to remind the reader that the articles were written over a period of 20 years. The most common notation occurs when the author referred to a recent time period. For example, an article written in 1992 that refers to "last year" has the notation added [1991].

Enjoy!

Gary Mokotoff
Bergenfield, New Jersey
February 2008

Potpourri

Freya Joins the Kahn Klan
by Freya Blitstein Maslov

Winter 1987

I was adopted at birth by my parents Harold and Sarah Kramer Blitstein. They brought me up in an atmosphere of happiness, love and dedication to my well-being.

While I was growing up, any questions I had about the circumstances of my adoption were always answered to my satisfaction. I was a much-wanted baby, the first in our family, and I was "chosen" from all the other babies at the hospital. I didn't need anything else—I had it all from my loving parents.

My interest in genealogy started in 1973, when a cousin of mine gave me all the information he had compiled about the Blitstein family 20 years earlier. This interest expanded to the point where I co-founded the Jewish Genealogical Society of Illinois in 1980. I never was motivated during this period to seek information about my birth family. A series of coincidences, however, caused me to try to get a copy of my birth certificate.

A genealogist knows that quite often you acquire information by luck, and that is how I managed to acquire my real birth certificate. In the summer of 1984, I requested it from the Cook County Board of Health, and apparently a clerk goofed and gave the document to me. (In the state of Illinois, adoption records are normally sealed.)

The certificate stated I was born the child of Wayne and Mary Blumenfeld Kahn. The record contained another piece of information that sent a chill through me. I was the fourth issue of Mary Kahn. A host of questions raced through my mind. Why was I put up for adoption after this couple had three other children? What happened to my three brothers and sisters?

The certificate was signed by Mary Kahn. From this, I surmised Wayne may have died, and perhaps that was the circumstance surrounding my adoption. I asked friends to help me look through the Chicago newspapers for an obituary for a Wayne Kahn.

A month later I received an excited phone call from one of my obituary-hunting friends.

"Freya! I have something to tell you. Get a piece of paper and write down the following."

I grabbed a pencil and paper, sat down and transcribed the information.

Robert (Jean)
Sid (Lois)
Phyllis (Irwin) Langer
Sande (William) Warsaw

Charles (Susan)
Judith (Phillip) Costa
Cheryl Johnson

Since we are both genealogists, I assumed he was giving me this information because he wanted me to do some research for one of his clients.

"Now for the source of these names," he said. "Freya, are you sitting down? I am reading from the obituary of Wayne Leo Kahn, died October 18, 1972, beloved husband of Mary nee Blumenfeld Kahn. Freya, I am reading your natural father's obituary. The names I gave you are the names of your natural brothers and sisters!"

I was in a state of shock! I didn't have three brothers and sisters. I had seven! How was that possible? How could I be the fourth of eight children of this couple and be put up for adoption when my brothers and sisters were not?

That night, when I got home from work, I called the funeral home mentioned in the obituary and asked for the next of kin. Two names and telephone numbers were given to me, the two oldest children, Robert and Sid.

Though still in a state of shock, I called Robert's number. It was disconnected, and calls were being referred to an area code 305 number (Florida). I thought for a moment and decided that this was not the type of telephone call that should be made long distance.

I tried Sid's number.

He answered. I took a deep breath, introduced myself as "Fran," and asked him if the date June 18, 1941, (my birth date) meant anything to him. He said, "No." This meant he knew nothing about a baby sister. My mind raced, grasping for a way of dropping the bombshell delicately.

"Sid, a baby girl was born on that date to a Mary and Wayne Kahn. She was ultimately given up for adoption," I said.

"But those are *my* parents' names," Sid replied.

"I know," I answered, "and I am that baby girl."

There was a long pause at the other end of the line. To this day, I do not know why Sid continued the conversation rather than slam down the telephone on this crazy person with a crazy story.

We agreed to meet at a local restaurant that evening at 8:30. By the time my husband Sy came home, I was a total wreck. I told him what had happened and asked that he accompany me to the meeting.

At 8:15, we arrived at the meeting place. As we pulled into the parking lot, a man was sitting on the fence in front of the door. I got out of the car and walked toward him. He turned to face me, and I stared at him. I thought I was looking in a mirror. Sid, or "Bud" as his friends called him, looked just like me. There was little doubt he was my brother.

The three of us sat down. Bud informed me he had called his mother, who now lived in Florida, and she had confirmed my story.

"But, why was I put up for adoption?" I asked. "Why me and not the other children?"

Bud informed me he recalled that when he was just six years old, his father abandoned the family. He, his brother and sister were put in the Jewish Family Home because his mother was destitute.

His mother later completed the story.

She was in the early stages of pregnancy. Her husband was not aware of her condition, and the children were too young to realize it. Because of her inability to support her three children, she was counseled to give up the unborn child for adoption.

Two years later, she was reconciled with Wayne and had four more children in later years. The pregnancy, birth and subsequent adoption had been her secret. Later, as my brothers and sisters were growing up, Wayne used to tell them at every family gathering to "always set an extra place at your table." They never really knew its true meaning until I entered their lives.

At this first meeting, Bud and I had a thousand questions to ask each other. We shared family pictures. I had forgotten my reading glasses and borrowed Bud's. I could see perfectly! We discovered we both had daughters names Marcy. Later, I found out they both shared the same middle name, too. My daughter's name is Marcy Joy; my niece's name is Marcey Joy.

Our meeting was brief. Bud wanted to call his mother with the details of this first meeting. It ended in the parking lot with a hug and kiss from Bud and a "Hi, sister."

Mary came to Chicago for Bob's surprise 50th birthday party in February 1985. I met her a few days later. We talked for hours, looked at pictures and asked and answered many questions. Mary moved back to Chicago a few months later, and we met several times. I learned all about my new brothers and sisters and felt that when I finally met them, I would already know them.

How to tell my three daughters?

After giving it much thought, I decided to tell them a story. Because of their hectic schedules, I was only able to get two of them together at one time. I told them I was doing genealogical research for a man who was adopted at birth and was searching for his birth family. I had managed to find that he had seven brothers and sisters. How would they feel if the situation was theirs? How would they feel if suddenly they had an additional 45 new family members? I wanted them to think not only about the immediate future but the far-reaching future. After some thought, they both said I should call him immediately. "After all, Mom," one of them replied, "it would be really neat for him to meet all those new relatives."

I then dropped the other shoe. "What if I told you I have been less than honest with you?" I said. "What if I said the story was true, but the family I found was mine? How would you feel then?" Their response made me proud. "Mom, you are kidding aren't you? We just told you how we feel. When do we get to meet them?" When I finally told my eldest daughter the next day, she reacted in the same manner.

How to tell my parents?

My mom was very ill—in and out of the hospital. I decided not to tell her yet, and I didn't want to tell only Dad. As her illness subsided and she became her old self again, I decided it was time. My mom's father died when she was young, in the influenza epidemic of 1918, and when her mother remarried, her stepfather adopted her. This was the only grandfather I ever knew. The day I went to her home to tell her the news, I turned our conversation to the genealogy of her natural father's family. We talked and the subject of adoption and medical histories came up. I slid my discovery into the conversation by saying I knew my own medical history. She listened and I watched her face. She later said she was a bit stunned but was not hurt. When Dad was told, he said, "Sarah, she isn't a teenager anymore. She is married almost 25 years and has three grown kids. She isn't about to run away."

How to tell my newly found brothers and sisters?

Bud and I decided to keep it from the rest of the family until Mary was ready. The meeting day was advanced when Bud accidentally disclosed my existence to his brother Bob. Bob was so excited that he wanted to pick up the telephone and call me immediately. Instead Bud called me the next day to ask if I would mind meeting Bob and his wife. Would I mind? What a question! I met my second brother the following Tuesday, June 18, 1985—my birthday. A few weeks later, our entire families got together. My children finally got to meet some of their new relatives.

How to tell the rest of the family?

Bob decided the disclosure should be a surprise at a meeting of the Kahn Klan. He called up each of his brothers and sisters and told them they had to come to his home that evening for a matter of utmost importance to the family. When they asked him what the matter was, he refused to discuss it. He said it was something wonderful and of such great importance that they had to cancel whatever plans they had and come to the meeting scheduled for 8:30.

He told me to arrive at 10:30. By that time they would have all arrived, and he would have had ample time to tell them the story of my existence.

I went alone.

As I pulled up to Bob's home, he was waiting in the driveway. He told me to sneak into the house through the garage and into the kitchen. "I don't want you to get stampeded." Once safely inside, he said, "Hang on, here goes." He went into his living room where his brothers and sisters were assembled and told them about my existence. He concluded by saying, "Do you want to sit there all night, or do you want to meet your new sister? She's in the kitchen!"

"Stampede" was an understatement. Bob had barely spoken those words when I suddenly felt what seemed to be a thousand arms hugging me. I was escorted into the living room, seated in a chair, given a drink and became the subject of an interrogation.

Whom did I look like? What were my likes? What were my dislikes? What was my childhood like? Where did I go to school? When was I married? When were my children born, and so on, and so on, and so on.

We talked of how our paths unknowingly crossed. Bud once had a business partner who was the son of the woman my cousin Arthur Blitstein married. One of my brothers-in-law went to the same grammar school and high school as I did. One sister taught bowling to children in Skokie, Illinois, about the same time we moved to neighboring Morton Grove.

There were differences. Most of them were Chicago Cubs fans; I was a Chicago White Sox fan.

For the next week, my telephone became a permanent fixture on my ear. If one called, the rest would call. One brother, Chuck, lived in Florida and, consequently, did not make the reunion. When he found out about me, he called to say he was packing his bags and he, his wife and two girls were on their way. When he found out my daughter Julie just had her 17th birthday, he sent her seventeen birthday cards—one for every year he had missed.

Julie was on her high school's varsity volleyball team. I happened to mention it to my newly found family. At the next game, they all came. Julie had her own cheering section. I wonder what the other fans thought of all the hugging and kissing that was going on. If they only knew!

October 16, 1985, was my 25th wedding anniversary; a day I will always remember. Mom was in the hospital again and wouldn't be able to go with us for dinner, a fact that made her feel very sad, because we always celebrated every birthday and anniversary together. Sy and I decided it wouldn't be right to celebrate it without her, so we arranged with the nurses to use a consultation room for a few hours. We decorated it and brought in Chinese food.

We stopped by mother's room before supposedly going out to dinner. It was obvious to us that she was upset she would not be with us. One of the nurses told her she would have to get up and exercise a little. They helped her walk down the corridor to the darkened consultation room where, to her surprise, we had our anniversary party. A restaurant is a restaurant; you can go to one anytime. But do you remember where you celebrated that special occasion? To Sy and me, it wasn't important where we had our 25th anniversary party. What was important was that we were all together.

My new family had planned an anniversary party for us three days later. All 45 members of the Kahn family showed up including Uncle Max and Aunt Ida (Mary's brother) from California.

On June 24, 1987, Mom finally met Mary Kahn. It was a meeting that took a long time for my sister Sande and me to arrange. I tried to put myself in my mom's position. What do you say to the woman who gave birth to your daughter? I also tried to understand what was going through Mary's mind. What do you say to the mother of the baby you gave up at birth?

My mom later told me that when she was alone with Mary for a few minutes, she thanked her for carrying me for them. She also told me later that "now meeting the rest will be easier."

I always felt that Freya Blitstein Maslov was a lucky person. Now I truly know it.

Freya Blitstein Maslov is one of the founders of the Jewish Genealogical Society of Illinois and one of its past presidents. At present she is co-coordinator of the Ukraine Special Interest Group (SIG) of JewishGen.

Epilogue

Freya and her sisters became very close. Their families became very close; close enough that Freya's daughter, Stacy, fell in love with her sister Sande's son, Daniel. They were married on October 16, 1988—which also happened to be Freya and Sy's anniversary. Picture the cast of characters at the wedding: The grandmother of the groom was the birth grandmother of the bride. Stacy and Dan are first cousins (first-cousin marriages are permitted by Jewish and Illinois law). When you marry your first cousin, your mother-in-law is your aunt. Both the bride and groom were heard during the wedding reception referring to their mothers as "Auntie Mom."

Evelyne Reclaims Her Identity
by Gary Mokotoff

Winter 2006

I am very involved in genealogy, both professionally and emotionally, but I do not like to do research for other people. Instead, I encourage people to trace their own ancestry so they can enjoy the rewarding experience that comes with this ever-growing hobby. There is one exception. If it is a Holocaust-related inquiry, I work free of charge to help the person with their research. My emotional involvement with the Holocaust comes from the fact that to date I have documented more than 400 members of the Mokotów family who were murdered in the Holocaust. I know of fewer than 30 survivors.

On October 1, 2004, I received an inquiry from Rachelle Goldstein of the Hidden Child Foundation in New York stating that the Foundation had received e-mail from Evelyne Haendel of Liege, Belgium. Evelyne was looking for a relative who lived in New York in the 1950s. Could I help her?

I e-mailed Evelyne asking for more information, and she informed me that when she was a child, her mother hid her with a Christian couple prior to the mother's deportation to Auschwitz. Hence, she was a part of the group of child survivors that became known as "Hidden Children." As she related it to me, "My parents were never heard from again." An aunt, Sasha, her mother's sister, survived Auschwitz. After the war, Sasha received copies of the Jewish *Forward* from Brooklyn, New York, sent by a man Evelyne believed was an uncle unknown to her—a brother of her mother. She was trying to locate this uncle.

When you do genealogical research for others, you need more than minimal facts. You often need to know about their lives. What makes you think he was your uncle? Give me a family tree showing names and dates. It required Evelyne to tell me more about herself.

Evelyne's Story

Evelyne was born in Vienna in August 1937, to Moses Haendel and Pessah Wolfowicz Haendel. Her father was a doctor and her mother was university educated. She and her mother fled Vienna for Belgium in December of that year, almost three months before Germany annexed Austria. Her father followed in 1938.

On May 10, 1940, Germany invaded Belgium. Her father was arrested by the Belgians and deported to France, because he was an Austrian and, therefore, considered an enemy alien (Austria was then part of Germany). When the Nazis started their anti-Jewish practices in 1941, Evelyne's mother received help from the owner of the house where she lived. He hid baby Evelyne with a Christian family. Finally, in 1942, when she was five years old, her mother was arrested in Brussels, and Evelyne resided until the end of the war with various Christian families for safe keeping. Meanwhile, her father was part of a roundup in France and was deported to Auschwitz in September 1942. Her mother was deported to Auschwitz shortly thereafter from Belgium.

In 1945, at war's end, her parents failed to return, and she remained with the owner of the house where her mother had lived. He and his wife eventually adopted her, changing her name to Colette Vandor. Fortunately, her adopted parents had rescued from her mother's apartment a good amount of memorabilia, including her parents' wedding picture, photos of Evelyne as a child and even some of her mother's jewelry—all items in her possession today. Even though she was brought up as a Catholic and given a new name, Evelyne always was aware of her true identity.

Wedding photo of Evelyne's parents, Moses and Pessah Wolfowicz Haendel, taken in 1932 in Vienna.

Her aunt returned from Auschwitz in 1945 and spent some time in Belgium, finally marrying and immigrating to Australia. It was the stepson of her Aunt Sasha, Harry Hollander, who told Evelyne, in August 2004, about this previously unknown uncle who sent Sasha copies of the *Forward*. Why didn't she have knowledge of such close kin? Because her knowledge of her family ended at the age of four when her mother placed her in hiding.

Over the next few months, Evelyne disclosed more and more information about her life. When she was in her 40s, she started to reclaim her identity. She legally changed her name back to Evelyne Haendel and started a 20-year quest to discover who she really was. She was alone in the world. The aunt had died a number of years before, but in reality, Evelyne had little communication with her after the aunt immigrated to Australia. She did find possible distant Haendel relatives in France, but was unable to determine how she was related to them. Evelyne had an uncle, Julius Wolfowicz—her mother's brother—who died in 1976, but he was always disinterested in her. The only daughter of Julius also wanted no contact. All of her grandparents died before World War II except her paternal grandmother, who was deported from France to Auschwitz with her son, Evelyne's father, and never returned.

The more I corresponded with her through e-mail, the more I became emotionally involved in helping her in two ways: to reclaim her Jewish identity and to find her uncle. Evelyne eagerly desired to do both.

Recapturing Her Jewish Identity

Early in our correspondence, I asked Evelyne whether she wanted to know more about her Jewish heritage and the response was "yes." There were a number of ways Evelyne could recapture her Jewish identity. I told her that every Jew had a religious name in addition to a secular name and that she undoubtedly was named after one of her ancestors, most likely a woman. Evelyne stated she did not know her religious name and could not think of any of her ancestors who had a name like Evelyne. So I chose a name for her. I told her to use the name Chava, which is Hebrew for "Eve" because it is close to "Evelyne," and Eve was the mother of us all. She readily accepted it. About a week later, I received e-mail from her informing me that, as she was reviewing her family tree, she found that she had a great-grandmother named Chawa Händel.

I made her aware of *yahrzeit* (memorial) candles as a way of remembering and memorializing the deceased—especially parents. Shortly thereafter, Evelyne disclosed to me the events surrounding her Aunt Sasha's family. Sasha's husband died of cancer in 1939, and her aunt and young daughter, Ursel, went into hiding after the Germans occupied Belgium. On June 6, 1944, the aunt and cousin were arrested in Brussels and were deported on the last train that left Belgium for Auschwitz. Both the aunt and 14-year-old cousin survived the selection and became prisoners at Auschwitz. On October 27, 1944, just 90 days before Auschwitz was liberated, her cousin, Ursel Fromer, was part of an in-camp selection by Mengele, and she was sent to the gas chambers. The following year, May 5, 2005, on *Yom HaShoah* (Holocaust Remembrance Day) Evelyne lit five yahrzeit candles; for her mother, father, aunt Sasha, Ursel and her grandmother, Jetti Haendel.

I was interested in helping her to know the Jewish holidays. This occurred shortly before Purim 2005. I described the holiday to her, that it is a joyous occasion, and encouraged her to go to the local synagogue to participate in the reading of the *Megillah* (Book of Esther). She was reluctant.

Passover was the next major holiday. Again I described the beauty of this holiday, how family-oriented it is, how people travel thousands of miles to be with family for the Passover *seders*. I suggested she go to the local synagogue and ask the rabbi to place her with a local family so she could attend a seder. Evelyne implied things like that were not done in her area. That night I spoke to my wife and suggested we invite Evelyne to our family seder and take her around New York to see the sites. The next day, I proposed it to Evelyne, and she leaped at the opportunity. I knew she would, because it wasn't merely participating in the seder; she would get to meet all my family members whom she got to know through our correspondence.

On April 22, Evelyne flew 3,600 miles—from Brussels to Newark Liberty International Airport—and the following evening participated in the first *seder* she had ever attended. She also was able to place a face and personality to the 23 people who were there.

Evelyne had a number of opportunities to be rescued from the Christian couple. Why didn't her aunt rescue her? I told Evelyne that my theory was that she would have been a constant reminder of her own daughter who was gassed at Auschwitz.

In April 2005, Evelyne asked me about a *mezuzzah*. I told her it is an object Jews placed on the doorposts of their rooms to fulfill the commandment of Deuteronomy 6:9 "that thou shalt place them on the doorposts of thy house and upon thy gates." She told me an interesting story. When she bought her apartment about 20 years ago, she saw a funny object on the entrance door. She asked the manager of the apartment complex, a Mr. Korn, what it was. He explained it was a *mezuzzah* indicating that the previous owner was Jewish. Evelyne disclosed she was born a Jew. Korn, who was Jewish, suggested that she leave the *mezzuzah* in place. She said to him that, no, she would remove the *mezuzzah* because, although

Evelyne Haendel, age 4, as a Hidden Child in Belgium in 1942. Behind her are her cousin, Ursel Fromer, and a Christian boy named Ivar. Ursel, at age 14, was arrested in Brussels with her mother and deported to Auschwitz on June 6, 1944. On October 27, 1944, as part of a routine camp selection, she was sent to the gas chambers. Her mother survived Auschwitz.

she was born a Jew, she did not feel it was proper to keep it up because she did not feel Jewish.

Evelyne sent me a picture of the tombstone of her mother's father, Joseph Wolfowicz from Dortmund, Germany. I read the Hebrew inscription which stated he was a Kohen, a descendant of the Jewish priestly class. In my next e-mail, I informed Evelyne that she was descended from the priests of the Temple that existed in Jerusalem, sort of Jewish royalty. "In other words, I am a Jewish princess," she jokingly replied.

Evelyne's birthday is August 22. The week before her birthday, my wife and I went to a local Judaica store and bought her a framed decoupage that had in the center the Hebrew word *Shalom* (peace). Today it hangs in the entranceway to her apartment in Liege.

Every Friday I receive e-mail from Evelyne. It contains only two words: *Shabat shalom* (peaceful Sabbath).

Finding Uncle Wolfowicz

Evelyne had done considerable genealogical research during the past 20 years to reclaim her identity. While most genealogists start their research by trying to find out more about their great-grandparents or perhaps even their grandparents, Evelyne's starting point was her parents. The last time her father was in her presence was when she was two years old. Her mother was deported from Belgium when she was five years old.

She accomplished much. Her father, Moses Haendel, was born in 1905 in Snyatyn, Ukraine, the son of Jacob and Jetti Hecht Händel. Her mother, Pessah Wolfowicz, was born in 1909 in Lódż, Poland, the daughter of Joseph and Malka Ehrlich Wolfowicz. Her parents met in Vienna where both were attending the university. She also determined the names of her eight great-grandparents.

Early Research

How do you find a man named Wolfowicz who lived in Brooklyn in the 1950s? To make matters worse, he almost certainly Americanized his name to Wolf. There was a small clue as to his given name. Evelyne had traced her Wolfowicz ancestors to their arrival in Dortmund, Germany, in the 1910s. In addition to her family, there was an Abraham Wolfowitz who arrived in Dortmund about the same time but lived at a different address. He left the city for Berlin in 1919. Evelyne dismissed this man as just a non-family member who had the same surname. To me it was too coincidental. Wolfowitz is a Polish-Jewish surname. Here we had two groups of people with the same surname arriving in a city in Germany at about the same time.

I used the Stephen P. Morse site to search the Ellis Island database that contains all persons arriving from 1892–1924. On my next trip to Salt Lake City, I also searched the microfilm index which covers that period and extends to 1942. No Abraham Wolfowicz or Wolfowitz matched the profile of a possible uncle of Evelyne's.

I searched the 1910, 1920 and 1930 census records located at www. ancestry.com for any person named Wolfowicz, Wolfowitz or Abe/Abraham Wolf. None met the profile. Abraham Wolf was too common a name to search other resources where minimal information is provided, such as the Social Security Death Index.

Major Breakthrough

In May 2005, I returned home to find a message on my answering machine. The message was nearly unintelligible, but I thought I heard the words "Wolfowicz found." Evelyne had been interviewed by a journalist about her experiences as a child survivor of the Holocaust. After hearing the story of her life, the producer told her there was a German Christian woman, Gisela Möllenhoff, who wrote a book about the Jews of Münster, Germany. Perhaps she could help her gain access to records in Germany. Evelyne wrote to her, and that led to Gisela finding a complete dossier on Evelyne's uncle, Julius Wolfowicz.

It was Julius' application for reparations caused by the events of World War II. The application was in German and Gisela translated excerpts from it. What it said made Evelyne very angry and caused her to cry. In the application, which had to identify all the heirs to the claim, Julius stated that Evelyne's mother never married, and the only heirs were himself, his sister Sasha and brother Adolph who lived at 169 Neptune Avenue, Brooklyn, New York. "It is as if they killed my mother a second time," Evelyne shouted to me. Julius was well aware of Evelyne's existence, and her aunt Sasha had lived in Belgium after returning from Auschwitz. Both chose to ignore that she existed.

This grief, however, was tempered by the information that her American uncle was named Adolph. Adolph would be more than 100 years old if alive today, so I went to the Social Security Death Index which lists virtually every American that has died since 1962. I found no Wolfowiczs, but there was an Adolph Wolf whose last residence was in the same zip code as 169 Neptune Avenue.

The 1930 census showed an Adolph and Bella Wolf living in Brooklyn at 222 Bay 34th Street, which is not far from Neptune Avenue. They had two children—girls named Pauline and Florence. Tracing women is difficult because their names change when they get married. Had either child been male, I would have looked for that person in the Social Security Death Index or an online telephone book.

An application was sent to the New York City Vital Records Department for Adolph's death record. When it arrived, it confirmed that we had the correct person, because it listed his parents as Joseph and Malka, Evelyne's grandparents. The informant was his wife, Bella.

A few days later, my wife, Ruth, and I visited the graves of Adolph and Bella. It was my intent to get the name and address of the next of kin from the cemetery office. Cemeteries normally do not give this information but will forward a letter to the next of kin. By a stroke of luck, when I went to the office and asked for the gravesite of Adolph Wolf, there were two men with that name buried in the cemetery. To make certain she was giving me the correct information, the clerk blurted out, "Adolph Wolf, whose daughter is Pauline Goldberg Frank?" Now I had the married name of their daughter, Pauline! [To protect their privacy, the names of Evelyne's cousins have been changed.]

Adolph's tombstone further confirmed we had the right person. The Hebrew inscription identified him as *Avraham bar Yosef HaKohen* (Abraham son of Joseph the Kohen). We returned to the cemetery office to give them the letter I wanted forwarded to Pauline Frank. In the hopes the clerk would be sympathetic to our quest, I let her read the letter and then asked if she would give me the address due to the circumstances described in the letter. She said she couldn't. "Can you tell me whether she lives in the New York area?" my wife asked. Her response was "No, Florida."

So now I was looking for a Mrs. Frank in Florida.

I informed Evelyne that evening of the find, but that there were too many Franks in Florida in the online phone directory, switchboard.com. Evelyne was so anxious to move the project forward that she called the cemetery and pleaded with them for a further clue. They told her the woman lived in Delray Beach, Florida.

Searching Florida

There were no Franks in Delray Beach in two online U.S. phone directories: switchboard.com and anywho.com. Very fortunately, in 1996, before the Internet was heavily used, I had purchased a CD-ROM national telephone directory. Searching the CD, there was an entry for a "C. Frank" at 5282 Magellan Way West in Delray Beach. With *Microsoft Streets & Maps* as a guide, I used the AVOTAYNU mailing list to locate a person who lived near that address. I called an AVOTAYNU subscriber, Dorothy Bernstein of Delray Beach, and asked her to find out the name and contact information of the homeowners association for that address. They would have information about the previous residents. She replied a few hours later with a phone number. When I called, I got a recorded message that the number was temporarily disconnected at the request of the owner.

I contacted Dennis Rice, president of the Jewish Genealogical Society of Palm Beach County, and asked for his help. He went to that address and interviewed the current resident. They did not know the previous occupants, so he went to a neighbor who stated she was very familiar with the family. Unfortunately, she was not cooperative, and, in fact, antagonistic. She informed Dennis that she would tell the family about Evelyne, but not to bother her anymore. They would contact him if they were interested.

This was unacceptable to Evelyne, and she called the woman (her number was listed in the online phone book). The woman was so furious she would not allow

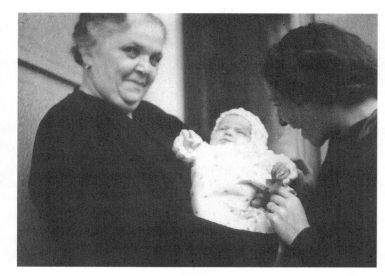

Baby Evelyne with her grandmother, Jetti Haendel, and mother, Pessah Wolfowicz Haendel. Both died at Auschwitz.

Evelyne to state her case and just slammed down the phone. Evelyne was distraught. This woman would undoubtedly contact Pauline Goldberg Frank and state some crazy woman was looking for her.

With that avenue shut, I decided to use another pathway—the professional genealogy community. Eileen Polakoff, a professional genealogist who shares my office, reminded me that Alvie Davidson, who is on the Board of Directors of the Association of Professional Genealogists, lives in Florida and his specialty is locating people in Florida. I am also on the Board of Directors, so I knew him quite well.

Week of August 22, 2005

The week of August 22, 2005, had to be one of the most significant weeks in Evelyne's life.

Monday, August 22. August 22 is Evelyne's birthday. For her 68th birthday, my wife and I had mailed her a framed decoupage that has the Hebrew word *Shalom* (peace) as its central theme. She received it on her birthday. It now was days since we heard from Dennis Rice, and I decided it was time to contact Alvie Davidson. An e-mail was sent in the morning to him asking if he could locate Pauline Goldberg Frank. After leaving the office for a short while, I returned to find two e-mails from Alvie. The first said, "I just got back to my office after a half day running errands. I will evaluate the information this afternoon and get you a current address for the person who lives in Delray Beach, Florida." Just 21 minutes later, Alvie sent the second e-mail. It stated, "I found Pauline Goldberg, widow of Isidore Goldberg, who has a connection to a female named Cynthia M. Frank." It included Pauline's current address and her daughter Cynthia's phone number. Pauline had moved only a few blocks from her previous address. I called Cynthia Frank's phone number and heard a strange message stating that the number did not accept any incoming calls. I called Dorothy Bernstein and asked if she would go to Pauline's home and speak to her armed with photos of the aunts and uncles Pauline shared with Evelyne. She consented, but stated it could not be done until Wednesday. Evelyne was impatient. To her, two days was a long time. I assured her Dorothy would act more quickly. Genealogists are compulsive when it comes to their research.

Tuesday. Dorothy called me in the afternoon. She had gone to Pauline's home and received a totally cold reception. Pauline said she was not interested, and when Dorothy offered to leave the documentation she brought with her, Pauline slammed the door shut. Evelyne was devastated. I was confident. We were too close to solving the problem to fail. If Alvie Davidson could so easily get the information he previously provided, maybe he could as easily locate the children of Pauline. I sent him another e-mail asking for information about the children. Two hours later, Alvie sent me the name, address and phone number of the son, who lived in neighboring Boynton Beach and the names of Pauline's two daughters, Mona and Cynthia.

Thursday. Evelyne and I were in the habit of using Microsoft Messenger instant messaging when it was necessary to discuss strategy at length. We both have web cameras and microphones to assist in the communication. That morning, as we were discussing the project, my phone rang. A man with a Scottish accent stated he was the son-in-law of Pauline Goldberg and was calling in response to our inquiries. He stated that he had checked me out, and it was obvious I was a prominent person in genealogy. "Why are you involved in this matter?" he queried. I told him that I rarely get involved in doing work for clients with one exception: Holocaust-related matters. I said I felt I had a moral obligation to help Holocaust survivors find family.

We had a 15-minute conversation where I knew I had to convince him that his family should make contact with Evelyne. I described Evelyne's life, the early loss of her parents, her being cut off from her roots, the change of her name, and her total ignorance of who her parents were. He ended the conversation with the statement that he would talk to his wife, and they would get back to me.

The most remarkable aspect was that Evelyne heard my side of the conversation because the microphone was still on. Evelyne, of course, got very emotional. I reassured her by saying it was likely they would call back. And even if they didn't, I would contact the family through Pauline's son.

That evening I received a phone call at home. The woman identified herself as Mona Goldberg, daughter of Pauline Goldberg. She had received a call from her sister, Cynthia, who lives in a suburb of London. Mona, who lives in Los Angeles, was excited about her newly found cousin. I told her virtually everything I had told her Scottish brother-in-law, but the conversation was more upbeat. I told her this was yet another love story about a Holocaust survivor being reunited with family. She gave me her phone number, cell phone number and e-mail address. I gave her all the information she needed to contact Evelyne, and she said she would call her the following morning. I e-mailed Evelyne immediately—it was now 2:00 a.m. in Belgium. Fifteen minutes later, I received a phone call from her.

Friday. Evelyne called me at my office to announce she had just completed an 82-minute telephone call with her newly found cousin in Los Angeles. Two hours later, Evelyne e-mailed me that she just had received a phone call from her cousin Cynthia. The call was brief, but they promised to talk at length the next day.

Saturday. Evelyne spoke to Cynthia for 105 minutes. As she was debriefing me about the conversation through Microsoft Messenger, the phone rang at Evelyne's home. It was Pauline Goldberg calling from Florida. She told Evelyne that her original fears that the initial inquiries were some sort of scam were overcome, and now she was excited to know that she had a first cousin that survived the Holocaust.

Yom Kippur

It was time for Evelyne to meet her cousin Pauline. I suggested to her that it be mixed with another dose of Judaism by recommending that she join my wife and me for Yom Kippur services before she and I flew to Florida to meet her cousin.

On Tuesday, October 11, Evelyne flew from Brussels to Newark and the following evening participated in her first Kol Nidre service. Before we left for the synagogue, the three of us lit five *yahrzeit* candles for my wife's parents, my father and Evelyne's parents. I prepared Evelyne for the service by informing her the synagogue would be packed with worshippers (there were about 600), that the cantor would sing the prayers in a manner that would be equivalent to listening to opera, and she would not understand the words, and that while most of the prayers would be recited in Hebrew, the prayer book included an English translation. I told her she would enjoy reading the prayers because they were like reading poetry that continually referred to God's love for us and our love for God.

Unknown to Evelyne, a week earlier I had written the rabbi a lengthy letter that started:

> *There will be an unusual person in your congregation attending Kol Nidre and Yom Kippur services this year. Her name is Evelyne Haendel, and she lives in Liege, Belgium. Evelyne is a child survivor of the Holocaust; a Hidden Child. When she was five years old her parents hid her with a Christian couple shortly before they were deported to their deaths at Auschwitz.*

It continued by telling the story of her life. At the beginning of the Kol Nidre service, the rabbi went up to the podium and told the congregation, "There is an unusual person in our congregation attending our service this year." He continued, without mentioning her name or asking to acknowledge her presence. "This Yom Kippur, she will, for the first time, participate in a Jewish religious service. It will be the first time she has heard Kol Nidre chanted. At the yizkor service, for the first time, she will say a prayer for each of her parents." Evelyne started to cry.

Midway through the service, one of the ushers approached Evelyne and told her that, when the service reached a specific page, she should come to the front of the congregation. I knew what was going to happen. The rabbi had decided to honor Evelyne by giving her an *aliyah*; allowing her to participate directly in the service. At the appropriate moment, Evelyne mounted the *bima* (platform) and opened the curtain to the ark in which the Torahs are kept. It was a total surprise to Evelyne, and when she returned to her seat she was beaming.

On Thursday, Yom Kippur day, Evelyne participated in the *yizkor* (memorial) service, and for the first time said *Kaddish* (prayer for the dead) for her parents and also for her cousin Ursel.

Meeting Rachelle Goldstein

We spent Friday evening at the home of Rachelle Goldstein, the woman at the Hidden Child Foundation who provided the initial link between Evelyne and myself. Rachelle also was a Hidden Child. Evelyne reminded me that Rachelle's initial e-mail to her stated:

> Dear Evelyne. I was born in Brussels and, like you, I was a Hidden Child. Had my parents not survived I would be in your position. Your quest, therefore, is very dear to my heart.

It was another joyous occasion for Evelyne. She later recounted the event by saying:

> The light of the candles, the warmth of our hosts, the sharing and immediate understanding and the delicious food made a wonderful Shabbat. This was yet another "first" in rediscovering my Jewish heritage.

JGSGW Anniversary Celebration

Meeting her cousin was placed on hold for a few days because many months earlier, AVOTAYNU editor Sallyann Sack asked me to be the speaker at the 25th anniversary celebration of the Jewish Genealogy Society of Greater Washington. Sallyann was the founder of JGSGW. Evelyne was thrilled. As she stated to me, she wanted to hear me give a speech. My wife, Evelyne and I drove to the Washington area on Saturday and stayed overnight at Sallyann's home. On Sunday, at one point in the celebration, Sallyann told the audience of Evelyne's presence and eventually asked her to come to the microphone and say a few words. I panicked. Sallyann was asking her to make extemporaneous comments. What she said was brief and quite remarkable. It included the statement, "You (genealogists) all know the significance of having family. I know the significance of not having family."

Meeting Family

Monday, Evelyne and I flew to Florida and met her cousin Pauline and her son. It was a joyous occasion for both women. Most of the talk was about Pauline's youth and her parents, especially her father—Evelyne's Uncle Adolph. Pauline served a "genuine Jewish lunch" of pastrami sandwiches.

The Saga Continues

Evelyne's new life continues to blossom. Some experiences are joyous, others cause pain mixed with joy. There are times I think she is the female Job. In September, she visited, for the first time, the grave of her maternal grandmother, Malka Wolfowicz, who died in 1938 and is buried in Antwerp, Belgium. To her amazement and horror, the tombstone on her grandmother's grave was for another person! Glancing along the row of graves, Evelyne noticed the identical name on another tombstone, indicating that when a second tombstone was ordered for that person, the wrong stone was replaced! Evelyne was in pain, but I turned the incident into an opportunity. I told her that now she would be able to honor her grandmother by selecting a stone of her choosing. Evelyne created a magnificent tombstone and added her parents' names, her paternal grandmother and Ursel's names at the bottom noting they died at Auschwitz.

מלכה בת יוסף ז״ל
נפטרה כ״א סיון תרצ״ח
ת נ צ ב ה

À MA GRAND-MÈRE
MALKA WOLFOWITZ
NÉE EHRLICH
1 MAI 1875 - 20 JUIN 1938

A la mémoire
de mes parents Moshe et Pessah Händel-Wolfowitz,
de ma grand-mère Jette Händel-Hecht
et de ma cousine Ursel Fromer
disparus à Auschwitz.
Evelyne

In late December, Evelyne expressed an interest in learning to read Hebrew. I mailed her a book geared for children that teaches Hebrew one letter at a time. I also mailed her the Conservative daily prayer book which includes the prayers in Hebrew and English. In February, we will start Hebrew lessons, 3,600 miles apart, using our web cameras, microphones and Microsoft Messenger.

Israel

In January 2006, Evelyne achieved another first in her return to being a Jew—her first trip to Israel. While there, she called my office and said that she had visited the Western Wall twice. She told me, "I feel like I am home!" On her departure from Israel she sent a text message: "Boker tov (good morning). In a few minutes I will be leaving our homeland."

Conclusion

At one point in this quest, Evelyne sent me an e-mail that sums up why I devoted all the time to this project. She wrote me, "In thanking you, I am thinking also of my father and mother. I am sure they would have been so happy—and grateful."

Gary Mokotoff is publisher of AVOTAYNU.

Epilogue

Evelyne's quest for family continues, and today her family tree contains more than 100 people. Her first cousin, Pauline, had two sisters. One was located in Texas; the other was killed in an auto accident in California. This sister had daughters that Evelyne was able to locate. In January 2007, a major breakthrough occurred when a book published during World War I listing Galician refugees was placed on the Internet. It included the name of a woman, Adela (Ethel) Haendel, whom Evelyne was able to demonstrate was her grandmother Jetti's sister. This led to locating paternal relatives living in Canada, Israel and the U.S. The Canadian relatives were not only aware of her existence, but had pictures of her parents and grandmother not in Evelyne's possession.

For her 69th birthday, my wife and I gave Evelyne a pendant which is her name in Hebrew: Chava (חוה). She wears it constantly. She regularly goes to Yom Kippur services in Liege to say *Kaddish* for her parents, Ursel and her grandmother. Since 2005 she has been a guest at my family's Passover seder service.

Evelyne is using the skills she developed in family history research to help others. This includes uniting descendants of Belgian Hidden Children with the descendants of those who saved the children. Using her expertise in 20th-century Belgian resources, she is helping other family historians find records of relatives.

Evelyne Haendel (left) at a Passover Seder in 2006 with the author, Gary Mokotoff, and his wife Ruth. On her left ring finger, Evelyne wears her mother's earring that she fashioned into a ring.

Photograph of Evelyne's parents, Moses and Pessah Haendel, was in the possession of the Canadian cousins she located in 2007. The picture was taken in April 1932 shortly before their marriage.

The Diary of Miriam Hanania
by Batya Unterschatz

Winter 1988

My friend told me about the diary when I invited her to my Jerusalem apartment for tea one evening. She had bought it in an antique shop in Amsterdam, Holland. It was the diary of a young girl written in 1938 and 1939. The girl must have been Jewish, she said, because there was Hebrew writing in one portion of the book. Would I help her find its owner?

The similarity between this story and the famous diary of Anne Frank, the Dutch teenager who died at Bergen Belsen concentration camp, made me shudder. Of course, I would help her.

My friend brought the book to me a few nights later. It was a leather-bound diary showing the wear of a book that was now nearly 50 years old. I opened it to look for clues about its owner and found it was not the kind of diary written by Anne Frank, which was a young girl's reflections on her life while hiding from the Germans. Instead, it was a collection of dedications written by the girl's friends to her. There were inscriptions in Dutch, French, and German and one sentence in Hebrew. All the entries were dated 1938 or 1939 in the Belgian city of Antwerp.

The owner's name was Miriam, but after going through the book, page by page, I had found no reference to her family name. No great obstacle. If the girl survived the Holocaust, she was undoubtedly married; therefore, it still would be difficult to locate her by her family name.

I am the director of the Search Bureau for Missing Relatives. For the past 16 years, my job has been locating people. I started to apply my skills to find the Miriam of the diary.

First, it was my hope that if Miriam survived the Holocaust, she, or some of her friends who wrote in the diary, immigrated to Israel. More than 500,000 survivors came to my country after the State of Israel was born.

Each article was signed by a friend of Miriam, most of whom were girls. I chose the only two names that were boys, Joseph Tannenbaum and Shmuel Schnitzer. Checking my records for persons named Joseph Tannenbaum living in Israel, I found three with that name. None were of the age that would have made them teenagers in 1939. I turned to the name Shmuel Schnitzer. There were five listed, but the profile of one made me feel he was the most likely. I called his home, and his wife gave me his business telephone number. It turned out he was the editor-in-chief of *Ma'ariv*, one of the largest daily newspapers in Israel. When he answered the telephone, I identified myself and asked him if he lived in Antwerp before the War. He said, "Yes." I was convinced I had found the right person.

The next day in his office, I showed him the diary and his signature as a young boy. He excitedly leafed through the pages. He told me the diary was about the interest he and his friends had in going to Palestine and fighting for freedom and possibly sacrificing their lives for their ideals. Joseph Tannenbaum, he said, was killed on his way to Palestine.

"Do you know who owned this diary about the girl named Miriam?" I asked.

"No," he said.

I persisted. He could not remember. I was insistent. "Look through the book again. Maybe you will see something that will make you remember."

Suddenly, Schnitzer exclaimed, "Kiki! Look, some of my friends dedicated their story to Kiki. I now remember that was Miriam's nickname. Her name was Miriam Hanania!"

I now had Miriam's full name.

Schnitzer now recalled that Miriam married a Jewish boy, came to Palestine, and settled in the Haifa area. I asked him for Miriam Hanania's married name.

Once again, he said, "I don't remember."

"I won't leave this office until you do remember," I said. He leafed through the book a number of times until he shouted, "Goldener! Yes, her married name is Goldener!" [Note: To protect the privacy of the family, the name has been changed—Ed.]

I was close to the completion of my adventure. Returning to my office, I looked for a Goldener family in the Haifa area. There was none. How was this possible? Schnitzer was so sure he had the right name. My experience in dealing with persons searching for friends or relatives made me realize that maybe he did not give me the exact married name of Miriam.

I checked other variations of Goldener and found a Miriam Geldman who was exactly the age of the person I was looking for. She lived in Givatayim.

I called her apartment excitedly. A man answered. "May I speak to Miriam Geldman?" I asked. There was a long pause at the other end. "Who is this?" the man queried. I identified myself and asked again, "May I speak to Miriam Geldman?" Again, a long pause at the other end.

"I am afraid that is not possible," the man said. "You see, we have just returned from her funeral."

I was stunned. Her husband wanted to know what it was all about. I explained about the diary, and he said he would be interested in meeting me and seeing the book. I waited until the end of *shiva*, the seven days of mourning, before going to his home.

There I showed him the diary. He cried and then told me about his wife and many of the persons in the book. He was so grateful for the book that a short time later I received a silver dish inscribed, "With appreciation to Batya from Miriam Hanania Geldman, of blessed memory."

Batya Unterschatz, while director of the Search Bureau for Missing Relatives, developed an international reputation for her ability to locate persons living in Israel or their descendants. She was born in Vilnius, Lithuania, to parents that both were Litvaks. She studied languages at Vilnius University and graduated with an MA degree in linguistics. In 1971, she immigrated to Israel and shortly thereafter joined the Jewish Agency's Search Bureau for Missing Relatives. She has helped thousands of people find lost family and friends. In 2002, Batya retired and the Bureau was closed. She still does research professionally when not enjoying her three children and 16 grandchildren.

A Priest in the Family?
by Annie Wolkin

Winter 1988

Several years ago, on my first trip to the United States from my home in Johannesburg, South Africa, I decided to look up my cousins, the Shulkins of Massena, New York. Our fathers had been half-brothers, but we had never met, and it had been many years since there had been any communication between us. Our name originally was Shulkin also, but a South African immigration official, mistaking the Russian *Sh* letter (Ш) for a *W*, made our name Wolkin. My father had been content to leave it that way.

Arriving in New York City, I sought assistance from the telephone operator, both of us initially assuming that Massena was somewhere in the New York City metropolitan area. Didn't all Jews live in New York City? After a little back and forth conversation, as the operator tried to be sure that she understood my accent, I was switched to long distance assistance. Then I learned that Massena was a small town upstate on the St. Lawrence River.

To my dismay, the only Shulkin listed in the Massena directory was one Father Eli Shulkin, a Roman Catholic priest! I didn't think he could be my cousin, but one never knows. After all, many years had passed since the brothers had written to each other. I called Father Shulkin. No, he was not a cousin, but he was able to direct me to one, the last of my Shulkins still in Massena, a married woman who, of course, had a different last name.

When I finally met the whole clan, I asked if they knew Father Shulkin and was told the following story:

Uncle Jake had owned and operated a large furniture store in Massena. One day he waited on a "greenie," a recent Polish immigrant who bought a houseful of furniture. Writing up the sale, Uncle Jake asked the man's name. "Shulkin," came the answer. Doing a double take, Uncle Jake asked, "How do you spell it?" "S-h-u-l-k-i-n," came the reply. "That's a pretty unusual name, isn't it?" continued Uncle Jake.

"Well, you know, my name really isn't Shulkin, it's really (and here the greenie gave a long, nearly-unpronounceable Polish Catholic name). We are new in town, and as we came over the hill and across the bridge, the first thing I saw was your sign, "Slavin and Shulkin Furniture." I said to my wife, "That's what we need—a genuine American name!"

And so it happened that a Polish Catholic family adopted a Jewish name from the very region of the world they had wanted to leave behind.

Children Under 16 Unaccompanied by a Parent: The Family Zuser

by Valery Bazarov and Marian L. Smith

Summer 2004

At the 2003 IAJGS Conference in Washington, DC, Marian Smith and Valery Bazarov presented "HIAS and INS Case Files," a demonstration of the relationship between records of the immigrant aid society and the government in certain immigrant cases. They transformed the lecture into a series of articles for AVOTAYNU, each of which offers lessons in immigrant research and records. Each case highlights how a representative of the government and a representative of the immigrant make different assumptions and follow varying research procedures.

The story of Wilhelmina and Anna Jentjes illustrates a common problem encountered at Ellis Island or other United States ports of entry during the late 19th and early 20th centuries. Immigration law barred the admission of children under the age of 16 who were unaccompanied by a parent. Even if a child traveled with an aunt, uncle or cousin, they might spend days in detention preparing guarantees for the child's safety. Unlike the masses of extended family groups who passed through Ellis Island each day unnoticed, the Jentjes girls caught the officials' attention and recently caught the attention of Valery Bazarov.

Valery Bazarov Comments

In New York, on the 28th day of November 1915, Hebrew Immigrant Aid Society (HIAS) representative Samuel Littman watched passengers disembark from a ship which had just arrived from Liverpool. The procession of passengers suddenly caused Littman's eyes to widen—he saw a Jewish woman with six children. Not an unusual sight, but two of the children were black. Who were they? What winds of fate threw the two black girls into the midst of a Jewish family?

Eighty-eight years later I was possessed with the same curiosity regarding this unusual case. The case went before the Board of Special Inquiry, which denied them admission. I soon located their file among the records of the HIAS Ellis Island Bureau (see "Records Used" at end of article). The group included Annie Zuser (or Zusser or Suser); her children Michael, Dorothy, Morris and Sara (ages 9 years to 11 months); and Wilhelmina and Anna Jentjes, ages 9 and 5. They were destined to Annie's husband, Mendel Zuser, in New York City. An appeal filed on behalf of the family by the HIAS representative indicated the family Zuser emigrated from South Africa with the two black girls.

The story of how these girls joined a family of Russian Jews was simple. Their mother worked for the family for many years. It seemed the father was never in the picture, and eventually the mother disappeared as well. Having no other relatives, the girls remained with the Zusers and lived with them for at least four years before immigrating to the United States. The Zusers would have adopted the girls, but South African law prohibited adoption of blacks by whites, and vice versa. In the United States, the family hoped to legalize the position of the girls. In South Africa, the only way to keep legal custody of the children was to register them as apprentices until the age of 21. Information in the HIAS file proved that Anna and Mendel Zuser's financial position[1] was more than adequate to establish themselves in the United States and take care of all the children. This being the case, why did INS officers deny the Zusers admission? Why did they need to appeal the Board of Special Inquiry decision?

Out of curiosity, I sent the case and my questions to Marian Smith, INS historian in Washington. She then sent me a package containing amazing information. It allowed me to be present at the Board of Special Inquiry hearing, where the fate of the Zuser family was at stake and to hear what the members of the Board heard. You, too, can judge whether to admit or reject the family Zuser:

Anna Zuser, a Russian Jew, answers the questions of the panel.

Q. Where are the parents of those colored children?

A. The father is dead. The mother, the last I heard of her she was in Cape Colony. She is a very poor woman and travels from one farm to another.

Q. What is her name?

A. Kaatje Jantjes.

Q. Explain to us how long you had these children?

A. For the past 6 years.

Q. You claim that they are your adopted; have you anything to show that you have legally adopted them?

A. Yes. (Submits indenture of apprenticeship showing that Kaatje Jantjes places the children, Mina and Anna, with Mendel Zuser until they are 21 years of age, to be brought up and educated by Mr. Zuser, and signed by the resident magistrate.)

Q. The papers you submit do not show that you have legally adopted them, but that they are indentured apprentices?

A. That is customary adoption there. You can't do it otherwise.

Q. Have you provided for them in the past 5 years?

A. Yes.

Q. Have they been going to school?

A. Well, there was no school near our farm, but I had an instructor come to my

---

[1] Detailed information, such as financial data, makes HIAS files a unique and rich source for genealogical researchers.

children, and he gave them lessons too.

Q. Are they to go to school in this country?

A. Yes.

Q. What was the purpose in taking these children?

A. I adopted them out of sympathy. Their mother had been in my service for a long while, and she begged me to take these children, because she knew they would be well taken care of.

Q. Have these children any relatives here?

A. No.

Q. Is it yours and your husband's purpose to provide for them as your own children?

A. Yes.

Now Mendel Zusser is called. He confirms all his wife stated before him and proves that he is a man of some means and has enough money to provide for his family. The questioning continues.

Q. How did it come that you took these children?

A. Their mother worked on our farm as a servant and their father died. They were very poor; the children were neglected. My wife felt sorry for them, and we took them and adopted them. We want to educate them.

Q. Are you going to send them to school?

A. Certainly.

Q. How long will you send them to school?

A. As long as the law requires.

Q. Will you assure us that you will send them to school until they are at least 16?

A. Yes.

Q. Will you also assure us that they will not be placed at work unsuited for their years?

A. I do.

Q. Are you to take the same care of these children as though they were your own?

A. Yes.

Q. The papers that have been submitted here show that they were not legally adopted but indentured to you?

A. That is the law in British South Africa. I am responsible for them until they are 21 years old. That is the adoption law there.

Q. Are you in a position to furnish a bond to insure the government against the likelihood of these two colored children becoming public charges, and that they will be sent to school until they are at least 16?

A. Yes. It states in the papers that I am to bring them up and educate them.

The Board took little time to come to a unanimous decision. They first excluded Wilhelmina and Anna Jentjes, then Annie Zuser, then all four of Annie's children. My questions remained. Why did the government deny them admission? Why did Annie Zuser need to appeal the Board of Special Inquiry decision? Again, I sent my questions to Marian.

Marian Smith Comments

After Valery sent me copies of the HIAS file documents, I was able to search for records of Wilhelmina and Anna Jentjes. Happily, indexes revealed a file number belonging to a series of records transferred some years ago from my agency to the National Archives and Records Administration (NARA) in Washington, DC. I took the number to NARA and requested the file from the INS Subject Correspondence and Case files (see "Records Used") and was relieved when technicians located the file. It contained 67 pages detailing the immigration case of the Jentjes sisters and the Zuser family.

HIAS helped Annie Zuser appeal the Board of Special Inquiry decision because the board decided against them, and an appeal would take the case to the Commissioner-General of Immigration and the Secretary of Labor in Washington, DC, who might overturn the board's decision and rule in their favor. Still, the Labor Secretary would have to wrestle with the law. Section 11 of the Immigration Act of 1907 excluded persons considered likely to become a public charge, a central provision of U.S. immigration law and policy since 1875. The Board of Special Inquiry decided Anna and Wilhelmina Jentjes were likely to become public charges for three distinct reasons.

First, "In view of their tender years they are incapable of self-support." The two girls were only 9 and 5 years old and obviously could not support themselves.

Second, "They have no one here who could be legally compelled to support them. They have no relatives here." While Annie and Mendel Zuser might promise to care for the girls as they care for their own children, the Zusers had no legal obligation to do so. Immigration officials learned from long experience that courts could or would not force people to fulfill such promises, and at Ellis Island, the officials' job was to ensure that children like Wilhelmina and Anna did not become wards of a state orphanage. In short, immigration officials would not be satisfied with any promise they could not "take to court."

Third, "While the claim is made by the elder alien that she has legally adopted them, the papers submitted show that they have been apprenticed to her." This section of the ruling obviously speaks to the question of legal obligation discussed above, but also raises a separate issue concerning children. Too often, immigrant children were found laboring in the sweatshops and factories of America. It was also the immigration officials' job to protect children who might be put to work soon after arrival. Thus, the Jentjes sisters were also excluded because they were "likely to be placed at work unsuited to their years." Given this situation, the Zusers presentation of apprenticeship papers did not help their case.

Children of such "tender years" could not be returned to South Africa alone, and the laws required that an "accompanying alien" be excluded with them. Thus, the board also excluded Annie Zuser. With that action, Annie's four other children were left as children under 16 traveling unaccompanied by either parent, so they were excluded as well. As the Zuser case shows, this "domino effect" of exclusion could happen when the board excluded either a dependent alien (a child or wife) or an independent alien (parent or husband). Sometimes, one child and one parent were excluded, and the rest of the family had to choose whether to remain in America or all return together. If those admitted could not afford to purchase return tickets, the family faced separation.

After the Board of Special Inquiry issued its decision, Annie Zuser had 48 hours to file an appeal. A HIAS representative, Samuel Littman, obviously thought he could get Annie's decision overturned and immediately drafted and filed the necessary documents. Littman understood the board's concerns, and he knew that the appeal process could generate the legally binding documents needed to overcome Wilhelmina and Anna's exclusion. Specifically, he correctly expected officials in Washington to overturn the decision on condition that the Zusers post a bond promising to send both girls to school (and not to work) until they were 16 years of age.

"Bonding" of excludable aliens was routine on Ellis Island, and issuing such bonds was a substantial portion of the business of many insurance companies, including the New York Life Insurance Company and Metropolitan Life Insurance Company. The government even had specific forms to be used in filing different types of bonds. The Zusers filed Form 579, Bond for Alien Children, with School and Public Charge Clauses. HIAS helped Mendel Zuser arrange for bonds issued by the Southwestern Surety Insurance Company. He posted $1,000— $500 for each girl—and the family was finally admitted to the United States.

Valery Bazarov Comments

The Zusers' immigration saga ended there. But we meet Mendel Zuser once again ten years later, in 1923. As we know, Mendel posted bond as a guarantee that the two girls would attend school until they were 16 years old. Mendel and his family settled in a nice neighborhood in New Jersey, and the girls attended a very good school with the other Zuser children. Yet, Mendel suddenly appeared on Ellis Island in 1923 with a very strange request. He wanted to change the age of Anna, the younger black girl, who in 1923 should have been 13, to 16. What happened? Anna was a model daughter, who completely integrated into the Zuser family. But she could not integrate into the family's suburban environment, which was hostile to her, especially in school. When Zuser explained the situation to the Ellis Island Commissioner, the bureaucrat became sympathetic to the delicate circumstances Anna endured and allowed the change. So Anna became 16 and the government canceled the bond.[2] The Zusers hired a private tutor to educate Anna at home.

Anna's sister, Wilhelmina, faced a different fate. When she was 16, she became a delinquent teenager, fled from home and disappeared into a large world.

Marian Smith Comments

Unfortunately, Wilhelmina's fate proved that the initial concerns of the Board of Special Inquiry were not unreasonable. After Wilhelmina left home in 1919, Mendel's bond was lost and the government collected the $500. In 1922, Wilhelmina was convicted of petit larceny and sentenced to a state reformatory. There, the New York State taxpayers spent more than $700 annually to keep her. By 1930, Wilhelmina was an inmate of the New Jersey State Hospital, where New Jersey taxpayers footed the bill.

Hers was a sad case, but it was not unusual. Immigrants of any race or ethnicity, who found themselves alone or alienated in America, often turned to or became the victims of crime, poverty or disease. Every day Ellis Island processed immigrants for deportation or return to their home countries. Most of the sick or destitute immigrants had arrived within the year. Deportations could be charged to the steamship companies, while "returns" were usually charged to the government's "immigrant fund." Not everyone found a good life in America.

Conclusion

Six days a week, all day long, families marched through Ellis Island toward a new life in the United States. Many of these were extended families, including parents, children, uncles, aunts and cousins. They usually came to join relatives already here, and would soon be followed by yet more relatives who would come to join them. Each wave of family immigration did not consist of a traditional nuclear family—a father, mother and their children. Migrant parties might be assembled from a variety of friends and relatives who would travel to America together, eventually reconstituting their family groups in their new home. Thus, many immigrant children did not arrive with both or even one of their parents. Many immigrant children arrived with an aunt and/or uncle, or an older sibling and his or her spouse.

In most cases, officials took no notice of these children. A couple with their two children and one nephew in tow claimed all three, and the inspector had no cause

---

[2] Unfortunately, even after the Bureau of Immigration canceled the bond requirement, Mendel Zuser battled the bond-holding insurance company until 1925, when the bond finally expired.

to doubt they were a family of five. Thus, the nephew immigrated with his uncle's surname and might be lost forever in the immigration passenger list records. If the passenger list identified the child as a nephew, and he was not traveling to join his parents in the United States, he might have also appeared before the Board of Special Inquiry like Wilhelmina and Anna Jentjes. And if the Jentjes sisters had looked like the Zusers, they might have marched through Ellis Island without a second glance from Samuel Littman, the immigration authorities or anyone else.

Records Used

Passenger and Crew Lists of Vessels Arriving at New York, NY, 1897–1957. National Archives microfilm publication T715.

HIAS Arrival Index Cards. Microfilm from 1909 arranged by year of arrival, port of entry, then alphabetically by surname. Ports of entry include (for different years) New York, Boston, Baltimore, Galveston, Philadelphia, Providence, San Francisco and Seattle. For 1940–64, they included Bradley Airfield (CT), Charleston, Gulfport, Laredo (TX), Miami, Mobile, New Orleans, Niagara Falls, Norfolk, Oswego, Portland, Rouses Point, Savannah and Wilmington (DE). Information includes: date of arrival, conveyance, names of all passengers traveling together, age, country of birth, sex, marital status, country of last residence, sponsor and sponsor's address. Some cards are illegible. Location: HIAS Headquarters, 333 7th Avenue, New York, NY 10001.

HIAS Ellis Island Records, 1905–23 (YIVO RG-245.2) include troublesome cases involving deportation, illness or detention requiring the services of the HIAS Ellis Island Bureau. These records consist of 26 rolls of microfilm, arranged alphabetically by name of person being detained or about to be deported. Location: YIVO Institute for Jewish Research, 15 W 16th Street, New York, NY 10011.

INS Subject Correspondence Files, 1906–56. Correspondence between INS headquarters and field offices, and between INS and other government agencies and with the public, concerning appeal cases; investigations; warrants; and other legal, policy and administrative matters. The estimated volume is ca. 750,000 files. The only available index (NARA microfilm T458) is by subject, not by name. Some HIAS files (above) will reveal an INS Subject File number. Location: National Archives, Washington, DC, Record Group 85, Entry 9.

Valery Bazarov is the Director of the Location and Family History Service at the Hebrew Immigrant Aid Society (HIAS) in New York City. Marian L. Smith, the former INS Historian, is now with U.S. Citizenship and Immigration Services (CIS), part of the Department of Homeland Security, in Washington, DC. Her writings do not necessarily represent the views of U.S. Citizenship and Immigration Services or of any other agency of the United States government.

Yes, Virginia, There Was a Sean Ferguson
by Gary Mokotoff

Winter 1989

What American Jewish genealogist has not heard the story of the poor-soul Jewish immigrant who wanted to change his name at Ellis Island and became so flustered when the immigrant officer asked his name, he blurted out in Yiddish *"Shayn fergessen"* (I already forgot). The immigrant officer dutifully recorded for eternity his new name, Sean Ferguson.

Is the story true, or is it the creation of some Borscht Belt comedian?

The answer is, there really was a Sean Ferguson...almost. The story is true...almost. AVOTAYNU tracked down what appears to be the origin of the famous story to a Syracuse, New York, attorney named Tracy Ferguson, the grandson of real Sean Ferguson, Samuel Forgotston.

According to Tracy, his grandfather, Samuel Forgotston, immigrated to the United States in the 1860s. He settled in upper New York State and either he, or one of his brothers, Americanized his name to Ferguson for some reason that has been lost in the history of the family.

In the mid-1930s, shortly after Tracy graduated Harvard Law School, he became active in raising funds for the Junior Division of the Joint Distribution Committee (JDC) by going around the country making speeches to various groups. His associates pointed out that his peculiarly non-Jewish name, Ferguson, might be a detriment to his fund raising ability. So Tracy turned disadvantage to advantage and invented a story.

He told his audience that his unusual name was derived in an unusual way. His grandfather, Samuel Forgotston, when he arrived at Ellis Island, in a moment of panic, blurted out to the immigration officer, *"Shayn fergessen"* to the question, "What is your name?"

The story brought gales of laughter from the audience, so Tracy continued to use it as a warm-up introduction to his appeal for JDC funds.

Tracy surmises that the story so caught the fancy of the public that it was passed from person to person until it became part of Jewish-American folklore.

People

Max
by Gary Mokotoff
Winter 1987

On January 25, 1985, an article appeared in the *Jewish Standard*, a northern New Jersey weekly, about my work in genealogy. Two days later, on a Sunday morning, I received a telephone call at home from a woman who identified herself only as Marilyn stating she saw the article in the newspaper. She was interested in knowing whether I was related to a man named Maximilian Mokotowski.

"Oh, you mean Max Mokotoff," I responded. "He's a cousin of my father, but we never talk about him, because we consider him the black sheep in the family."

"I can believe that," Marilyn replied.

I told Marilyn that I had never met Max but recalled that in my youth, in the late 1940s, my mother showed me an article in the New York *Daily News* about him. He had been indicted for embezzling the life savings of a woman to whom he claimed he was a very rich Polish count.

Marilyn confirmed the story; the woman was her mother.

She then related her version of the events. In 1949, when she was 10 years old, her divorced mother met Max and fell in love with him. Her mother's family was suspicious of Max, but her mother was a headstrong woman and insisted he was a good man. She married Max in 1950. A few months after the marriage, the family discovered that Max was a bigamist; he had never bothered to divorce his previous wife.

"They almost killed him," Marilyn said. "They beat him up and threw him down a flight of stairs."

In the conversation that followed, Marilyn mentioned that her mother became pregnant during her brief "marriage" to Max but miscarried. That statement triggered in my mind the recollection of a genealogical loose end in the Mokotoff family tree.

"Marilyn, I have news for you. I don't think your mother miscarried. I think she had the child, a boy, and put it up for adoption." I explained to her that Mokotoff is a unique name. As a consequence, about a year earlier, at the New York Public Library, I went through the annual birth indexes for New York City from 1905 to 1970, recording every Mokotoff born in the city. In 1950, I told her, there was an entry for "Male Mokot," born November 28. I recalled from the newspaper article that Mokot was one of Max's aliases.

Marilyn was dumfounded! "Gary, I am an only child and now you tell me that I have a brother."

Marilyn told me that her mother was dead, but she had aunts living in Florida who would certainly know if my theory was correct. I offered to make inquiries through my family. Another cousin of my father, a cardiologist living in Middletown, New York, had commented to me some years earlier that he thought Max might still be in prison. The hospital where he practiced served the prisons in the area, and a guard claimed that there was a Mokotoff at his institution.

I asked Marilyn to give me her telephone number so I could contact her in case I found out any information. She declined to give it to me stating that, if nothing came of the matter, she would rather remain anonymous. I respected her privacy and told her to call me at my office the following day (Monday).

That evening I called my father's cousin in Middletown, who confirmed the story he had related to me earlier. He wasn't sure which prison it was, but guessed it was Wallkill Correctional Facility. He would contact them.

Monday afternoon at 4 p.m. Marilyn called me. "Gary, the story is true. My mother did have a child that she gave up for adoption. I called my aunts and confronted them with your story. At first they denied it, but after pressuring them, they finally admitted it. Gary, how do I find my brother?"

I told Marilyn of an organization in New York that assisted adopted children looking for their birth families or persons trying to find adopted relatives. I had forgotten the name and offered to call the president of the Jewish Genealogical Society who would know the name of the group. If she still wanted to remain anonymous, she could call me the next day at my office. She chose to remain anonymous.

I called Steve Siegel, the JGS president, who informed me the name of the organization was ALMA.

On Tuesday, again at about 4 p.m., Marilyn called me, and I gave her the name of the organization.

"Now I have news for you," she commented. "Would you believe I know his last name. It's B_____." By interrogating her aunts further, Marilyn discovered that, while her mother had a tremendous revulsion for Max and did not want to keep his baby, she was compassionate enough to place the child for adoption privately through a lawyer. Apparently, she wanted to make sure the boy was given to a good Jewish family. Marilyn indicated that a rabbi from upper New York State may have adopted her brother.

I told Marilyn now that she knew a rabbi was involved and knew his last name, she could make inquiries through the rabbinic organizations to locate the man. I also told her that since we knew her brother's adopted surname, his date of birth and that he might live in New York State, I would do a check of the Department of Motor Vehicles (DMV) to see if a man with that description had a driver's license.

Tuesday evening at about 8 p.m. I called an uncle of mine (mother's side) who is on the New York City police force and asked him to do a DMV check for me.

Tuesday evening at about 9 p.m. the phone rang.

"Hello, Gary. This is Marilyn S_____."

"Who?"

"Marilyn S_____. You know, Marilyn."

"Marilyn," I exclaimed. "You told me your last name!"

"Yes, I know. Would you believe I found him? In fact, I just got off the telephone with him."

"Marilyn," I said. "Do you realize you just set the world's record for locating an adopted brother? Just two days ago you were an only child, now you have a brother."

Marilyn was elated. She determined her brother was adopted by a rabbi in Maine who was since dead, but the widow was still alive. She called the home and told the *rebbitzen* (rabbi's wife) that she was a friend of her son and asked for his telephone number. He lived in a suburb of New York, only 30 miles from where she lived.

That Saturday evening, Marilyn and her husband traveled to the home of her newly found brother and met him and his wife. Two weeks later I met Marilyn and her half brother for the first time at her home. At the end of the evening, I turned to my second cousin and told him he was a lucky man.

"Do you realize that if you are a success in life," I said, "people will say, 'What do you expect from the son of a rabbi?' If you turn out to be a failure, people will say, 'What do you expect from the son of Max Mokotoff?'"

Some weeks later, I was contacted by an official at Wallkill Correctional Facility who informed me there was no Max Mokotoff at the facility, and no person with that name was ever incarcerated there.

A week later, the official called me and embarrassingly stated that, indeed, Max did serve time, under a different name. More specifically, in 1950 he was sentenced to eight to ten years for obtaining money under false pretenses.

The man started reading from the file in front of him. Max had married six times between 1934–1957; four times consecutively and twice concurrently. It noted two children, Lawrence, in 1934 (I knew this from another cousin) and Marcia, in 1937 (a name in the New York birth index I never was able to identify). He was paroled after six years, and the last item in his file was an invitation to his sixth wedding.

Marilyn tried to develop a relationship with her brother, but he was cool to the idea. She invited him to a family gathering a few months after they met, but he declined. Although very interested in meeting Max, he shows little enthusiasm for fostering a brother-sister relationship at present.

Gary Mokotoff is publisher of AVOTAYNU.

Epilogue

The incident motivated me to find Max and his two other known children. His daughter, Marcia, was found easily through the wife of Max's half brother. She knew Marcia's phone number. Finding Max's eldest son, Lawrence, is a story worth another article in this book.

Veteran genealogists will tell you that sometimes you do not find answers to your family history; sometimes the answers find you. Martha Lev-Zion is president of the Jewish Genealogical Society of the Negev. She lives in a suburb of Beer Sheba, Israel. A neighbor of hers was Larry Daugherty. One evening, in 1998, Martha steered the social conversation toward genealogy and told Larry all the work she had done tracing her families' histories. Larry commented that he knew nothing about his family; that he was an only child. He said to Martha, "I was not born Larry Daugherty. That was the name of my stepfather who adopted me. I was born Lawrence Mokotoff." Martha immediately located a copy of AVO-TAYNU, pointed to my name in the masthead and said "If you are related to Gary Mokotoff, he can tell you all about your family history."

On December 21, 1998, I received my first e-mail from Larry asking if we were related. My response to him was "Are we related? Your name is Lawrence Mokotoff. You were born on June 18, 1934. Your father's name was Max Mokotoff and your mother's name was Mary Sears. I have been looking for you for 15 years. Oh yes, you have a half sister and half brother who live in the New York City area." Needless to say Larry was dumbfounded.

Larry had craved family all his life; now he had two siblings. His mother was still alive living in Brooklyn, so the next time he came to the U.S. he contacted Jonathan and Marcia and the three became close—primarily through the efforts of Larry.

What happened to Max? I spent 11 years trying to locate Max. I was even able to get his military records from World War II. Private Mokotoff was dishonorably discharged from the service. The reason is part of his military records.

> *Specification 1: ...unlawfully pretend[ed] to said Florence Butcher that he was un-married and would marry her...and by means thereof did fraudulently obtain from the said Florence Butcher, the sum of $40.00.*
>
> *Specification 2: ...did wrongfully, unlawfully and feloniously marry one Pauline Rosenberg, he, the said Private Mokotoff, having at that time a lawful wife, living to wit, Lillian Mokotoff...*

He was sentenced to seven years hard labor.

Max died on 24 September 1996 in Jersey City, New Jersey, just about 30 miles from where I live. Even in death he was up to no good. He died destitute in a Jewish nursing home. After his death, his daughter Marcia received a phone call from the home and was informed that, since she was the only known next of kin, she would have to pay for Max's funeral. Marcia refused stating she had met her father only once in her adult life, and it was not a pleasant experience. The home relented and paid for the funeral. Marcia attended, as she told me, so she could have closure. His obituary, printed in the *Jewish Standard* on 4 October 1996, from information apparently provided by the nursing home, stated:

Maxwell Mokat, 84, of Jersey City, died Sept. 24. Born in New York City, he was a self-employed attorney before retiring in 1974. He was an Army veteran of World War II.

Tracings of an Unlucky Man
by Judith Saul Stix

Winter 1991

The purposes of the Ladies Hebrew Benevolent Society of Columbia City, Indiana, were spelled out when it was founded in 1874: "To assist the neety and help does in distress [sic]." The membership was never more than 10, and dues were on the order of 25 to 50 cents a month. My great-grandmother, Caroline Schloss Lipka, came from the same circles as the ladies, among them her cousin by marriage, Hattie Mier. Far from being a member of the club, Caroline and her husband Nathan were objects of its charity.

In September 1877, the society had $11 in its treasury. On October 24, 1877, the minutes include this notation, "Paid Lipke $2.25." (Variations in the spelling of this name are the rule, not the exception. I take the numerous spellings as an indication that Nathan and Caroline were illiterate in English and spoke it poorly.) The lists of amounts headed "Paid to Poor" include such disbursements as 75¢, $2.25 and $2.75. The only name listed on that occasion is that of Lipke. To illus-

trate the magnitude of the amounts paid out, the society another time gave "to a poor woman, $1; to the same for lodging and breakfast, 50¢."

The ladies may also have bought goods from Lipka, who almost certainly was a peddler. One page shows a February 1879 entry "O[r]der (?) of Libky, $15." Earlier, the ladies had bought yard goods, silk, wool and cashmere totaling $24. The payment to Lipka may have been a comparable expenditure.

On January 10, 1880, the minutes show the budget. At the top of the list is "Paid out as to order." The first two items are to "N. Libky." Each is identified by a word in parentheses. The first seems to be "Band"; the second, difficult to read, may be "Poor," or may be "Prov" [provisions?]. The two items total $15. Following that are five items under the heading, "To Poor," and the fourth has the additional notation "Lipky." The payment was $1.25.

These five entries are the only ones that mention Nathan Lipka, who is undoubtedly the man referred to. He and Caroline were married in New York City in 1876. Their two daughters were born in Columbia City in 1877/8 and 1879. The family moved to Cincinnati in 1880, where they were recorded by the U.S. Census in June of that year.

Nathan died in 1891 and Caroline four years later. They were buried in the "Old Ground" of the Walnut Hills Jewish Cemetery in Cincinnati. Their two stones, a few rows apart, are the smallest and poorest in the cemetery and are almost illegible. The thin limestone slabs have "Nathan Lipka" inscribed along the top edge of his, "Mother" in the same place on hers. Seeing these stones moved me, their senior descendant, deeply. The stones conveyed as nothing else could that Caroline and Nathan were among those immigrants who did not find in America fabulous luck and streets paved with gold.

It was the day after visiting their graves that I found the pathetic record of the charity meted out to them on a microfilm at the American Jewish Archives in Cincinnatti.

Nathan Lipka seems to have been unlucky all his life. He was born in the small town of Graetz bei Posen, Prussia, present-day Poznań, Poland, in 1824. When he was 11 years old, he and his older siblings, Rachel and Elias, were orphaned, as first their father and then their mother died within a few months. Nothing is known of their lives until Nathan appears in the New York City directories of the 1860s and early 1870s. During those years, he was a peddler, a porter, a seller of slippers and an undertaker. During this time he became a U.S. citizen.

When he and Caroline were married, he was 51 years old. The record shows that he had been married before. Nothing is known of his first marriage, whether he was widowed before coming to America or whether he might have had an earlier set of children. Caroline was 38 when they were married; she had not been married before.

Their daughters, Belle and Hattie, both died in Baltimore, Maryland. Death certificates show that they were born in "Columbia, Indiana" and "Columbia City, Indiana" in the latter 1870s, several years before vital records were kept in Indiana. The charity records and purchases from Nathan Lipka in the Benevolent Society minutes dovetail neatly with the previously known dates.

After he moved from Columbia City to Cincinnati, Nathan continued to work as a peddler. The family lived on Fifth Street, sharing a duplex with the family of a mulatto whitewasher. Then they moved to Sixth Street, where they lived either in the very busy market block or the next block west of it. (Although far more affluent, my husband's ancestors lived nearby on West Fourth Street. All of their houses have vanished.)

Writing a century after Nathan's death, I contemplate how very nearly all knowledge of his fate, and even his name, were lost. Left to me by my mother (his granddaughter) was the half right mention of his name, as "Isaac Lipke," in a family tree that she wrote down when I was born—and which, after five years of research, I now know contained numerous other errors.

My mother thought that Nathan's wife's name was Karen and that she had been born in Ligonier, Indiana; both of these pieces of information now have been proven wrong. When I found my great-grandmother's family, they did in fact have many roots in Ligonier, which is about 25 miles from Columbia City. I also found an extensive family tree that had been prepared by a cousin, Jim Ackerman, but the Lipkas and their descendants had fallen off the tree and been forgotten.

Caroline's birth in Lindenshied, Hunsruck, Germany, in 1838 and her membership in the Schloss/Stiefel family have been established definitively through civil records obtained from Germany.

Still alive is a second cousin, Estelle Greenberg, who had known my mother in Baltimore and who knew part of the story of my grandmother's early death, a few days after my mother's birth. Although Estelle did not know the names of Nathan or Caroline, she did know that their two daughters had come to Baltimore from Cincinnati to live with their aunt, Johanna Schloss Frank, Estelle's grandmother. It was Estelle who told me that they spelled their name "Lipka."

With that much to go on, I quickly found Nathan and later Caroline, widow of Nathan, in Cincinnati directories from 1880 to 1895. Soon the implied dates could be confirmed by their death certificates. Their grave sites were located on the second try by the cemetery, where the name had been read in cemetery records as "Libza."

Finding them in the 1880 census was difficult because they were recorded as the family of "Emil Lipker," the final "r" putting them into the wrong soundex category. The address, however, was confirmed as correct by the city directory listing for Nathan Lipka.

Perhaps it is possible to think that in his descendant's finding these faint footsteps of his wandering life, Nathan had had a bit of luck after all. Surely, it was nothing but luck that made me look for him in New York City directories, for there had been nothing to indicate that he had ever lived there. His constantly misspelled name became almost a confirmation in itself.

Finding him in New York led to locating his citizenship papers (under the name "Lippko") and the marriage record. I had sought the latter intensively in Indiana where Caroline had had numerous relatives and where their children had been born. The excellent New York marriage record, unlike those in Indiana, provided Nathan's birthplace, his parents' names as Simon and Theresa and the fact that he had been married before.

Again, our luck—his and mine—held. From a microfilm borrowed from the Mormon Library, I was able to read one document from Graetz bei Posen, the town where he was born. It was a record of Jewish deaths in the town in the early

19th century. Strangely, only the right-hand pages of the book had been filmed, giving the names of the survivors of each deceased person listed. The left-hand pages, presumably with the names of the deceased individuals and other information about them, were not there. It had not been possible to locate the original record book. [When using the LDS German vital records films, readers should always look through the whole microfilm. Some books were filmed in a sequence where all left (or right) pages were filmed first and then the book was turned and the facing pages were filmed—Ed.]

The Graetz death records, in which the name is consistently spelled "Lipke," enabled me to learn that my great-great-grandparents were Simon and Treina Lipke and that Treina's maiden name was Jacob. From one step further back into the mists of time, her mother's name appeared, Genendel Jacob, and his mother's name, Rachel Lipke.

Everything that I have learned about my great-grandparents indicates that they were among the poorest of the poor in their lives in America. In addition, one can guess that Nathan, who was orphaned at the age of 11, must have had a very hard struggle even before he came to America. Now his dozen heirs can honor his memory and place their pebbles on his humble gravestone, as I did a century after his death.

Judith Saul Stix is a poet and biographer who lives in St. Louis, Missouri. Until she began her genealogical research, she thought that she was 100% Litvak; now she knows that she is one-quarter German Jew.

Grandpa Didn't Tell the Truth
by Sallyann Amdur Sack

Winter 2002

A well-known passage from the musical play *Fiddler on the Roof* illustrates how 19th-century Russian Jews felt about the czar:

Rebbe, is there a blessing for the czar?

A blessing for the czar? Of course....

May the Lord bless and keep the czar—far away from us!

Techniques that our ancestors used to escape detection by the Russian government are legend. Old habits die hard; apparently some of them even carried over into the new country following emigration.

My mother's father was my only grandparent still living when I was growing up. I knew that his name was Benny Steinsnider and that he had come to the United States from Poland while a very young man. When I started to trace my genealogy, Grandpa told me that he had come from a place called Plotsk (Płock, in Polish) and had gone first to Toronto, Canada, where he married and where my mother had been born. From his marriage record at Holy Blossom Synagogue in Toronto, I learned that his real name was Wolf Baer Steinsnider. Then I discovered that Grandpa had taken out citizenship in both Canada and the U.S.— but had told different stories about where he had been born. His Canadian naturalization papers recorded Łódź as his birth place. His youngest brother, Sam, by then living in a nursing home and reportedly not a reliable source ("You can't believe anything Sam says," Grandpa explained), insisted that the family had come from "Vishkovo"—a place I couldn't find. The U.S. citizenship application said Plotsk.

One day, I took myself to Miami to interview my by-then very deaf, 90-some-year-old grandfather again. Out of the blue, he suddenly announced, "Ya know, the name isn't really Steinsnider." Doing a double take, I demanded to know what he meant. The dialogue went something like this:

"It's Dubner," he proclaimed.

"I never heard that," I protested, "and neither has my mother or any of her brothers or sisters."

"Don't you remember I told you that I was running away from the czar's army?" Grandpa demanded.

"Yes, yes, I remember, I remember. You told me that—with a loaf of pumpernickel under your arm. You told me many times. So what?" I wanted to know.

"Well, I bought papers from a guy named Steinsnider!" the old man announced in an isn't-it-obvious tone.

"But Grandpa, that was 1905; this is 1979; how come you never told?" I spluttered, as I thought that he might have died and I would have been fruitlessly chasing Steinsnider.

Waving a bony finger under my nose, my grandfather fixed me with a stern eye and triumphantly announced, "Ya never know!"

"Ya never know" has sent many Jewish genealogists down false trails.

You might think that was the end of the story. Oh, no. This canny immigrant really didn't trust government officials—or his family either, apparently. Remember, he wrote Łódź as his birthplace in Canada and Plotsk in the U.S.—but he told me Plotsk. Certain that he would not lie to his eldest grandchild, I figured that I now knew his real name and his real birth place, the two indispensable bits of data without which no one can search for records across the ocean. The knowledge didn't help me much at that time, though. Poland was still a communist country, the Mormons had not filmed Jewish records from Plotsk, and I couldn't find a way to get the records I wanted.

Some years later, I came to know Jerzy Skowronek, the late Polish State archivist, who offered to look for records of my Dubner relatives in Plotsk. After an impatient wait of two or three months, a letter arrived from Skowronek. It began, "Dear Madame, I regret to tell you that there is no evidence that anyone named Dubner ever lived in Plotsk."

Benny had done it again. Favorite granddaughter or not, Grandpa had lied once more. By then Benny had died—and he had taken to his grave the secret of where he actually had been born. Back to square one—until I was rescued by the wonderful Jewish genealogical network.

Do you remember a best seller named *Turbulent Souls*, written by a young man from Upstate New York named Stephen Dubner? He wrote about having grown up Catholic, the son of parents who had been born Jews and converted.

Sometime before the book appeared, Stephen Dubner telephoned and introduced himself. He was planning a research trip to his grandparents' birthplace in Poland. Steven Siegel from the New York-based Jewish Genealogical Society told Dubner that I also was researching Dubners and suggested that he speak to me.

"Where in Poland are you going?" I asked.

"Pultusk," he replied—and a thousand-watt bulb went off in my head.

Plotsk—Pultusk; they don't sound very much alike, at least not to my ears, but if you look carefully, you see that the consonants are exactly the same: PLTSK! Could my grandfather have been born in Pultusk? Discouraged about ever tracing Benny, I had never bothered to look at JRI-Poland lists. I did now and saw that, indeed, lots of Dubners lived in Pultusk. And what about "Vishkovo, " the place Grandpa's unreliable brother Sam insisted was the family's home? A short distance down the road from Pultusk is Wyszków, also with many Dubners. In fact, Fond 98, *akt* (document) 16 shows the birth in 1885 of one Wulf Dubner—the exact year of birth that Grandpa listed on all of his records. Wulf Dubner from Wyszków, aka Benny Steinsnider from Lodz or Plotsk—I had found his trail at last.

Sallyann Amdur Sack is editor of AVOTAYNU.

Three Cousins
by Gladys Steinfeld Krongelb

Winter 1990

How could I have imagined on that spring afternoon in 1982 that the information I was about to receive would launch me on an exciting voyage of discovery? My adventure began in the parlor of my cousin Julia's apartment in New York City where my husband and I sat taping stories that Julia was relating about my dad's family.

Dad and his five older siblings were born in Bucharest, Romania, to Joseph and Elisa (née Feldman) Steinfeld. My cousins and I had been fed fragmented, unrelated tidbits about the family's life in Bucharest. Grandpa had been a tailor, grandma a seamstress. One of grandma's sisters had sewn fancy dresses at the Royal Court. My grandmother's family had come from Turkey originally; my father's oldest brother had fled military conscription; the family name Steinfeld may have been Gherman originally.

In 1910, the last members of the immediate family landed at Ellis Island. My father was then 10 years old. One brother sought his fortune in Indiana. The rest of the family settled in Jersey City, New Jersey, except for Fanny, the oldest and only sister, who remained in New York.

On that fateful spring afternoon, Julia, who was sharing some family treasures with us, had just finished telling about her stepmother Fanny's schooling in a convent near Bucharest. Reportedly, the education offered there was far superior to the one available to girls in the public schools, and Fanny had not been required to attend religious courses or services.

"Look what I have for your collection," Julia announced, pulling out three photographs from an envelope. The first, marked "Romania, Januarie 1949," was a snapshot of four people.

"Who are they?" I asked. None of the faces in the picture was familiar to me.

"Don't you know?" Julia queried. Pointing to a gray-haired woman, she explained, "This is your grandfather's sister, Ana. And this is her son, her daughter-in-law and her granddaughter." The latter appeared to be about ten years old.

"Grandpa's sister?" I inquired excitedly. "Wasn't Grandpa an only child? No one ever talked of family in Europe."

"It has been so many years since I've thought of them," Julia sighed. "A few days ago I was looking over some of Fan's things that I have kept and I found these photographs."

"Are any of those people still alive?" I questioned.

"I don't know. Fan and I sent CARE packages to them after the war. Over the years we lost contact. I don't have any more information." Sadly, Julia added, "I can't even remember their last name."

| Antoinette | Olga | Gladys |

Seeing the look of disappointment on my face, Julia hastened to add, "Maybe these two pictures will help. They're of Ana's daughter, Hermine Klarreich, and her family." The first, taken in Romania and dated 1935, was a stylishly posed photograph of two people whom Julia identified as Hermine and her young daughter, Antoinette. The second, snapped on a Warsaw street in the early 1940s, showed a teenaged Antoinette, wrapped in a warm coat, hat and fur muff, standing next to her father Leon.

"What can you tell me about them?" I asked, encouraged that at least their last name was known.

"Leon Klarreich was a Polish citizen," Julia replied. "In the early 1940s, he was deported by the Romanian government. For some reason Antoinette went with him. I was told that they were both killed in the Holocaust. I don't know what happened to Hermine."

My appetite had been whetted. I determined to search for more information about my two newly discovered cousins, Antoinette Klarreich and the young girl (Ana's granddaughter) in the 1949 photograph. The first course of action would be to try to find that girl who might still be alive, but with only a 30-year-old snapshot and the one name "Ana" how was I to find her?

During the next few weeks, I looked through the information I had already acquired about Grandpa. The passenger list for the Hamburg Line's *Kaiserin Auguste Victoria* on which Grandpa had arrived at Ellis Island on September 26, 1910, provided the most promising lead. The relevant entry beside his name was in the column headed, "The name and complete address of nearest relative or friend in country whence alien came." Grandpa's answer was "bi/lw Daniel Alter, Bukarest." I had seen this entry before, but had assumed that Daniel Alter had been married to one of Grandma's sisters and that he had remained in Europe. Now I wondered, could this be Ana's husband?

I wrote a letter of inquiry to all Alters listed in the most recent Bucharest telephone directory available in the New York Public Library. One person answered.

Mrs. Mendel Alter replied that no one in her husband's family either recognized anyone in the pictures of Ana's family or knew of a Daniel Alter. Her next step had been to telephone the Jewish Federation about my questions. They had given her information about three Alter families, all unrelated to her husband. She had invited them to her home. Mrs. Alter was sorry to tell me that none of them could provide any information. The friendliness and concern with which she had treated my request were echoed in her closing remarks (translated from the Romanian).

...if you are going to come to our country we would enjoy it if you would visit us and we would consider you as relatives. Although we do not know your language, we could find a way with a little bit of Yiddish.

Neither further perusal of Grandpa's memorabilia nor talks with cousins suggested any other path for exploration. Almost two years passed before I resumed the search for Ana's family. In May 1984, my husband and I attended the first International Seminar on Jewish Genealogy in Jerusalem. One of the sites visited was Yad Vashem, a complex erected in 1957 on Har Hazikaron in Jerusalem in memory of the six million Jewish victims of the Holocaust. In its Hall of Names are housed records of the martyred, registered on memorial pages from testimonies of relatives and friends. Although the files were then in the process of being microfilmed, seminar participants had access to any records that were readily available.

Focusing on the information that Julia had supplied, we searched for the name Klarreich and found a large stack of testimonies signed by a Kalman Klarreich. The page for Ana's son-in-law was among them. It included the following information: "Klarreich, Leon; relationship-brother; place of birth-Poland; minor children killed-Antoinette Chana, age 15." No place or time of death was entered. The testimony was dated 15.4.56 and showed Kalman's Haifa address.

To determine if the Kalman Klarreich listed in the current Haifa telephone directory was the same person as the one at the 1956 address, we consulted Batya Unterschatz at the Jewish Agency Search Bureau for Missing Relatives in Jerusalem. Batya is a remarkable lady who runs a one-woman office and has access to a variety of records for Israeli residents. She confirmed that this was the same Kalman Klarreich. There was no answer to our repeated telephone calls to him from Jerusalem. On our arrival in Haifa a week later, we called again. No answer. We went to his street and knocked at his ground-floor apartment door. Again, no answer. A couple living upstairs, hearing our knocks, invited us to their apartment.

Over a *glassele tey* (glass of tea) and freshly baked *mandelbrot*, they conversed with my husband and me in Yiddish. Kalman, they informed us regretfully, had died two months earlier. The closest relative they knew of was a cousin of Kalman's in Haifa, whom we contacted at their urging. He knew nothing about

Leon's fate, or whether Leon's wife, Hermine, was still alive. He could give us no new leads. We were disheartened that the only information we had obtained about the Leon Klarreich family was the stark confirmation of Leon's and Antoinette's deaths, handwritten on that single Page of Testimony at Yad Vashem.

Toward the end of our visit to Israel, we learned about a Romanian-language newspaper, *Revista Mia*, printed in Tel Aviv. We inserted a notice in this newspaper relating all the information we had about Ana's family. We never received a single reply. Our three tries at finding living relatives of Ana's had failed. Wasn't it time for our luck to change?

About six months after we returned home from Israel, we placed a second inquiry in *Revista Mia*, this time including a copy of the 1949 photograph of Ana's family. Months passed. We had almost given up hope when a letter came from Israel. The writer identified herself as the sister of the younger woman in the picture, Ana's daughter-in-law. The daughter-in-law's name was Belina Rosenfeld, and she was still living in Bucharest with her daughter, Olga Solomon, the young girl in the picture!

I sent Belina's sister the information we had received from Julia plus some facts about Grandpa's descendants and asked her to relay them to her niece, Olga. I did not know if Olga, a stranger to me and a resident of a Communist country, would want to be contacted by me directly. After what seemed like an interminable wait, I received a reply from Olga. It had been almost three years since I had first learned of her existence. The letter read in part (translated from Romanian):

> *Dear Mrs. Gladys,*
>
> *...I had a pleasant surprise to read in the letter I received from my aunt in Israel that somebody asked about us through an Israeli newspaper....We would be very glad if you would write us directly. I would like to know how is Aunt Fanny and Julia?...My grandmother, Ana Rosenfeld, died in 1957 and my father in 1983. Thank you for thinking of me. I am married and have a twelve-year-old son. We are well and eagerly awaiting the answer to this letter....*
>
> *Affectionately and with love, Olga"*

I had found my cousin! And she too was excited that we had made contact.

In subsequent letters, which she insisted on writing in English for practice, Olga answered some of my questions. Yes, she thought she remembered Fanny's CARE packages; no, she did not know a Daniel Alter; no, her family had not been able to find out the whereabouts of her father's sister, Hermine Klarreich. She informed me that the family's original name had been Gherman, not Steinfeld. I had not mentioned Gherman in any of my letters to her. Olga's statement corroborated both the rumor that had been passed around among my American relatives as well as the fact that Olga was indeed my long-lost cousin. Only a relative would know that surname.

Olga also sent a family chart on which she provided astounding information.

While, indeed, Ana was Grandpa's younger sister, there had been six siblings in between. Most of their descendants had made *aliyah* (immigration) to Israel. Grandpa's small family here in America had suddenly expanded to include a huge *mishpacha* (family) in Israel.

After writing this story, I sat back to reflect upon the fates of three girls growing up during the Holocaust: Olga, Antoinette and me. By the luck of the draw, two survived; the third became a statistic in one of man's most horrible experiences. Olga was too young to remember much, but as Jews in Romania, her family had been lucky to remain alive. Some of my recollections, those of a little girl living in a country physically far removed from the war, were as follows: savings stamps and food ration stamps, knitted squares for soldiers' blankets, air raid drills, articles that I clipped out of the newspapers about Allied victories, letters to my older cousins in the Armed Services. As for Antoinette, all I had to speak for her were photographs and a Page of Testimony.

My brief encounter with her life had moved me deeply and inspired me to compose the following:

> *I stare at your frozen image*
> *Cousin I'll never meet.*
> *Wrapp'd snugly in winter garb,*
> *You pose on a Warsaw street*
> *Smiling, so innocent*
> *Of the fate in store—*
> *Snuff'd out ere womanhood,*
> *Soon to be no more.*

Over the years I have continued to correspond with Olga and with two other cousins to whom she introduced me. In the fall of 1987, Olga sent me a jubilant letter from Israel, written in Romanian this time, to be sure that she would be understood. It included the following declaration, again from translation, "My family and I have made *aliyah*. Now I can write to you whatever I please. I am a free person in a free land."

I was so excited that I telephoned her at her absorption center and spoke with the aid of a friend who is my Romanian translator. After a brief conversation with him, Olga insisted on speaking with me personally, in English. We had a short, emotion-packed encounter. It was, and continues to be, one of the highlights of my life.

Gladys Steinfeld Krongelb pursued genealogical research with her husband, Sol, since the late 1970s with the hope that her grandchildren would one day enjoy the fruit of their grandparents' labors. She lived in suburban New York and died in 2004.

Three Benzions, Three Normans
And the Devastation of World War II
by Michael Richman

Winter 2005

Two of my great-great-grandfathers, Benzion Pargamanik and Neach Leyb Rycher, died during the second decade of the 20th century. As a result, three grandsons who were named for each during the 1910s and early 1920s came of age just before or during World War II. Here is the story of how that war affected each of their lives.

Benzion Pargamanik was a grain merchant who lived most of his life in Belaya Tserkov. Like the rest of the Jewish community of Ukraine, he suffered through the major pogroms of 1905, which prompted his eldest son, my great-grandfather, to leave Russia and another son to leave a few years later. Sometime between 1906 and 1910, Benzion moved to Kiev, where he died on Erev Rosh Ha-Shanah, 1913. We know this because his death was reported in a letter dated September 22, 1913, from my great-grandfather's brothers who remained in Russia. He appears in the Duma list of 1906 as living in Belaya Tserkov; in a 1910 letter to a niece he gives a Kiev address.

The first grandson named for Benzion was born in December 1913 in Belaya Tserkov. This grandson, also Benzion Pargamanik, grew up in the town and went to work on a collective farm, driving and maintaining tractors. The second grandson, Benjamin Pargh, was born in New York City in May 1919. Growing up during the Great Depression, he joined the Civilian Conservation Corps, one of the government programs designed to train workers and provide employment, where he learned to work with machines. The third grandson, Bernard Pargh, was born in Oklahoma in 1920. His father's business failed during the Great Depression of the 1930s, which resulted in his family moving to be closer to his mother's family in Nashville, Tennessee.

Benjamin Pargh and Bernard Pargh probably met at one time or another while growing up, because their fathers kept in touch. At some point, the two American brothers lost contact with their brother in Ukraine, so Benjamin and Bernard never met and possibly were not even aware of their cousin Benzion. (I only learned about their cousin Benzion a year and a half ago from Benzion's grandson, who emigrated from Ukraine to the United States five years ago and found me through the JewishGen Family Finder.)

Neach Leyb Rycher was born in Śniadowo, Poland, in 1858. In the mid-1880s, he moved to the nearby larger town of Ostrów Mazowiecka, where his wife's family lived. His family and his wife's sister's family ran a bakery, which

Benzion Pargamanik   *Benjamin Pargh*   *Bernard Pargh*

gave them access to food and enabled them to survive World War I. Neach Leyb died about 1919.

The first grandson named for Neach Leyb was another Neach Leyb Rycher, born in Ostrów Mazowiecka in May 1920. He immigrated to New York at age eight, taking the name Norman Richman. The second grandson was Neach Leyb Wajnkranc, born in Ostrów Mazowiecka in 1922. Although his father went to Cuba, he, his mother and his sister remained in Poland. The third grandson was Norman Wertel, born in the Bronx in 1925. Norman Wertel knew his cousin Norman Richman growing up, but never met his cousin Neach Leyb Wajnkranc.

World War II

Then came World War II.

Benzion Pargamanik of Ukraine, having experience working with tractors, was drafted to serve in the Soviet army tank corps. He died in a tank battle before the age of 30. His wife and two children, who had fled from Belaya Tserkov and spent the war moving from town to town trying their best to survive in central and southern USSR, were never able to learn the details of his death. What I do know comes from Benzion's grandson who now lives in Baltimore, Maryland. Meeting him and learning the family story prompted me to write this article.

Bernard Pargh joined the U.S. Army Air Corps and served as a navigator on a bomber. He survived the war in Europe, despite having to escape from behind enemy lines after his plane was shot down. When his airplane was returning to the United States, however, it crashed in bad weather over Scotland, and he died at age 24.

Benjamin Pargh served in the U.S. Army. Because of his experience working with machinery, he became a tank mechanic, like his cousin Benzion. He fought in the Battle of the Bulge. Unlike his cousins, he survived the war. He was involved in the liberation of the concentration camps and for many years carried pictures with him to show people that the Holocaust had really happened. He died in 1984, survived by his wife, daughter and two grandchildren.

Norman Richman and Norman Wertel both served in the U.S. Army during World War II. Norman Wertel, age 19, died in combat in Belgium in January 1945, in the aftermath of the Battle of the Bulge. Norman Richman survived the war, but was permanently affected by it and ultimately ended up in a psychiatric hospital. He died in 1981.

Their cousin, Neach Leyb Wajnkranc, his mother and sister perished in the Holocaust in Poland. I have been unable to learn the details of their fate.

These stories are a stark illustration of the effects of World War II on a whole generation, using six examples spread over three countries and two continents. First cousins born in the 1910s and 1920s who grew up and made their way through difficult times—the Great Depression and the Stalinist regime in the USSR—had their lives irreversibly changed. Of the six individuals I have described, three perished in combat during the war, and one other, while he survived physically, was unable to lead a normal life in society. A fifth perished in the Holocaust. Only two of the six have surviving descendants today.

Norman Wertel

The casualty count among these cousins may be higher than that of many other Jewish families in the United States—my grandmother (the elder Benzion Pargamanik's granddaughter) had three other first cousins who served in the U.S. military and survived the war, and I am not aware of anyone who perished in my mother's family. But many Jewish families in Poland, like the Wajnkranc family, were never heard from again, and thousands of young men in the Soviet Union of the younger Benzion Pargamanik's age, Jewish and non-Jewish, perished during the four years of fighting with Nazi Germany. The juxtaposition of these U.S., Polish and Soviet relatives demonstrates the extent to which so many Jewish families were affected.

Michael Richman, an attorney in the Washington, DC, area, has been researching his family history since 1975. He has been a member of the Jewish Genealogy Society of Greater Washington since 1982 and also has been involved in the Suwalki-Lomza Interest Group and Jewish Records Indexing-Poland.

Leonard
by Gary Mokotoff
Winter 1988

Early in my research into the history of the Mokotow family, I located a fourth cousin living in Brighton, England. In the course of our correspondence, he related the following story of the Holocaust to me.

In 1937, while living in Portsmouth, my father received a cable from Berlin—a desperate plea. It was from his cousins, the German Mokotows. "Please would you look after our 15-year-old son, Leonard." So Leonard Mokotow came to live with us in September 1937. When the war began in 1939, the government decided that enemy aliens had to live at least 20 miles from the coast. (Portsmouth is the largest naval port in the country.) Seventeen-year-old Leonard was, they decided, an enemy alien. My father arranged Jewish lodging and work in a large Jewish factory. The owners promised to look after Leonard. The location was in the outskirts of London.

On the 11th of September 1940, a German bomber miles off target discharged its bombs. They exploded on the shelter where my 18-year-old cousin was. He was buried in the West Ham cemetery in London. My parents were distraught. Leonard was an only child; his parents had entrusted him to their care.

We survived the war. In 1945, my father had a letter from Leonard's parents. They had escaped to Vichy, France, where they had been hidden by friends. They, too, had survived, but both were very sick. They wanted their son. All through the terrible war years, they at least felt happy that their son was safe.

Leonard Mokotow

My poor father had to tell them the truth. I believe they died shortly afterwards. My father had a stroke three years later, I am sure partly from this. The rest of his life was spent as an invalid until his death.

At the Seventh Summer Seminar on Jewish Genealogy held last June [1988] in Washington, DC, I heard that there were State department visa application records located at the National Archives. All records concern people denied permission to enter the United States. I sent a letter to the Archives asking for a list of all persons named Mokotow in their index. They replied with six entries. One read:

Leonard Mokotow, December 10, 1937

I stared at the listing and thought how different it would have been if they had let this teenage boy into the United States. But then, there are 5,999,999 other stories about the Holocaust.

Gary Mokotoff is publisher of AVOTAYNU.

Gustavo
by Chava Agmon

Winter 1989

My telephone rang one cold February morning this past year. On the line was a volunteer at the Dorot Genealogy Center at Beth Hatefutsoth in Tel Aviv. She informed me of a young man who had been referred to them as a possible source of help with a problem.

He was Gustavo Jose Caro from Buenos Aires, Argentina, age 22, who had spent a short time in Israel and had only a few days before returning home. The Dorot Center was unable to help him, but they thought of me and my close connection with the Caro family and its genealogy. We fixed a time to meet at my home on the same day.

I realized this was a rare case and planned the meeting carefully by preparing a list of documents, records and other historical data which he would have to see in order for him to make the best out of this short, but fateful, opportunity.

Over hot coffee and cake we got acquainted and, after dispelling his initial shyness, Gustavo told me what brought him to Israel. He comes from a Catholic family, originally of Granada, Spain, but he felt Jewish and at the age of 17 converted to Judaism in an orthodox conversion.

Gustavo finished high school, spent some years in England to learn the language and returned to Argentina. He came to Israel in the framework of a Jewish Agency program which includes spending time on a kibbutz and was referred to Beth Hatefutsoth because he wanted to search for his roots. Thus, he gently landed on my doorstep.

After a short introduction into the Jewish Caro history, no easy task as it includes Ashkenazim, Sephardim, Oriental Jews, and of course, Marranos, I proceeded to present Gustavo with the documents I had prepared and marked for him to read. From time to time I heard him whisper "fantastic, fantastic." There was one, very special letter which I kept for the end. After he finished reading that, he looked at me speechless.

The letter was from Jose Caro, professor of endocrinology at the South Carolina School of Medicine, in which he states having been proudly told by his father in Granada, Spain, of their connection to the famous Maran R. Joseph Caro of Toledo, Spain[1] (1488–1575), author of the *Shulchan Aruch*[2] and progenitor of the

---

[1] Since publishing this article, it has been determined that R. Joseph Caro was born in Zamora, Spain.
[2] The *Shulchan Aruch* is a codification (written catalog) of Jewish law and is considered one of the greatest of Jewish works.

family.

There was just not enough time for all the questions I wanted to ask Gustavo, because I felt that it was more important for him to read about what must have been the prime motivation for his visit to Israel, his search and the baring of his Jewish roots.

Chava Agmon was born in Germany and immigrated to Eretz Yisrael in 1936. At the time of her marriage, her mother gave her an old list, in German, of her Caro ancestry. Years later, she inherited the Gothic-script manuscript "Familien Chronik des Hauses Caro" (Family Chronicle of the Caro House) which initiated her genealogical trek.

Serendipity Answers
"Who Was Benny Ross?"
by Rick Liftig

Winter 2006

I suspect that, for most of us, the spark for genealogical research lights early in life. All four walls in one room of my parents' house were covered with pictures, but the sepia-toned icons of a hundred years ago looked nothing like real people. Although my ancestors looked young in these photographs, the poses, dress and hairstyles made them appear far older. Historical is the word that comes to mind.

One picture stood out, a publicity shot of a man named Benny Ross. Obviously, he was an ancestor of note, but I had never seen him at any family gatherings; none of my relatives called him on the phone. When asked about Benny, my mother would say, "He was a cousin of your grandfather's and played in vaudeville." My grandmother had little to say about Benny except for a brief, "Eh." We noticed that she frequently removed the photograph from the wall, only to find that my brother had replaced it several days later.

Benny resembled my grandfather; I had learned to recognize the profile from looking through old albums. For years, my brother commented that we should attempt to find Benny, but Benny lived in California, and I would have been unable to do research before the days of the Internet because I lived in Connecticut. With no leads and the likely futility of searching on the name "Benjamin Rosenberg" (the name before it was Ross), I didn't feel like knocking myself out.

Fast forward to the fall of 1997. The PBS American Masters Series produced a documentary entitled "Vaudeville," and I watched its premiere. Midway into the show, the title "Ross and Stone" appeared with the familiar profile. "That's Benny Ross!" I shrieked. To find an ancestor on paper is one thing, but actually to see this ancestor living, breathing and plying his craft was nothing short of miraculous. I had found a "famous" relative; what could be better for a genealogist?

That night I sent a letter to KCTS in Seattle, the station that had produced the series. Within three days, I received a call late on a Friday afternoon:

> *Hi, Mr. Liftig, I have some good news for you. We were hoping that someone would recognize a face in the program, and you were the first to contact us. We don't have much information here, but the gentleman who provided us with that video clip has more.*

This was the fabled moment that every genealogist hopes for. The golden egg has just landed in his lap, and the goose is whispering, "You ain't seen nothing yet." As promised, I was put in contact with Ron Hutchinson, whose brainchild,

Benny Ross and Maxine Stone taken from 1934 film.

"The Vitaphone Project," had re-united the film of Benny Ross and his wife Maxine Stone with its audio record for posterity. The project had started in 1991 and was resurrecting many of the early "talkies." Ron graciously sent more complete copies of the video he had along with his source information.

This remarkable stroke of luck led to the next discovery. Ross and Stone were the third act on the bill. In the vaudeville tradition, they were the headliners. With this fact in hand, my brother and niece visited the New York Public Library's Billy Rose Theater Collection at Lincoln Center. It took very little time to find a mother lode of clippings about Benny Ross and his wife Maxine Stone's career.

The proof of their fame was undeniable. Right next to such headliners as Count Basie, Kitty Carlisle and Henny Youngman were Ross and Stone. A headline from a London paper reported, "The Duke and Duchess of Kent Paid a Special Visit to See Them." They had played internationally and had enjoyed a long and success-ful career during the 1920s, 30s and 40s, but like many other vaudeville stars, the jump from the stage to film and television was difficult, and they were forgotten.

Like many genealogical stories, the trail suddenly grows cold here. Hints of fur-ther searches await. Even though the couple had no children, Maxine Stone's obituary noted two brothers and a sister; Benny Ross' obituary lists him as Robert Ross. In an early persona of Ben Rosenberg, he had created an act with a dancer named Maude Weaver—Maxine Stone's real name, perhaps? So like all of our explorations, these clues will get placed into that big database for me or maybe one of my descendants to ponder and follow.

A new joy has been found. I am beyond the collecting dead people phase of my genealogical searches. Now each ancestor has a life waiting to be fleshed out. Who was this person; why did they leave Europe? How am I like them? I suspect the answer to the last question has already been answered.

Rick Liftig became interested in genealogy 15 years ago when a friend asked, "Are you related to the Liftigs on the memorial at Beth El." Despite the rarity of his surname, he didn't know the people and had to find the answer. He says, "The rest is history."

I Never Heard My Grandmother Sing
by Harry D. Boonin
Winter 1987

Did she have a beautiful voice? My paternal grandmother Matle Boonin died in 1911, 25 years before I was born. She lived, died and is buried in Russia. My father was six years old when his mother died, so even if he had lived a long life, he could have related little to me of his mother. My father died when I was 10 years old, but one of my father's brothers, in the early 1940s, wrote a short history of the family. Describing his mother with love and affection he wrote:

> A song which was most impressive and full of sadness was the traditional song of the surrender of Jerusalem and the burning of the holy Temple by the Romans. Mother would put much feeling and expression into its interpretation and the sad memories which this song awakened in every Jewish heart.
>
> The dark bedroom where my mother was singing and the slow, monotonous, sound of the rocking cradle added much to the gloom of the song. Sometimes the rocking cradle would center on some loose boards of the floor, and its squeaking sound made an almost perfect imitation of the sound of a crackling and flaming wood fire.
>
> My own reaction and emotion to the above song can not now be described, because the details of that painful event were then fresh in my young mind through the study of the Bible, and its effect on me was so thorough that I could close my eyes and imagine visions of the flaming Temple.

Oh God, I too can hear the flames crackling.
I hear my grandmother singing in a language I do not understand.
The Temple burns.
The flames rise.
Get the men of the city. Put out the flames!
Everyone is running. Jerusalem burns.
Oh God, why have you burned your city—and the room is dark and warm.
And my grandmother sings.

And her notes are pure and true. And her words are soft, but strange.

I must get up. I must get up and go.

How long will the flames burn? How long will the ashes glow? How long will the ashes glow?

How can she sing so beautifully?

Where did my Grandmother learn so much? Who taught her?

Did she ever see the flaming Temple? Was she there?

I am getting sleepy.

But I must stay awake. I must listen! I must learn!

I must learn what Grandmother knows.

Surely her song will explain everything to me. I will know why the Temple was destroyed.

I will learn why the people were attacked by their God.

I will understand everything. But Grandmother must continue to sing.

Grandmother died and was buried in the cemetery on Zarettse Gasse.

And who visited her grave?

Her children, immigrants in an immigrant's world, left her.

Who said Kaddish? Who says Kaddish for the abandoned ones?

The Bolsheviks? The Mensheviks? The Bundists?
    The Communists?

And her grave became overgrown and neglected.

But the sweet birds sang above her in the Spring.

Oh, how she loved the birds.

They sang songs she would have loved to learn.

She was alone—and undisturbed.

The vines did not bother her.

The weeds lay moist and wet above her after a storm.

And there was always another sun.

And a song was in her heart—until June 22, 1941.

Strange noises were heard on Zarettse Gasse. Where is everyone running? What has happened?

What are those low rumbling noises?

And so many others now joined her. There wasn't room for everyone.

They all couldn't fit.

They would have to lay next to each other.

They would have to lay on top of each other.

How would one know where to stand to say Kaddish?

They were too close. Bones were getting mixed up.

...I must get going. I must.

There is music to learn. And songs to sing.

My heart is gay and cheerful. The sun shines. And I read books.
Many books.

I know words on a printed page.

But the pages do not sing.

And the room is comfortable, but not warm.

And I listen for a voice to sing to me.

I long for that voice to tell me how the Temple burned so many years ago.

But the voice has been stilled.

And the notes, the clear notes that for years brought sadness and tears and joy to
her children, are gone.

Harry D. Boonin is the founding president of the Jewish Genealogical Society of Philadelphia, author of The Jewish Quarter of Philadelphia and the recently published The Life and Times of Congregation Kesher Israel, a book about the immigrant synagogue in Philadelphia and the surrounding neighborhood.

The Last Mokotowski in Poland
by Gary Mokotoff

Winter 1998

For more than 150 years prior to the Holocaust, there were Jewish families named Mokotow or Mokotowski living in Poland, primarily in the Warsaw area. The Holocaust ended that. More than 400 descendants of my great-great-great-grandfather, Tobiasz Dawid Mokotow, were murdered in the early 1940s. Those who survived, no more than 30 of them, left Poland in the late 1940s during the anti-Semitic period that followed World War II.

Do any remain in Poland to this day? This was a question I wanted to answer. There were reports that women named Mokotow had remained and married, but an advertisement in the Warsaw Jewish newspaper seeking them out produced no results. A Chaim Mokotowski registered with the Jewish Agency in Chelm after the war, but I have never been able to locate him.

In 1990, a Polish professor published a book, *Slownik nazwisk wspolczesnie w Polsce uzywanych* (Dictionary of Surnames Currently Used in Poland), that listed all surnames in Poland, the frequency with which each name appeared, and the *wojewod* (county) in which the name appeared. The source was official government records. Not one person was named Mokotow, but remarkably there were two persons named Mokotowski—one in Łomża, the other in Gdańsk. A Polish-born friend recommended that I write a letter to the cities of Łomża and Gdańsk asking for additional information.

Within two months I received responses from both. Łomża claimed there was no person named Mokotowski living in its region. Gdańsk provided me with the name Ryszard Tadeusz Mokotowski of Gdynia, a suburb of Gdańsk.

Could this be a missing relative? A letter was sent to Ryszard with no response. My Polish-born friend wrote to her sister who lives in Gdańsk. She went to the apartment building in Gdynia to visit Ryszard. He was a man in his twenties who looked like a punk rocker. She mentioned the reason for her visit, but he was not interested.

I sent a second letter, which he finally answered. He disclosed he was a Polish Catholic who had assumed the name Mokotowski. Ryszard's real name was Germanic. His father had been abusive to him and to his mother. He came to hate his name, partly because of his father and partly because it was not Polish. He decided to acquire a Polish name and chose Mokotowski because of its association with the Polish capital of Warsaw. Mokotów is the southern district of Warsaw; therefore, Mokotowski meant "of Mokotów." The town name is the origin of my family surname.

Ryszard was concerned. He had not realized that Mokotowski was a Polish-

Jewish surname. He offered to change his name back to his original name, because he did not want to get in trouble with the authorities. I wrote back to him:

> *Thank you for your kind letter explaining how you acquired the name Mokotowski. Do not feel embarrassed or stupid about the name change. Please keep the name. I agree it is a fine Polish name; one that existed in Poland for nearly 200 years.*
>
> *As the only person named Mokotowski in all of Poland, if you have sons who will bear the name, perhaps 200 years from now, your descendants will be able to trace their ancestry to a man who once lived in Gdynia and changed his name from a German one to a fine Polish name.*

Gary Mokotoff is publisher of AVOTAYNU.

Family

The Vagaries of War
by Carol Davidson Baird

Winter 1993

My grandfather, Hugo Davidsohn, faithfully and diligently served the German Fatherland in World War I, as did about 100,000 other Jews. They represented 17 percent of the total troops in the German forces. At that time, Jews represented 1–2 percent of the total population. His role model was his father, Jakob, who served in the Franco-Prussian Wars in the Second Army Corps, 4th Division, 8th Infantry Brigade, 4th Pommeranian Troop Regiment No. 21, 1st Battalion (Conitz) from 1860 to 1895. I know all this because I have his military papers saved from the fires of the Holocaust, as were those of his son.

In fact, my grandfather actually served from 1910 until 1919. He, as well as most other Jews in the German military forces, remained faithful to their Judaism, as well as to their Fatherland. They conducted religious services on the front and even in foxholes. I have pictures of my grandfather celebrating Chanukah in the trenches and helping conduct a Passover *seder* while in the Somme region of France.

Hugo received the Iron Cross, Second Class in the field on July 20, 1916, while in the Reserve Infantry, Regiment 110, 9th Company. Of the 100,000 Jews in the German forces, 1,500 received the Iron Cross, First Class; 10,000 the Iron Cross, Second Class for bravery; about 12,000 lost their lives in the war. My maternal grandfather and two great-uncles also earned the Iron Cross.

Hugo Davidsohn

Two other military awards that Hugo Davidsohn earned are noteworthy because of their dates. The citation for the first reads:

> In the name of the Fuehrer and Reich's Chancellor, businessman Hugo Davidsohn of Stuttgart is awarded the Iron Cross for Front Line Combat by Reich's President Field Marshall von Hindenburg, based on an edict of July 13, 1934, in memory of the World War 1914/1919.

The other medal came with an official document stating that businessman Hugo Davidsohn of 37 Johannesstrasse, Stuttgart, is awarded the "wound stripe" in black (akin to the American Purple Heart given those wounded in battle) for army service, given in Stuttgart on May 18, 1936. What is amazing is that the wounded-in-battle document has the official Nazi stamp with swastika. Only two years later, that Nazi stamp appeared on Hugo's business closure documents, his arrest and deportation orders to Dachau the day after *Kristallnacht*, his eventual passport, and his revised birth and marriage certificates, to which had been added the name all German-Jewish males were required to carry—Israel.

The reason I have emphasized Hugo's military service is because that duty and his friendship with comrade-in-arms Heinrich Wicke is the reason my father's family survived the horrors of Nazi Germany.

Hugo married a young lady he met while stationed in Kassel, Germany. From the time of their marriage in 1920 until 1933, they always attended a yearly Christmas-time reunion of my grandfather's military regiment. My father recalls these parties well since he also was in attendance, and he remembers them as being "so much fun." They always had a raffle, and one year my grandparents won a rattan sofa and love seat. Jews and Christians partied, did business together and lived in harmony for the most part. In 1933, when Hitler came to power, Hugo's friend, Heinrich Wicke, approached him and said, "If you should ever need help, please come to me." There is a saying, "Hindsight is 20/20 vision." If my grandfather knew then what Wicke meant, as he later did, I am sure he might have tried to leave Germany immediately. In 1933, however, he still had his business, my father still was enrolled in school, they still went to synagogue every week and life was the same as for all other Germans suffering from the Depression.

The High Holy Days of 1938 proved to be a nervous time. My grandfather felt it unwise to leave the *shofar* (ram's horn) he blew in the synagogue, so he took it home with him until he could blow it again the following year. *Kristallnacht* came on November 9, 1938. There was no following year. The Stuttgart synagogue was burned to the ground. Also destroyed were my dad's and grandfather's prayer books, yarmulkes and top hats, prayer shawls, and most of all, their dreams. The *shofar* survived to be blown once again, a half century later, by Hugo's great-grandson, my son, Geoffrey Baird.

The following day, my father hid under his bed by order of his parents. The Nazis came to Hugo's apartment, put his hat on his head and led him to a truck in the street below. Wolfgang Amadeus Fackenheim—later known as William Frazer (the brother of Emil Fackenheim)—saved his life right then by giving him some bread to get him over a severe ulcer attack. Hugo was taken to a satellite camp of Dachau called Welzheim. What happened there I never knew; what happened after that was a miracle. What I learned last year was amazing.

Right after my grandfather was hauled off, my frightened little grandmother boarded a train alone and went to see Herr Heinrich Wicke in Heilbronn. After all, he had said to come to him if the Davidsohns ever needed help; now they did. She learned that he was the Police Commissioner of Heilbronn and went to plead

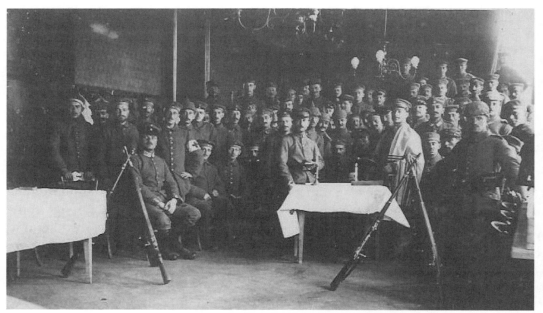

Hugo Davidsohn (standing center) conducting Passover services May 10, 1916, in Baupaume, France.

for her husband's release from Welzheim. Wicke listened and sent her home to wait.

After a month, Hugo returned to Stuttgart. He had been required to sign papers promising to leave Germany within six months. The family had, in fact, earlier applied for visas to leave, but had not yet received them. There they were, having to leave, but having no place to go. Then came papers officially ordering Hugo to close his business by December 31, 1938. Times were impossible; they were not allowed to shop, buy food, go to school or socialize. Visas came and Dad, age 17, left Germany alone, at midnight, crossing the Dutch border and vowing never to slink away from anything ever again. His parents left a month later and met their son in London, where they had to wait one year for visas to the United States.

In June 1992, my father returned to Stuttgart for a reunion of former Stuttgart Jews sponsored by the city and chaired by the mayor, Manfred Rommel, son of Field Marshall Erwin Rommel. My parents have always done genealogical work for me during their travels to Europe, so I asked Dad to find out about Herr Wicke, since no one ever knew what had become of him. I think Dad would have liked to thank his children if he had any.

The amazing part of this story is what my father learned. He was given a copy of a page in *Die Wuerttembergische Polizei im Dritten Reich* (Wuerttemberg Police in the Third Reich), published by the *Historisches Institute der Universitaet*

Stuttgart (Stuttgart Historical Institute) in 1989. This was a curriculum vitae for Wicke, Heinrich, *SS-Sturmbannfuehrer* (SS battalion commander), *Polizeidirektor* (police chief) in Heilbronn! Wicke was a member of the feared and hated SS! His birth, World War I military service and work at the Automobile Club in Stuttgart started off the summary. He entered the NSDAP (National Socialist Democratic Workers' Party) on September 1, 1930, and the SS on April 17, 1931. He became a *Sturmfuehrer* (company commander) in September 1934, *Obersturmfuehrer* (one degree above company commander) in November 1934 and *Sturmhauptfuehrer* (two degrees above company commander) in April 1935. By January 1936, he was *SS-Sturmbannfuehrer* and by September of that year was one step higher.

By September 1938, Wicke was *SS-Obersturmbannfuehrer* (regimental commander) and police chief of Heilbronn. From 1942 to 1945, he was *SS-Standartenfuehrer* (division commander) in Erfurt, and in 1945, was *SS-Oberfuehrer* (rank above division commander) and chief of police in Stuttgart. In 1947–48, he was incarcerated in Hohenasperg (a prison) and in March 1948 was sentenced to 600 days of special work detail.

After that, Wicke disappeared; no one knows the date or place of his death. He was childless after 40 years of marriage, and there are no known relatives. What is known about Herr Heinrich Wicke is that he helped more Jews than just my grandfather. Despite his membership in the SS, he repeatedly aided the escape of anti-Fascists and victims of the Nazi tyranny. In 1989, according to the Stuttgart city archivist, a Mrs. Oppenheimer from the United States spoke to him, suggesting that a tree be planted in Wicke's memory at Yad Vashem. According to the archivist, however, Yad Vashem considered it inappropriate to plant a tree in Israel in memory of a long-time, high-ranking member of the SS—despite his acts of righteousness.

Finding answers to our questions about Wicke only generated more questions. Was he a "righteous Gentile" playing a Nazi only to aid Jews? Did he have a guilty conscience? Or was he displaying loyalty to a former comrade-in-arms? Regardless of his motive, my family still is grateful for his help. I would not be here today, if not for him. Such are the vagaries of war.

References

For a city by city listing of German-Jewish military men killed in World War I, consult *Die Juedischen Gefallenen Des Deutschen Heeres, Der Deutschen Marine und Der Deutschen Schutztruppen 1914–1918, Ein Gedenkbuch* (Jewish Casualties in the German Army, German Navy, and the German National Guard 1914–1918, A Memorial Book), published by the Reichsbund Jüdischer Frontsoldaten in 1932. U.S. Library of Congress call number DS135 G33 R272. Each man is listed by name, birth date and place, date of death, service number, and rank and casualty report number. There is an index of names.

Chapters regarding Jews in the German military may be found in:

1. "Jews in the German Armed Forces," *Ashkenaz: The German Jewish Heritage*, 1986–87 exhibit at Yeshiva University Museum, ed. Gertrude Herschler, 1988. (U.S. Library of Congress call number: DS135 G3 A6 1988).

2. "The Jews During the First World War," in *The Jews in Germany From the Enlightenment to National Socialism*, by H.G. Adler, 1969 (U.S. Library of Congress call number DS135 G33 A293), University of Notre Dame Press.

Carol Davidson Baird, the only child of German Holocaust survivors, was past president of the San Diego Jewish Genealogical Society and North San Diego County Genealogical Society, lectured at International Association of Jewish Genealogical Societies and National Genealogical Society conferences, researches internationally, writes for genealogy journals and newsletters, and lectures in her community based on her 35 years of research experience.

Epilogue

The Germans did not exterminate Jews from 1933–1938. After the synagogues were burned on Kristallnacht, men were arrested and their wealth confiscated the following day. They were sent to labor concentration camps for the purpose of frightening them into leaving Germany. The Nazis' object at this point was to exert pressure on the Jews and their families to emigrate from Germany within the shortest possible time. Thus, in the winter of 1938–1939, 9,370 Jews were released after their families, as well as Jewish and international organizations, had made arrangements for their emigration. (My grandmother obtained sponsorship from cousins in London, where her family would wait one year until visas came for their emigration to Brooklyn under the sponsorship of other cousins.) When they would not or could not find places to emigrate, another plan needed to be devised and hence, The Final Solution.

Therefore, Herr Heinrich Wicke, the kind and helpful SS officer, actually knew in advance that Jews would be rounded up and sent to concentration camps to be released within about two months. When he told my grandmother on November 11, 1938, that her husband would be home in a few weeks, she assumed that he was "pulling strings" to make that happen. In actuality, he was not altruistic. Now I understand why Israel denied planting a tree in his honor.

Finding a Family: A Tribute to My Father
by Kathy Markell Britton

Winter 1998

In 1928, my grandfather, Jacob "Jack" Markell, died as a result of an automobile accident that occurred while he was traveling on business through the mountains near Kenova, West Virginia. A native of Baltimore, my grandfather had met my grandmother, Floy Alline Havens, in her native Louisiana in the years just before World War I. Eventually they settled in Kentucky, where Jack worked as a traveling salesman. In his late thirties when he died, my grandfather left behind not only a wife, but also two sons, my uncle Walter Markell, who was 12 years old, and my father, Harold Markell, who had just turned 7.

These were the only facts that I knew about my grandfather when I was growing up. As a child, I would ask my dad questions about his Markell family, but he could not give me any answers. After his father died, his mother did not stay in touch with his father's relatives, and he knew nothing about that part of his family.

My grandmother, who lived near us in Sacramento, California, did not seem eager to give me any further details about her husband's family. When I asked her about the Markells, she either said she could not remember, or she would change the subject and tell me something cute my dad had done as a child. The one bit of information she did give me was that the Markell name was "French Catholic," which seemed logical since we were all raised as Catholics. But my father did not even know where his father was buried. Although he had been curious for a long time, he decided not to press the issue with his mother, and instead did some of his own research—especially looking up Markells in telephone books for years—without success.

In the spring of 1984, my husband and I were expecting our fourth child and decided to name him Jacob after my grandfather. I was curious to know if my grandfather had had a middle name and began once again to delve into the history of the Markell family. Soon my curiosity widened, and I became interested in finding out as much as I could about my grandfather and his background. Although I did not know it, I was beginning a search for my family that would take me 13 years and reveal a cultural and religious background I had never suspected.

I sent to West Virginia for my grandfather's death certificate. It listed his birth date—1892—and his father's name, John Markell. His mother was listed as "Unknown." At my local genealogy library, I looked for the family of John Markell in the 1900 federal census for Baltimore, Maryland; I knew my grandfather had come from that city. Delighted, I found a record for my grandfather's family that not only provided the name of his mother, Annie, but the names of his brother and five sisters. Other Markells, presumably relatives, were listed in the census. They lived on or near the same street in South Baltimore as my great-grandparents and their children.

The census windfall allowed me to begin my genealogical search in earnest, and over the next 12 years I checked every record I could find for more information about my grandfather. I obtained his marriage certificate, his World War I draft registration record and many other documents. None of them gave me even a hint of the middle name that I had been curious about originally or any other, more significant information about him. I had started a filing cabinet with documents, but I still did not have any real insight into who my grandfather was, where he was buried or what happened to his brother and sisters.

Finally, I sat my dad and uncle down and asked them to tell me everything they could remember about their father. As a result, I got three pieces of information. They said that, after his death in West Virginia, my grandfather's body had been transported back to Baltimore for burial. Because they were very young, they had not been allowed to attend his funeral; instead, while the ceremony was going on, a cousin in a military uniform took them to play in a park. Finally, my uncle remembered the name "Simond" stitched on the cousin's military uniform.

With the information that my grandfather was buried somewhere in Baltimore, I mailed more than 200 self-addressed postcards to every cemetery listed in the telephone book. I received answers from all of them, but Jacob "Jack" Markell was not buried in any of them. Neither were his parents, his siblings or any of the other Markells listed in the census as living near my great-grandparents. This was such a mystery to me, but I remained convinced that my grandfather had to be buried in the Baltimore area.

Reevaluating Evidence

A break came in the spring of 1996 when I began to look closely again at some of the documents I had found when I first started to search in 1984. Poring over the pages I had copied from the 1900 Baltimore census, I looked carefully at all the names, ages and occupations. I had a deep feeling that I had missed something when I found these records years before. Reading line by line, I finally looked at the family listed as living next door to my great-grandparents. I was amazed to find a man named Wolf Samuelson whose occupation was listed (and misspelled) as "rabi." I knew that a rabbi would probably live in a community largely populated by Jews. Then I noticed that almost everyone on the page, including the rabbi and my great-grandparents, had been born in Russia. Could my grandfather's family, whom I had always been told were French Catholics, really have been Russian Jews?

I had been using the Internet in my genealogical research and had noticed a

Jewish genealogy forum sponsored by JewishGen, although I had never had any reason to explore it. Now, with a possible Jewish connection in my family, I looked more closely and began to read all the information it had listed. Luckily, I found a reference to the Jewish Museum of Maryland, located in downtown Baltimore, which has a large collection of materials pertinent to Jewish genealogical research in the area. I telephoned the next day and requested the special search packet they offered for genealogists. When filling out the questionnaire, I gave them all the information I had on the Markell family, and I made sure to mention that Rabbi Wolf Samuelson had lived next door. Exactly six days later, I received a letter from Dianne Feldman who handles genealogical research for the museum. She had been able to determine that Samuelson was the rabbi of Congregation Anshe Emunah, a synagogue of Lithuanian Jews located on Hanover Street, not far from where my great-grandparents had lived. After a quick telephone call to the congregation's cemetery, she was able to confirm that my grandfather was, in fact, buried there. She had found Jacob "Jack" Markell's burial place.

I had wanted so much to give this information to my father for his 75th birthday, but I could not wait. I called him and reported that his father was buried in the United Hebrew Cemetery on Washington Boulevard in Baltimore. My father was dumbfounded that his father was buried in a Jewish cemetery, but he was so excited. Next, I called the manager of United Hebrew, Joel Frankel, and asked if he had any records. Kindly, he read to me over the telephone the names of all the Markells buried in his cemetery. Not only were my great-grandparents buried there, but so were some of the other Markells I had found in the census records. I sent Mr. Frankel a disposable camera, and he photographed all the headstones for me and copied all the records.

Jacob (Jack) Markell

Armed with this information, I hoped that perhaps I might find some of my father's living relatives. Buried next to my grandfather was a Solomon Markell and a Fanny Kahntroff. From the census records, I knew that Solomon Markell was not from my grandfather's immediate family, but my grandfather did have a sister named Fanny. I sent for her death certificate which listed a Mrs. Leonard Levy as the informant. Several Leonard Levys are listed in the Baltimore telephone directory, but only two Kahntroffs. I tried my luck and wrote to Dr. Brian Kahntroff, who turned out to be Fanny Kahntroff's grandson. He kindly passed the letter on to his aunt, Norma Kahntroff Levy, the informant listed on the death certificate. Soon after, I received a telephone call from Norma, and I asked her what seemed like a million questions. She gave me a wealth of information on her mother's Markell family, but it turned out that her mother was not my grandfather's sister after all. I was sure that Norma and I were related, but I had no idea how.

Frustrated, I turned again to JewishGen on the Internet, which had originally led me to Dianne Feldman and my grandfather's burial place. I posted a message asking anyone with knowledge of the Markell family to contact me. I also mentioned a possible relationship to a Simond family—the name my uncle had remembered seeing on his cousin's uniform the day of his father's funeral. Incredibly, the next morning I had three messages from the same man in New York, Eric Goldstein, telling me that he was the great-grandson of my grandfather's sister.

My Grandfather's Story

The Simond name was really Simon. Eric knew the entire story of how my grandfather had been killed in a car accident and that he had left a wife and two sons. He told me that my grandfather had left Baltimore around 1915 to help his sister, Jennie, and her husband, Aaron Simon, run their general merchandise store in the small town of Merryville, Louisiana. Eric's grandfather, Fred Simon, had told him many stories about Uncle Jack, who had a very warm relationship with all the Simon children. According to Eric's grandfather, Jack had eventually married a non-Jewish Merryville girl, Floy Havens, and had two sons.

The story—down to my grandmother's maiden name—corresponded perfectly to the little I knew of my grandfather's past. According to Eric, after Jack and his family moved to Kentucky and Jack was killed in the car accident, Jennie Simon had tried unsuccessfully to find out what had happened to her two nephews. When Eric began his own genealogical search years later, his grandfather Fred had asked him to try to find these two long-lost cousins. Now we had both ended our searches and found one another. I was ecstatic; my father was beside himself. He finally had a family.

During my conversations with Eric, he told me that one of Jennie Markell Simon's sons, Walter, was living only about an hour from us in California. At this time, Walter's brother, Melvin, was visiting from Louisiana and Mel's two daughters were due to come for a visit from southern California. I made plans to take my dad to visit his cousins. During the visit, Walter, who was in his nineties, mentioned that he had graduated from West Point the summer my grandfather died. He was the cousin who had taken my father and uncle to the park during their father's funeral.

My search for my father's family culminated in June 1997, when my parents and I flew from California to Baltimore to meet the rest of the family. Norma and Leonard Levy met us at the airport. I cannot put into words the joy I felt at seeing their smiling faces. My father said his heart was pounding. We met several other cousins that night. Eric came from New York the next morning, and we spent four wonderful days meeting other relatives and touring the neighborhood where our family had lived. We also visited the Jewish Museum of Maryland and had a private tour. I was able to thank Dianne Feldman in person for the wonderful research she had done for us.

In a remarkable coincidence, it turned out that Dianne herself was a cousin to Eric Goldstein on another side of his family. Most importantly, my father finally got to visit his father's grave at United Hebrew Cemetery. We had a new monument erected to replace the simple footstone that had marked the grave for the past 70 years. With the help of the cemetery manager, Joel Frankel, we were able to determine that my grandfather's Hebrew name, which had been omitted from the original tombstone, was Yakov. We had it placed on the new monument. For my father and me, the trip to the cemetery was the single most meaningful moment of the entire trip.

Over the next several months, Eric and I stayed in close contact, sharing a growing fund of information about the Markell family. My father continued to be delighted with each new discovery. Eric told me that John and Annie Markell had immigrated to Baltimore in 1883 from Raseiniai, a town in western Lithuania. An inquiry to the Kaunas Archives in Lithuania revealed that John Markell was originally Kasriel Merkel. In addition, a number of family lists and tax lists from the archives revealed that the Merkels had originated in the town of Kedainiai and gave us family information stretching back three more generations to the mid-1700s.

We discovered that Kasriel/John had a twin brother, Nokhem/Newman Markell, who was Norma Levy's grandfather and the ancestor of the other Markells whom I had found in the Baltimore census all those years ago and who are buried at the United Hebrew Cemetery. Another mystery solved. My contacts with Eric and Norma were more than just inquiries into the family story. We were not just correspondents sharing arcane historical facts; we had become true family.

In counterpoint to my father's great joy over our new discoveries and deepening connections to his family, his health began to decline steadily in the months after our return from Baltimore, and he died on March 23, 1998. Four days before his death, I asked my father if he were afraid of dying. He looked at me and replied no, that he now had a huge wonderful family waiting for him. We talked about the family resemblances he shared with his cousins and the fact that we both felt connected to our newly found family. One thing my father told me was that he had been thrilled to hear his cousins say how their parents had always wondered what had happened to him after his mother took them from Baltimore following his father's funeral. I felt connected in a different way. I had always been close to my mother's family and had many cousins right here in the Sacramento area, but I felt a bond with my new cousins that made me feel complete.

Kathy Markell Britton has been gathering genealogy information since 1983. In 2002, she graduated from college with a degree in nursing. She and Pat, her husband, have been blessed with five grandsons, the youngest named Jacob after his great-great-grandfather.

The Quest for the Topf Family
by Sophie Caplan

Winter 1987

I s it possible several decades after the Second World War to find traces of an Eastern European family that vanished into the whirlpool of the Holocaust? It is, if you have at least a few scraps of information such as names and pre-war places of domicile and if you are determined and logical in your search. Having photos of some members of the family also helps, as well as a basic knowledge of contemporary European Jewish history.

I never knew my father, who died suddenly in Nazi Germany the year that I was born. I knew little about his family, whom I met only as a child of two when my mother took me to Poland to show me to my grandparents. My parents came to Germany in the early 1920s from different parts of Poland. My father came from the small town of Wiślica, in the district of Pińczów of the province of Kielce, formerly under Russian domination after the partition of Poland. My mother came from the Ruthenian village of Nowica, near the town of Kałusz, in the district and province of Stanislaw (also Stanislawów/Stanislau), formerly under Austrian aegis.

My father was fleeing military conscription for the Russo-Polish War in 1920. My mother came to join two uncles and to improve her lot as the eldest daughter of poor farmers in Galicia. They married in Germany in 1929, but my father's parents could not afford to come to the wedding, so my mother did not know his family very well.

In the late 1930s, my mother remarried, and we fled Germany at the eleventh hour. In Belgium and then France, under wartime conditions, my mother thought it best if I had the same surname as she, so I lost even my father's name. The only reminders of my father's existence were about 20 photographs of him, his parents, siblings and their spouses, and cousins in Wiślica taken between 1920 and 1937.

When we fled Belgium during the German blitzkrieg, my mother took clothes, documents and all the family photos. These were hidden and saved, for a fee, in one of our trunks in the house of a French family during our incarceration in Vichy French concentration camps and our close calls with deportation.

After World War II, when postal communications between countries were reestablished, my mother wrote to all the relatives in Poland. No answers came, or else our letters were returned with the stamped message "unknown at this address." We eventually heard details of their fate from two surviving male members of the family who spent the war years in Asiatic Russia with the Polish army, first as prisoners of war, then as allies. They returned home to Nowica, Kałusz,

Stryj and Rożniatów to find that most of the family were shot by a German Einsatzgruppe (special killing squad) in a ditch in the Kałusz Jewish cemetery. Other family members were killed singly by the local Ruthenian (now Ukrainian) peasants.

For the Topfs of Wiślica, there were just the returned letters saying "unknown at this address" in Polish, and nothing else. We knew of no relatives in countries of refuge, and although my mother put their names into "Lists of Relatives Being Sought" put together by Jewish organizations, nothing turned up. As far as we could tell, all the Topfs of Wiślica were dead.

As a child at the end of the war, then a teenager and young adult, I did not want to participate in any search. I wanted to be like everyone else, with a known mother and father, not with a string of dead relatives. Consequently, I never told my friends that my stepfather was not my real father.

We immigrated to Australia where I continued my schooling, studied, married an Australian-born Jew and had three children. I did not know there were Topf relatives, also new immigrants, right in my home town of Sydney; they were females with a different name. I knew one of them, whom I discovered thirty years later to be a second cousin.

It was only as a woman in my thirties that I began to feel the gap in my identity in not having known my father and his family. The need to know more about them began to gnaw at me. By then I knew everything there was to know about my mother's family, the Hausmanns of Nowica, and others came to me for information. I knew practically nothing about my father's family. I questioned my mother closely, until it irritated her, to find out all she knew. I wrote down names and perused photos at length. I then placed advertisements with local and international Jewish organizations seeking "the descendants of Joseph Topf of Wiślica." Total silence.

Joseph (Yossel) and Yentl Topf were my grandparents. Their children were Abraham, my father; Hershel, who married Rosa; Max (name of wife unknown); Dvora, who married Israel Buchman; and Tova, whose husband's name was no longer remembered by my mother. Dvora and Israel Buchman had two sons in the 1920s, Meyer and Schmuel. We had photographs of all of these, and also of some Topf cousins whom my mother did not know by name.

Whenever I look at those photographs, I am conscious that these are probably the last earthly remains of people who were wiped out and whom no one now remembers. At the back of one photo it says (in English translation) "In remembrance of your cousins B. CH. and F." I often speculate whether it might have been Bella, Chanah and Fanny. All my mother knew was that one of them was my father's childhood sweetheart. This is why I always urge people to label photographs fully on the back with names, dates and places.

The photographs were taken in the 1920s and 30s. Some my father must have taken with him when he fled Poland, or they were sent on to him. Some were taken with a Kodak Brownie box camera by my mother's brother on his 1937 visit to Poland.

In 1976, my husband gave himself a sabbatical from his Sydney law office. We spent it in Israel where many of my mother's relatives live. Although I had met most of them on previous visits, I still managed to find new ones. For instance, when I went to Tel Aviv to purchase the Rożniatów *yizkor* (Holocaust memorial) book from a man called Friedler, he asked me why I was interested. On hearing the name of my maternal family, he asked whether I knew about Utzi Strassmann. I did not and hot-footed it by taxi to the distant suburb of Tel Aviv where he lived. I was greeted warmly as the first relative he had seen since 1934. He told me his story and that of his whole family, and I later inherited some of his family photos.

Yentl and Joseph Topf in Wiślica, 1925, with their two youngest children, Tova and Max, and eldest grandson, Meir Buchman. Only Meir survived the Holocaust.

My husband, who has several hundred relatives in his hometown of Sydney, could not understand what he called my obsession with finding more relatives. I decided to be discreet and avoid being ridiculed in the special task I set for myself in our sabbatical year. My secret goal was to find some trace, however faint, some relative, however distant, of my paternal family.

My mother knew of no Topf relatives, except my father, who in pre-World War II immigrated to any country outside Poland. I reasoned that any survivors from a ghetto or concentration camp, or from the Polish army in Russia, probably would have immigrated to Israel after 1948, or after 1968, when most of the remainder of Polish Jewry left Poland for Israel.

Searching for Topf Relatives in Israel

My first tool was the English edition of the three telephone books covering all of Israel. After taking months to acquire these books, I systematically phoned every Topf and every Buchman in Israel, opening with a little phrase in Hebrew: "I don't speak *Ivrit* (Hebrew) well, but I speak English, French, German, Yiddish and Spanish," which actually covered every eventuality. Most opted for English, German or Yiddish.

Unfortunately, out of the 50 or 60 entries under those names, I only struck pay dirt once. Avigdor Topf referred me to his father, Herschel Topf of Ramat Gan, who turned out to be, not my uncle, but a very distant cousin of my father. Herschel Topf, 69 years old and the sole survivor of his family, was born in the town of Dzialoszyce, also in the district of Pińczów. He recalled as a boy being told by his grandfather that the Dzialoszyce Topfs originated in Wiślica two generations earlier, and all the Topfs in Wiślica were of the same descent. This very simple man did not know any more, except he was named after his great-grandfather, Herschel Topf, and he thought a descendant of my grandfather Yossel Topf had survived. Where and who he was he did not know, but this gave me hope to go on.

Visits to the Jewish Agency Search Bureau in Jerusalem yielded some Topf names and addresses abroad, as well as the address of the president of the Wiślica *landsmanschaft* (townsman society). The addresses obtained were all circa 1952, and all letters came back unopened. The office of the Association of Jews from Poland in Tel Aviv, *Igud Yotzei Polin*, yielded absolutely nothing.

Less than a month before our time in Israel was up, I went to Yad Vashem Archives. I wanted to ascertain the dates on which the small Jewish towns and villages to which the various branches of my family had belonged were destroyed, either by deportation or by mass shooting. As I was waiting for assistance, I espied on a wall of the research room a map published in Germany in September 1944 and titled "*Der Deutsche Osten*" (The German East). It included East Galicia, my maternal home territory, and showed me, for the first time, the geographical relationship between the various villages and townships which were part of my maternal family lore: Kalusz and Rożniatów, Nowica, Zawadka, Krechowice, Stryy, Dolina, Landestreu and Perehińsko and Stanislaw, all on the tail end of the Dniester River.

I made a quick sketch in my notebook and took note also of the map's publisher, Justus Perthes. Back in Australia, the West German Consulate Economic Section supplied the present address of the firm, and I wrote asking to buy a copy of that map. They replied denying they ever printed a map with this title but offered me a large scale map of any district in Eastern Europe. Thanks to that, I acquired a map of the Stanislaw area so detailed that my mother was able to identify the position of her parental house in the native village. It also showed physical contours and land use. As the map and its companions were composed in 1888, it suited my purpose perfectly. It is the *Generalkarte von Mitteleuropa* 1:200000, or General Map of Central Europe 1 cm to 2 km.

When the Yad Vashem research fellow came, he was able to read me a handwritten eyewitness account of the massacre of the Jews of the Kalusz ghetto into which most of my maternal family has been herded. Then he told me there was a *yizkor* book put together by the survivors of Wiślica in Israel, and he took me to the Yad Vashem library to look at that book. To my disappointment, it was in three languages, none of which I could read fluently: Polish, Yiddish and Hebrew without vowels.

I decided to go through the book anyway to look at the photographs of the town, its people, family groups, individuals and Jewish clubs. Perhaps I would be lucky and find some familiar faces. First, I asked the librarian if she would kindly help me find my family among the Hebrew alphabetical list of Holocaust victims of the town, which is a feature of most *yizkor* books. She found the Topfs for me, confirming various names, but claimed she could not find the Buchmans. Later I found them myself. Other *yizkor* books generally have lists of Holocaust victims in both the Hebrew and Latin alphabet. This can also be a source of family names.

Contact with Family

As I started turning the pages and studying the Wiślica street scenes and the faces in the photographs, I was suddenly startled. On page 74, the photograph of a man's head and shoulders looked familiar. It was, on spelling out the name, my uncle Israel Buchman. The librarian translated the legend under the photo, revealing my uncle had been a hardware merchant as well as the Jewish representative on the town council.

I knew concentration camp survivors could not keep photos or documents and survivors who lived under false identities would only have photos of their nearest and dearest. I wanted to reach the editor of the book, a book prepared by a committee of non-historian lay people, like most *yizkor* books. Luckily, the Yad Vashem librarian was able to supply me with the address of the committee member who assumed editorial responsibility, and I rushed home to phone him.

His daughter answered and informed me that the photo on page 74 was supplied by Israel Buchman's son. Was he alive? Yes. He lived in Haifa. The reason he was not in the Haifa telephone directory was because he had changed his name, not to a Hebrew form, but to the Polish *nom-de-guerre* (war pseudonym). Under this

Israel Buchman
(from Wiślica yizkor book)

name he received false papers, joined the partisan peasant battalions, and gained some renown as a partisan. This is why I phoned every Buchman in Israel without being able to find him.

Israel Buchman (extreme right) with his wife and two sons. All died in the gas chambers of Treblinka.

The first conversation with my first paternal relative in 40 years was very cautious until I established, to my satisfaction, it was indeed my first cousin to whom I was speaking. On both sides it was a moment fraught with emotion. My cousin, who was at the Hebrew *gymnasium* (high school) in Kraków when I visited Wiślica as a toddler, had not met any relatives on his maternal side since October 3, 1942, when his parents, brother, grandparents, uncles, aunts and cousins were herded into trucks on their way to Treblinka killing camp. He was held back with a few other strong young men to help the Germans carry their loot from Jewish houses. That night he and three companions escaped from their drunken supervisors, and so started his life as the solitary survivor of the Topfs of Wiślica.

After the war, he married a fellow survivor, also the sole remaining member of her family. He spent some years in the immediate postwar Polish administration, then ran his wife's family's recovered business, which later was forcibly acquired by the Polish government. After years as a leading Polish journalist, he secretly visited Israel in 1958 and decided to emigrate. His wife took longer to persuade, but he wanted his children to know their Jewish heritage, which he and their mother kept secret from them in postwar anti-Semitic Poland. Today, his two daughters occupy leading positions, one in Israeli industry, the other as a very senior army officer; each has two children.

Thus I found, nearly 32 years after the end of World War II, the saved remnant of my father's family in Wiślica, together with his wife, children and grandchildren. From him I learned the names of other relatives. It helped that his father's mother was also a Topf in Wiślica, the sister of our joint great-grandfather, Eliezer. Eliezer's younger brother, Herschel Topf, was still alive during the Nazi occupation and was the last head of the Wiślica *chevra kadisha* (burial society) for over 40 years.

From Meir Buchman, alias Marian Bielecki, I learned some of the family tree, including the prevailing first names. As a young boy he spent most of his adolescence at the Kraków Hebrew *gymnasium* and later at the university in Kraków studying economics; therefore, he did not know as much about the family as I would have liked. We shared our histories, and he told me how he acquired the photo of his father by taking a copy of a photo of the pre-war Wiślica city council. He did not have photographs of any other members of the family. I made copies of all the photos in my mother's possession, and I was able to supply him and his daughters with likenesses of his mother, brother, grandparents, uncles and aunts for the first time since 1942. Unfortunately, he did not recognize "B., CH. and F." He did not know my father, who left Poland the year of Meir's birth.

I was eager for anecdotes and any details of our family history. Two years later, in January 1979, during my next visit to Israel, I again entreated him to tell me more. He then told me our grandfather, Yossel Topf, was not actually brought up by his own parents, but by his grandparents. His parents, Eliezer Topf and his wife, were sent to Siberia. After serving a punishment sentence somewhere in Eastern Siberia, they established a raw pelt collection and fur export business in Irkutsk, became very prosperous and bore three more children, two sons and a daughter.

Meir did not know their names. He did recall, as a child, the whole family being excited by a letter received from the Topers from "a large city in China to which they fled after the Russian revolution." He was told the Topers were the brothers of our grandfather, born in Irkutsk, and they were still in the fur business.

He recalled that letters came from time to time, perhaps even parcels. One of the brothers settled in Japan, the other in North America. Presumably, to a child in prewar Poland, the vast North American continent was all one. That is all my cousin knew, and he never attempted to find out more.

Further Research

Could one find relatives lost such a long time ago? And with so little data? We figured out, from what our grandfather's age must have been in 1942, that he must have been born in the early 1870s and his parents exiled in the mid-1870s. I even worked out that the date of birth of the next child, born in Siberian exile, must have been approximately 1880, which turned out to be "spot on," as we say in Australia.

My mother then recalled that my father had told her of the Siberian relatives. They had written that one of them would visit Wiślica in the summer of 1914 and bring my grandfather some of the family inheritance. No one ever turned up, and nothing further was heard until my father left home in 1920. My mother forgot all this until her memory was prodded by my cousin's recollections. I was determined to find this lost part of the Topf family. But how? Had I recalled in time something seemingly unconnected, my quest would have been much easier. In 1964, I joined the Australian Jewish Historical Society, and I often went home on the same route as an elderly gentleman of Siberian birth. From time to time he would reiterate a question that seemed an obsession with him, "Do you have relatives in Russia?" I always answered in the negative and took the question not at all seriously, but as a sort of conversation sustainer on his part.

On one occasion, I recalled much later, on our trip home I told him my stepfather once had relatives in Russia in the fur trade and also that my birth name was Sophie Topf. He then exclaimed, "Sophia Toper, that's who you remind me of." "Do you mean I remind you of her physically or in personality?" "You are just like her. You remind me of her both physically and with your personality."

I must confess at that time I took these remarks not at all seriously, but as a form of heavy-handed flirting by the lonely elderly towards the young. Later, I was to regret bitterly my light-hearted dismissal. When he died in September 1979, aged 86, I discovered anew he was born in Irkutsk, and by then I was seeking people who might have known my relatives. It turned out the Sophia Toper the old gentleman compared me to was the only sister of my grandfather, even though the two siblings never met.

The first resource I used in trying to find the traces of my relatives from Siberia was the Australian immigrant community of so-called Far Eastern Jews. They started to arrive early this century via Manchuria and Japan until World War I, and then again after World War II from Shanghai, Tientsin and Harbin. Those Jews from Shanghai included many former German and Austrian Jews who were deluded into buying the fake Shanghai visas in 1938–39 for which many Jews paid large sums, although Shanghai was then a "free port" and anyone could settle there.

From Tientsin, Harbin and Shanghai, came the Russian Jews who settled in Manchuria and in China after the Russian Revolution, coming from European Russia in some cases, but mainly from Siberia. My own research into the day-school movement in New South Wales showed how the pre-World War I Far Eastern immigrants stuck together and supported each other for decades afterwards. I also had many friends whose parents and grandparents, and sometimes they themselves, were of Far Eastern Russo-Jewish origin. I started asking them if they knew of a Toper family from Irkutsk. Unfortunately, it seemed no one knew them, but I later discovered it was because all the people I asked were from Shanghai. Eventually, I happened to ask a Far Eastern White Russian non-Jew, who told me which of the Far Eastern Jews in Sydney would be able to help me "because he knows everybody." The man in question was the late Bob Drisin, unofficial and unelected but effective President of the Far Eastern Jews in Sydney. He did not know the Topers personally, but he was able to tell me who did. Thus,

I discovered there was even a Toper in Sydney, a married lady in her early seventies named Sarah.

When I rang her, very excited at finding a long-lost relative so close, she was unimpressed and reluctant to tell me the slightest thing. When I learned her married name, I realized immediately I knew one of her sons. He had been my contemporary at the Zionist youth *moadon* (meeting hall) which he and I, my husband and so many of our joint friends had frequented. This made her even more suspicious. Eventually I obtained Sarah's agreement to visit her at her home. She reluctantly showed me the photograph of her father, Pavel Toper, born in 1880 in Siberia. I presumed that he was my grandfather's brother. The facial and physical resemblance to my grandfather, Yossel Topf, was striking, even though one was dressed as a Russian of the merchant class, the other as a religious Polish Jew with a beard and a shiny black capote. This resemblance was only visible to me, and to refute my argument she brought out photos of her brothers, all very different.

I was immediately struck by the appearance of her brother, Grisha Toper, who strongly resembled my father at the same age. The other brothers were Abraham and Samuel, while Pavel's brother was Max (Moshe) and his sister none other than Sophia Toper, the woman of whom I reminded Solomon Stedman. It was extraordinary, but Sarah would not permit any assumption of a possible family link between us.

Sarah would not give me the addresses of her relatives overseas to whom I wanted to write, assuming them to be my relatives, too. She did not know either Pavel's or Grisha's Hebrew names, and she was firm in stating that her grandfather was Lazar Toper, nothing else. She believed her grandparents "came from somewhere in Poland or in Lithuania, I don't know where," but she heard of "Wiślica." Since it is a very small town, even unknown to many former Polish Jews who tend to mix it up with Vinnitsa, I was heartened. How could a Siberian-born lady, raised in China, who never was in Europe, have heard of such a small town? She wouldn't have unless the place was meaningful to her family in Siberia and China, because it originated there?

Analyzing Given Names

My basic knowledge of Hebrew names and the particular forms which first names take in several European languages, made me surmise that Pavel would be Paul in English, which is often Pinchas in Hebrew. Similarly, Lazar would be the Russian form of Eliezer and, since Russians do not use the letter *H* which they replace with *G*, would it not be possible that Grisha Toper might be Hersh or Hirsh Zvi in Hebrew? All these names, plus Abraham, Samuel and Moshe, the names of her other brothers and her uncle, were also present in my immediate paternal family. Of course, these names are all very common indeed, but here the precise cluster of names in the Toper family corresponded exactly to the cluster of names used among the Topfs of Wiślica. This suggested to me that both sets of people were named after the same ancestors.

My great-grandfather was Eliezer Topf, and I believed he was the same man as the person she knew as her grandfather, Lazar Toper. Eliezer Topf's two brothers who remained in Wiślica, I learned from Meir Buchman, each called a son Pinchas after their grandfather, Pinchas Topf. Was it not possible, and even likely, Eliezer Topf, alias Lazar Toper, called his first son born in Siberia Pavel Pinchas after the same grandfather? Lazar had another son Moshe, or Max, as did my grandfather Yossel. Yossel called his older sons Abraham and Hersh, just as I believed Pavel Pinchas Toper, whom I believed to be his younger brother, had done. Sarah asked me to prove my assumptions. What she meant were certified government documents, I suppose, and these were destroyed in the Holocaust. I had no documents to prove anything. I set out to prove things in other ways.

Eliezer Topf

Some of my Far Eastern Jewish informants told me that Grisha Toper died in Tokyo in recent years, but was buried in the U.S. The former rabbi of the Tokyo Jewish community, Rabbi Marvin Tokayer, had recently published a book called *The Fugu Plan: The Untold Story of the Japanese and the Jews During World War II*. I assumed, since the Japanese Jewish community was small, he might remember Grisha Toper, put me in touch with his descendants and also tell me if Grisha's Hebrew name was Hirsh Zvi. It took one-and-a-half years and many letters, as I sought Rabbi Tokayer around the world, but at last my hunch was confirmed. Grisha Toper was indeed Zvi Hirsh ben Pinchas, but, alas, he left no descendants.

Further Research

Meanwhile, I also tried other avenues of contact with my other putative Toper relatives. This was mainly through Far Eastern Jewish contacts but also through the international telephone system. How hard it was to get any response. Evidently Jews in China and in Manchuria were a close-knit and persecuted community, because there was immense mistrust, and tight-lipped silence met many of my endeavours to find my relatives.

Being used to the openness and volubility of Eastern European Jews on the subject of *mishpochology*, I could not understand what was happening. It seemed like the *omerta* (code of silence) among Sicilians; no one wanted to tell me anything, and some people were actually warned not to talk to me.

Whenever I did trace a friend, acquaintance or distant relative of the Toper family, it seemed my motives were automatically distrusted. Often, after much trouble in tracing someone, my detailed letters were answered with a few terse lines stating the recipient was either ill, incapable of writing or had not known my relatives well enough to answer my queries. The rabbis of the Tokyo Jewish community, past and present, were a pleasant exception. Many letters were never answered, and I wondered if they reached their recipient or had been lost in the mail despite having a return address.

One day this problem was resolved. I knew Samuel Toper was the one son of Pavel Pinchas Toper still alive and living in North America. But where? I decided to take a chance that he might live in the Greater New York area. I asked our Telecom telephone system to find Samuel Toper for me in New York, since I believed it to be the most likely place. If this failed, I would have tried Los Angeles, Chicago, Miami, Montreal, Toronto, St. Louis, Cleveland, etc., in descending order of Jewish population, but I was lucky.

After finding myself connected to a young lady in New York called "S. Toper," I hit the jackpot. I had Samuel Toper on the line in New York at 8 p.m. on a Thursday evening, a civilized time to ring a long-lost relative from the antipodes, at my cost. I had never attempted to contact him before, but he was not pleased now. When I introduced myself to him, his first words to me were, "You are too persistent!" He made it clear that he did not care to acknowledge any relationship. Nevertheless, our short, sharp conversation proved to me my letters had indeed reached their recipients, been communicated to my putative relatives and were deliberately left unanswered.

My Siberian Relatives

I slowly built up additional information about my Toper relatives, for I became convinced they were indeed the Siberian descendants of my great-grandfather. I found an old gentleman who told me some family stories which might explain why certain relatives did not want their family linen washed in public. My persistence in pursuing the Far Eastern Jewish connections eventually gave me a background of whom and what my family had been.

After some years in the far northern settlement of Ustkut, where their children Pinchas, Moshe and Sophia were born, Eliezer and his wife, whose name may have been Toba,[1] settled with their children in Irkutsk. Here they founded the firm of "L. Toper and Sons," fur traders, which prospered greatly. The home of

---

[1] It has since been determined that his wife's name was Raizel Klainer.

Eliezer Lazar also served as a Jewish house of prayer, although there were neither rabbis nor any way to give the children a proper Jewish education.

Whatever Jewishness the parents were able to pass on to their children was obviously diluted in the third generation, although Eliezer's grandchildren all married Jews. Not so the "Siberian" great-grandchildren, although it varies.

Pavel Pinchas Toper fought in the Russo-Japanese War at the side of Joseph Trumpeldor, and apparently there used to be a photo of them together at Port

Raizel Klainer Topf

Arthur. It was also Pavel who, with his wife, made a trip westward on the Trans-Siberian railway to Poland and possibly other parts in the early summer of 1914. Disappointed by the relatives they met in Warsaw, they did not bother to contact his brother Yossel and his family in Wiślica.

They were the visitors who never came and who never brought my grandfather's part of the inheritance. Their mother had died, and it is possible Eliezer was already dead too, or else he died the next year. After the Russian Revolution in 1917, the younger Topers moved to Manchuria, to Harbin, but for some years apparently the business and some family members remained in Irkutsk. The family continued to deal in fur pelts, and Sophia Toper's husband, Preisman, joined the firm. Some members of the family became interested in the theatre and even in actresses; some moved to Tientsin, others to Shanghai.

Grisha Toper fell out with his father and moved to Yokohama in Japan, and his hobby became amateur theatricals. He is remembered as having been very active raising large funds for various charities, together with his cousins and friends. Apparently, he also visited Sydney once or twice in the 1950s, and our paths may even have crossed when I was invited to supper and dancing at the Russian Social Club for some twenty-first birthday celebrations.

Despite having gained much information, I still wanted the satisfaction of knowing more about my family, of meeting my father's surviving cousins and my second cousins, and of being acknowledged by them as a relative. For a few years it seemed an impossible dream.

Eventually there was a breakthrough. My non-Topf half-sister married a Far Eastern Jew. His aunt came from Los Angeles to visit her relatives in Sydney. She knew the Topers in Harbin and Tientsin, and she advised me to write again to someone I had written to two years earlier without eliciting any answer. This letter had also been read by Samuel Toper. Now I wrote in some anger, perhaps even with some bitterness, instead of the friendly open tone I used two or three years earlier. This time there was an answer accepting my conclusions about our relationship and giving me the addresses of several other relatives. Providentially, this letter came a month or two before my first visit to New York. I wrote to my second cousin, Arnold, grandson of my great-uncle, Moshe Toper, and received an invitation to dine with him at his home in Great Neck.

I wrote back requesting him to bring out the family photographs. As an only child of an only child, I surmised he would have the family photos of his branch of the Topers. He did. After dinner, in company with Tamara, another joint second cousin, we dipped into a vintage silver-plated Russian photograph album. Among the many photos, mostly unlabeled, were those from a photographic studio of an elderly couple, circa 1900. There was an imprint in Cyrillic script which Tamara deciphered as "Irkutsk." Were these our joint great-grandparents, Eliezer Topf, alias Lazar Toper, and his wife Toba? For me it was an emotion-laden moment, particularly when Arnold generously offered to loan me these photos to get copies made back home.

There has never been a certified verification of these photos. A leading photographic expert in Sydney, author of several books on the "mechanical eye in Australia," has dated them for me. They are from 1890 at the earliest and 1910 at the latest, and the photograph of the elderly lady may be copied from an older photo. Judging by the age of the people in the photos, it can only be Lazar Toper and his wife. When my mother was first shown the photos, she exclaimed, "But that's your grandfather, Yossel!" and then, "No, the beard is too long, but it looks like him." So, if not Yossel, surely it must be his father.

There is also a striking resemblance with one of my children, and this has helped me to understand why my great-grandfather was exiled to Siberia. For, if this particular son of mine ever lived under an oppressive regime, he might also fall foul of the authorities. He cannot tolerate injustice, irrationality or hypocrisy.

After that breakthrough in mid-1981, I gradually met many of my "Siberian" relatives on different trips to the U.S., and we have become friends. The exception is Samuel Toper. He is obdurate and does not want to know me. I guess it is his loss. In 1983 when we passed through San Francisco, one of my second cousins advised me to visit some relatives on their other side who are older than anyone else left alive and who have known the Toper family over nine decades. We did visit them, and so a final piece of the puzzle was solved.

The wife of this couple had a brother who died the previous year, aged 93. This brother had recalled the times in Irkutsk and Harbin when Pinchas and Moshe Toper sent letters and parcels to a brother left in Poland. Strangely enough, the younger generation was never apprised of this fact, which is why they could not bring themselves to believe there were relatives left in Europe.

Genes however have longer memories than fallible family tradition. Apart from my middle son's facial and surmised temperamental resemblance to my great-grandfather, there are other Topf-Toper interfamily likenesses. My father-in-law, seeing a photo of Tamara's son, thought it was my youngest boy. Last year, when my eldest son was working in a hospital in another city, a nurse working in the same ward commented how much he reminded her of a friend of her parents in his way of speaking, his mannerisms, his sense of humor. It was an older man, also a Jew, a man my son has never met; my second cousin Sarah's son, named after our great-grandfather Eliezer.

In my own photo album, my grandfather, Yossel Topf, is at last reunited with the parents from whom he was separated in early childhood and the brothers he never met.

In Israel last January, I spent several hours quizzing my stepfather's elderly niece, Dora, about the family background. As a direct result of what I learned that day and my own applied genealogical efforts since then, I have just found the second set of lost relatives in four weeks, the daughter of my stepfather's older half brother who went to the U.S. pre-World War I.

I heard of this legendary "uncle in America," but none of us knew where he might have settled—New York, Chicago, who knew where? All it took was a request to copy some of Dora's family photographs, inherited from her mother who reached Palestine in 1938 or 1939, and who, as the eldest sibling, had a photograph from Pesach Kempinski in the U.S.A. I looked at the back of the photo and it said, "H. Brodkin, Art Photographer, 3-5 Temple Street near Main Street, Paterson, New Jersey."

I wrote the Australian Jewish Welfare Society, our local equivalent of and corresponded with HIAS and the "Joint," and gave them the information. This morning in the mail I received a note with the name and address of the daughter of the half brother in Clifton, New Jersey. Just now, writing the above, I decided to telephone her. I woke her, not realizing the time on the U.S. East Coast, but we had a very happy telephone reunion. At last, the mystery of why there was no contact between my stepfather and his brother was explained.

In 1933, Uncle Pesach developed a brain tumor. Although he survived until 1943, he was plagued with recurrences of the tumor for the rest of his life. I now know my stepfather's two siblings who escaped the Holocaust both died before the end of the World War II, one in the States and the other in Palestine in 1944, which is why family ties were cut.

Dora, in Israel, also told me one of her cousins survived by going to Siberia. He later settled in Denver; now he was dead. He had children, but she did not know either their names or their addresses. I contacted the local U.S. Information Service through the U.S. consulate and asked for the name and address of a Denver Jewish newspaper. When they gave it to me, I wrote a short letter to the editor.

This resulted twelve days later in an excited call from Denver. The relative there also knew she had "an uncle who came to the States before World War I," but did not know where he lived. Now I can put her in touch.

Sophie Caplan is founder of the Australian Jewish Genealogical Society and was its president until 2002. She is a child survivor of the Holocaust from France and has worked in both Australian Jewish history and Holocaust history. In late 2004 she became president of the Australian Jewish Historical Society in Sydney and continues today in that position. Her work has been published in anthologies and journals in English, French and German. In 2000, the Australian government awarded her the Medal of the Order of Australia for her work with survivors, day school students and genealogy.

On Helping a Relative Find His Father
by Wayne Pines

Winter 1988

The letter was like a plea. It came from Phillip Pines, a 44-year-old electrician in Athens, Georgia. It was a form letter, sent to all people with the surname Pines in the northeastern United States.

Phillip Pines was seeking his father. The letter explained that he was looking for Lester Pines. Born in Pittsburgh in 1936, Phillip had been brought up entirely by his mother, Ada Notter. Phillip's parents had separated when he was only three. He wrote, "I believe he returned to New York City which was his home. We have not seen or heard from him since that time."

Now in 1980, Phillip's daughter was getting married, and he was wondering about his family. Was his father still alive? Could anyone find Lester Pines?

I had just completed a genealogy of my branch of the Pines family and knew of no one named Lester Pines, but something about the name did ring a bell. My grandfather's sister, Dora Pines, had married Samuel Eikov, and among their children was a Lester Eikov. Lester was regarded as the black sheep of the family. Apparently, he was a drifter all his life. Even his own brothers and sisters were not sure if he had died or if he had a family.

With the possibility that Lester Eikov and Lester Pines were the same person, I called Phillip Pines seeking more information. At first, he said that he had none since his mother, still alive, refused to talk about his father. Finally, Phillip sent me two documents. One was his own birth certificate which listed his parents as Lester Pines and Ada Notter. The second was his parents' application for a marriage license. This document proved to be the key to the mystery.

Again I called Phillip Pines, this time to relay my strong suspicions and to ask if he could send anything else. A few weeks later I received a small photograph of Lester Pines photocopied into a corner of a piece of paper. It was a copy of the only photograph that Phillip's mother had of his father.

I sent a copy of the photo to Lester Eikov's sister, now living in a nursing home in upstate New York. "Is this your brother?" I asked. It was no surprise when she said that it was. She told me that Lester often had used his mother's maiden name, Pines, in his various pursuits.

Before calling Phillip with the answer to his quest, I wondered how he would receive it. Phillip's mother was a devout Methodist and had brought him up in that religion. How, I wondered, would a Methodist electrician from Athens, Georgia, react to being told that his father was Jewish with a large extended family in the United States, England, Israel and Russia, many of whom were quite religious?

Needless to say, Phillip was astonished but also grateful that his search had been successful. When I told him of his ancestry and his living family members, he immediately began to correspond with them. I have since lost touch with Phillip and do not know how he is relating to his new-found family. One of Phillip's aunts, Lester's sister Helen, wondered whether I had done him any favor. "I feel sorry for this Phillip; his father didn't even leave him his own name," she wrote. "Far better," I wrote back, "to know than not to know." I am sure that Phillip Pines agrees.

Wayne Pines started Pines family research in the 1970s. In 1978, he published a book, The Sermons of Jerome Martin Pines with a Partial Genealogy of the Pines Family, which included sermons by his father, a rabbi. Wayne continues to seek to connect the many branches of the Pines family.

Ain't Nothing Like the Living Thing, Baby!
by Debra Katz Klein

Winter 1999

I am much more comfortable in a research library than making a cold call to a distant relation. I am darn good at archival research, often surprising family and even myself at how much I am able to piece out and puzzle together. Yet it is only when I have pushed myself to follow that classic advice—find and talk to living relatives—that I have unearthed the kind of pure gold no repository can hold. Let me offer just a few examples of things I have learned from relatives I had never known before getting into genealogy. Note that almost all started the conversation with "I really don't know much...."

Saved by Runaway Sam

My husband's grandfather, Middy, died young, but my mother-in-law gave me the name of Middy's brother, who responded to my letter of inquiry with warmth and great details about my husband's ancestry. This great-uncle then gave me the address of a cousin who had moved to Israel. I wrote to the Israeli cousin, and his reply, along with many wonderful tidbits, included the following story:

Great-great-grandmother Chava and her five children left Taurage, Lithuania, in 1888 to join her husband, who had immigrated to Philadelphia a few years earlier. After sailing to Liverpool, Chava bought tickets for the next boat to New York. The family was standing around the docks waiting for their ship to depart, when Chava suddenly noticed that her youngest son, Shmuel, was missing! He was only three years old and prone to wandering off, but now he was nowhere in sight. Chava panicked and began scouring the dock area for a sign of him, all to no avail. Hours passed and it was time to board the ship. Chava had no choice but to remain on the docks and continue searching for little Shmuel.

The ship sailed, and much later Shmuel was finally found. Chava did not have enough money for new tickets, so she had to wait for her husband to send more. Meanwhile, Chava learned some news that made shivers run down her spine—the ship that they had missed boarding had just sunk at sea, and most of the passengers had drowned. Little runaway Shmuel had inadvertently saved their lives. My husband's family (descendants of Shmuel's eldest brother) still cannot believe how much they owe their existence to this incredible twist of fate.

Dying to Get Out of Russia

My grandmother saved old letters, including several from Israel. These letters were written in the 1950s and were mostly in Yiddish, which I could not read. I decided it would be worth the postage to take a chance and write to the return address. I simply asked if the current occupant had ever heard of anyone with my family surname. As fate would have it, the current occupant was the son of the original letter writer—and fluent in English. From him and from the other relatives with whom he connected me, I learned about a huge Israeli branch of the family.

Better still, I discovered an amazing amount of information about the family *shtetl* in the Ukraine, information that was equally relevant to my American branch, but had not been passed along by relatives here. For example, I learned about political activism in both branches:

The police in the Berdichev district were keeping close tabs on the Katz family. Benjamin Katz was the regional leader of the Zionist organization. Benjamin's brother had two socialist sons who had to run off to Siberia to escape capture. Benjamin's sister had a socialist son, Abram, who was not so lucky; he was thrown into jail for his activism. Abram's father was fairly influential, and by knowing and bribing the right people, he was able to smuggle Abram out of the prison as a corpse in a coffin.

Not the least bit dead, Abram went into hiding at a cousin's house (a girl he later married), but he knew that the police were hot on his trail and he had to get out of Russia fast. Someone had the idea that he should dress up as a woman, which he did, and in that disguise he traveled all the way to London. Then Abram became a "man" once again and boarded a ship to Boston—and his freedom.

Butcher Bornstein Goes Overboard

I'd always known that my great-grandfather William Goldstein had been a sausage maker. I'd also heard that Goldstein was not his real surname, but had never been able to discover where he was from, his original surname or how he got into the delicatessen business. One day I decided to try an Internet search for one of William's nieces. Her father was William's youngest brother, and she was the youngest child in her family, so maybe she was still living. An old wedding invitation gave me her rather uncommon married name. I found a listing for her husband and soon was in contact with a very much alive, alert and enthusiastic 82-year-old lady. During our fourth telephone conversation, after apologizing for not knowing much about her Uncle William, she said, "Oh yes, there was one little story:

The Bornstein family was from Ratno, Ukraine, originally, but when the patriarch died in 1877, his wife moved to Odessa with her three sons, the eldest of whom was William. Like so many others, William ended up leaving Odessa to escape army conscription and somehow made his way penniless to Liverpool. Exhausted, William was leaning against a tree outside a butcher shop in the Jewish quarter when the butcher spotted him. After a short chat, he offered William a job as his apprentice, and William soon learned both English and the butchery trade.

Eventually, William realized that the butcher was planning for him to marry his daughter, something William did not want to do. So, when William overheard some sailors at the docks talking about how their ship's butcher had just quit, he seized the opportunity to get away. He asked the sailors to take him to their captain, and William talked his way into the job. As ship's butcher, he set sail for New York a few days later.

Whether he had planned it all along, or just got the idea at some point during the voyage, no one knows, but William decided he wanted to stay in America. When his ship sailed into the harbor, he jumped overboard unnoticed. Somehow he made it ashore and past immigration officials. Having heard about Chicago's meat industry, William headed to the Windy City. There he got a job as a butcher in the elegant Palmer House hotel — and he adopted a new surname, Goldstein, just in case the Russian army authorities — or the boat captain — ever came looking for him.

It's an Incredibly Small World

I had hit another brick wall trying to trace one of my maternal lines, so I turned my attention to my father's family. I wanted to find his cousin Bob, who I knew must still be alive. Bob's mother had died when he was born, and Bob's father had remarried soon after, never speaking of Bob's mother again. But Bob's aunt — my paternal grandmother — had kept some contact with her nephew over the years. From her old address book, I got an idea of where to start looking for him. Again, I used the Internet with great success.

My grandmother, who had basically raised her sister and loved her dearly, had kept dozens of photographs and other memorabilia of her. When I discovered that Bob did not even know what his mother had looked like, I sent him a package of mementos for which he's never stopped thanking me.

A few months later, I was bemoaning to my mother and uncle how I couldn't find any more leads on their Wolkin line. My uncle casually remarked that he vaguely remembered some descendants from that line who by coincidence had lived next door to my father's cousin, Bob. Did I have any idea how to reach Bob he asked? Did I ever! I immediately called Bob and sure enough, he had grown up next to a Wolkin descendant with whom he'd been very close, so close in fact that more 40 years later he still had a current telephone number. A few more calls and I had opened the door to a wealth of information and leads on my Wolkin ancestry.

The Bottom Line

These anecdotes are but a few examples—I have dozens more—of the amazing tales, incredible coincidences and heartwarming moments that come to light when you follow the genealogist's golden rule:

Contact relatives and, through them, your ancestors will contact you.

Debra Katz Klein, a native Californian, has been playing family history detective since 1990. Originally told her ancestors were "from Russia," she since has been able to trace nine ancestral lines back for centuries into shtetls from Riga to Odessa. And thanks to her more recent forays into genetic genealogy, Debra claims that she has linked her lines to ancient Israelite priests, Fulani tribes in Africa and Mediterranean peoples that hobnobbed with Neanderthals. What an adventure!

So You Think It Is Impossible
by Carol Rombro Rider

Winter 1992

E lie Wiesel said it best in his story, *Testament of a Jew in Saragossa*: "I did not know it when I arrived, but someone was awaiting me there." The only difference was that his storyteller traveled to Saragossa, and this writer journeyed to Salt Lake City in the summer of 1991.

My grandmother, Mary Kushner, was the youngest of four children, born a short time after her father died. She was the first of her immediate family to emigrate from her hometown of Dunayivtsy, or Dinovitz, in Ukraine. She settled in Baltimore and was followed by a brother, Isaac, who continued on to Los Angeles to seek his fortune. Another brother, Leib, came to America but decided to return home where it was more *frum* (traditionally Orthodox). The last brother, Bernardo, left the *shtetl*, not for America, but for Argentina. Sometime in the distant past, Mary lost touch with Bernardo and his family. She died in 1959, never having been able to locate him.

The only clue was that Bernardo lived in Buenos Aires and had four sons. I assumed that one of the sons would have been named in memory of Bernardo's father, who died before Mary was born, so I decided to add a possible Moshe Kushner to my list. That was all I had, that and an address in Argentina written on old, crumpled paper at least 50 years ago and barely legible.

It was in Salt Lake City at the LDS (Mormon) Family History Library, sitting behind the Information Desk on the European floor, that I found him. I first approached with a question about my maiden name. "Could the name Rombro be Spanish?" I asked, and with it began an animated discussion about referrals to Italian sources. His name was Egeo Gabasa, and he was assisted by his wife, Claribel. "Where are you from?" I asked, "And where did you learn so many languages?"

The reply came back, "Argentina," and I was aware that my mouth had dropped open. He laughed when asked if I could show him an old address, and I ran to my briefcase to locate the copy I had made.

As he looked at it, a smile of amazement came over his face, and he mumbled, "I haven't seen anything like this in years!"

"What does it say?" I demanded.

"I just haven't seen anything like this in years," came the reply again.

The address was from times past, a station on a train stop from days gone by. The closest thing to it I could imagine was an address in the Old Wild West on a stagecoach line. He clearly made out the name of the town of Ceres, with a population of only 2,712 in 1921. The energy that the Gabasas put into finding the town on a map and locating detailed information made my head spin. There was no question the gap of years was closing, but there were still a few more left.

Now the detective that lies dormant in every genealogist sprang to the surface. How do you close a gap of so many years? To whom do you write? Years before, my sister had tried writing to every Kushner (spelled Kusnir in Argentina) in Buenos Aires, but received few replies. At least I now knew why. Part of the story handed down was mistaken—Bernardo had settled in Ceres, not Buenos Aires. That's like looking for relatives in Chicago, not knowing that they had settled in Indianapolis.

Among the books I keep in my genealogy collection is a little gem called *The Jewish Travel Guide*, published yearly by the *London Jewish Chronicle*. My copy was from 1982, already nine years old. Never mind. Located at the end of the article about Argentina was a list of small Jewish communities throughout the country. One was listed for Ceres, with an address. I sent off a generic—and I do mean generic—letter in Spanish to the address. On the wings of an angel, the letter I sent ended up in the hands of an older gentleman, Elias Volcoff. He wrote back to tell me that not only did he know my great-uncle, but also named his wife, four children (and, yes, the eldest was Moshe) and gave details of the family. I assembled my father and his sister and, with the help of a relative who spoke Yiddish, we called to speak to Volcoff. More details were supplied; grandchildren and great-grandchildren were scattered across Argentina. We succeeded in doing what my grandmother had wished for in her last years. A puzzle was put together, and a large, new branch was added to the tree.

As in Elie Wiesel's story, mine, too, will end in Israel. Next year we hope to travel there, and on the "must do" list is the important one of locating and meeting the great-grandchildren of Bernardo Kushner, who made *aliyah* (immigration to Israel) from Argentina.

Ah, that Elie Wiesel. He sure knew how to tell a story!

Carol Rombro Rider began doing genealogical research in 1977 when she read Dan Rottenberg's pioneer book, Finding Our Fathers. She was at home with a newborn baby and needed something to do. Something to do became a full time obsession. Rider lives in Baltimore, Maryland.

Uncovering the Real Family Name
by Paul H. Silverstone

Winter 1994

We of the Silverstone family are heirs to a curious chain of circumstances that led to our inheriting this surname. According to family lore, our grandfather, Harris Silverstone, changed his name from an unpronounceable name to Silverstein (and later to Silverstone) upon immigration to the United States—a not uncommon Jewish story. As a result of genealogical research, we have been able to uncover the real facts.

The family story handed down to us is that when Harris arrived in New York, the immigration inspector asked his name, which Harris gave, and then the inspector asked how it was spelled. Afraid that he would be turned away, Harris gave his wife's maiden name, Silverstein. His daughter later wrote, "One had to cough to say the name, so father took my mother's name." A pretty story. How many families have stories about how their name was changed when they arrived in America? How many families have the same surname on both sides?

Another story was uncovered. Harris's brother Jacob, upon his arrival, took his new surname because the original name meant horseradish in Polish, and it was distasteful to him. He also took the name Silverstein because that was his wife's maiden name as well. She was Harris' niece by marriage.

Having discovered my grandfather's true surname, I now know that these stories are substantially true. On the gravestone of Harris' father, Ezra, in Maków Mazowiecki, Poland, the family name is given as חזשאן. On his wife's tombstone it is spelled חשאן.

Alexander Beider, author of *A Dictionary of Jewish Surnames from the Russian Empire*, has confirmed that these letters are phonetically equivalent to the Polish word for horseradish, *chrzan*. Beider writes in a letter to me:

> *Rz is normally pronounced as zh as in pleasure, but close to the unvoiced consonant rz is the pronunciation as sh. This is the case for chrzan as the Polish ch (like the English ch in loch or chaim, designated usually as kh in transliterations) is unvoiced. Thus, the English versions might be Khzhan, Khshan, Chzhan, Chshan or Hzhan and Hshan. The Russian passport of another brother, Boruch, gives the name as Хрзан, which is transliterated Khrzan.*

When Harris arrived, an uncle of his by the last name of Cherry, was already living in the United States. Last year, my aunt, Estelle Silverstone, chanced to meet Barbara Eisenberg, whose maiden name had been Cherry and whose grandfather, Charles Cherry, is buried next to my grandfather, Harris Silverstone, in the Makower section of the Acacia Cemetery in Queens, New York.

Barbara remembered that the maiden name of her grandmother Bryne had been Shann. From Bryne's death certificate, I learned that her father's name had been Jacob, the same name as Harris's great-grandfather (the father of Ezra). In fact, on that death certificate, dated 1972, his surname is given as Silverstein—an example of a retroactive name change. From all this, we learned that Bryne Cherry was, indeed, Harris's aunt, and hers was the family to whom he had come upon arrival in the U.S.

Many members of the Silverstone family had used a dentist named Harry Cherry, the sixth child of Charles and Bryne Cherry. (The family's original name had been Vishnick, the Polish word for *cherry*.)

Barbara told me that she had cousins who were the grandchildren of Bryne's brother or sister. Eventually, I called one, Edith Charet, whose grandmother, Friede Hinde Lichtenstein, had been Bryne's sister. Photographs taken in 1927 of Harris and his wife Esther, when they visited their native town of Maków, show them standing next to the gravestones of Ezra and his wife. With them are Itche Meier Lichtenstein and his wife, Friede Hinde. Until I spoke to Edith, no one in our family had known who the second couple was. Another mystery was solved.

Now we know that Jacob Chrzan, who died before 1883, had at least three children: Ezra, the father of Zvi (Harris Silverstone); Bryne (Shann) Cherry; and Friede, later Friede Hinde Lichtenstein. The key was finding the Cherry family, long out of touch with the Silverstones. The question of how to pronounce the name on the gravestones was solved by learning Bertha Cherry's maiden name and connecting it with Alexander Beider's analysis. The telephone call to a totally unknown collateral cousin produced the identity of the unknown couple in the old photograph.

As with most genealogical research, the solutions of these problems produced further questions. The necrology in the Maków yizkor book, written after the Holocaust, lists three Chrzan—Ezra, Friede Hinde and Moshe. Although we do not know as yet who they were, their given names suggest that they were descendants of our Ezra. They perished, as did Friede Hinde, Itche Meier Lichtenstein and almost all of their family.

Paul Silverstone, a resident of New York, is an author of books on warships and naval history. In addition to his interest in genealogy, he has researched the clandestine immigration of Jews to Palestine during the years 1938–48.

The Cortissoz Diary
by Gail Greenberg
Winter 1989

Beshert. The older I get, the more I believe in that wonderful Yiddish word that means fate or fated.

Two years ago, I took a course on American foreign policy. One of the required texts concerned the Jewish mercantile class in Europe during the 16th to 18th centuries. Much to my surprise, my mother's family name, Cortissoz, showed up not once, but twice, in this text, although it was spelled Cortissos. Was it possible that there was any relationship between the Marranos of the book and my mother's Marrano ancestors? My heart leaped at the possibility, but at the time, my sister and I were preoccupied with our mother's battle with cancer and her subsequent death, so I did not pursue the matter.

When it became necessary to sell our parents' home, my sister rediscovered an old family diary of my mother's in the basement where it had been shelved along with dozens of other old, musty books. We had known they were down there, but had dismissed them as more of "Mother's old junk." A true child of the Depression, she had collected old magazines, empty bottles, etc.

This time we read the diary. The first time I read it I sat in my kitchen transfixed, tears streaming down my face at the recitation of *brits* (circumcisions) and of infant deaths, of massive loss of life due to plague (Malta, 1810), and of unsuccessful commercial interests. It was as if my ancestors were at my shoulders, standing around me as I read this amazing chronicle which begins in 1774 with my mother's great-grandfather, Abraham Haim Simah Cortissoz, on the island of Saint Eustatius in the Dutch West Indies. It details journeys from Amsterdam to London and Malta, to Surinam and Jamaica and Saint Thomas. Eventually, one branch of the family arrived in New Orleans in 1848, and some went immediately on to San Francisco. This incredible piece of history is about my ancestors, my mother's parents, grandparents and great-grandparents.

That was about six months ago. Last month, while casting about for a project topic for completion of my bachelor's degree at George Mason University in Fairfax, Virginia, I suddenly had a flash. What if I could persuade my advisor to permit me to research my family pedigree, starting with the Cortissos brothers mentioned in the textbook, Joseph and Manuel, through the diary to the present? Not only would this require extensive research and historical reading, but it would also provide intense personal satisfaction. I have even wondered whether my interest in the diary at this time is part of the cathartic process necessary in grieving.

I presented the proposal to my advisor: to research the information surrounding Joseph and Manual Cortissos of the textbook; to develop a line from them to the diary; to unearth information regarding the people, lives and times of the diary; and to present it all, possibly in an article for publication. I could see the goose bumps raise on her arms as I showed her the diary. There is something almost metaphysical about this book, not quite holy, but sacred somehow. That a personal chronicle of my ancestors should have survived this long seems truly remarkable. To have this diary and to read a text mentioning two Cortissos was more than coincidental to me. While the project request was highly unusual, the historical significance was deemed worthwhile and my advisor agreed to the proposal.

This fall [1988] I joined the Jewish Genealogy Society of Greater Washington (JGSGW). Members told me about St. Eustatius records filmed by the Mormons at the American Jewish Archives. I learned about a publication of the Dutch Jewish Genealogy Society detailing Sephardic *ketubot* (marriage contracts) in Amsterdam. In the JGSGW library, I found an index to all articles published by the Jewish Historical Society of England. To my amazement it listed several pertaining specifically to the Cortissoz family.

Yesterday, I spent five hours in the genealogy and local history room of the U.S. Library of Congress in Washington, DC, tracking down several articles from the Jewish Historical Society of England's volumes, as well as following up on leads in other articles and books. Not only did I discover extensive background on the Jo-

Page from the Cortissos family diary

seph Cortissos of the textbook, complete with a picture of the portrait which hangs in London's Bevis Marks Synagogue, but I also found evidence of a pre-Revolutionary branch of the family in Charleston, South Carolina.

However, the most exciting discovery was a family tree showing several generations and marriages of the Joseph Cortissos family. The diagram ends at the bottom of the page with one of the sons, Emmanuel Cortissoz marrying Leah da Costa Mesquita. On pages seven and eight of my mother's diary it says:

Amsterdam, 25th Dcbr., 1800. On this day which Corresponds to the 6th Tebett 5561 Providence was pleased to call to Eternal Glory my Good Mother, Mrs. Leah

Cortissoz Da Costa Mesquitta at this city, at abt. the age of 62 years, Leaving three sons and two daughters to lament her loss.

So there I have it. According to Charles Rubin, author of the Jewish Historical Society article, my great-great-grandfather, Abraham Haim Simah Cortissoz, was the son of Leah da Costa Mesquitta and a descendant of the Manuel Cortissos of my textbook. I can now trace my family in a direct line seven generations back to Emanuel (Isaac) Cortissos, brother of Joseph Cortissos.

Furthermore, Rubens quotes something entitled "Genealogy of My Family," a document written by the grandson of the above Joseph Cortissos about 1780. It contains a short account of his ancestry and of the activities of his grandfather. There is an endorsement, which reads, "Your great-grandfather being grandson of the Marquis de Villa, a Grandee of Spain." In other words, it appears that my ancestry can be traced back, without a missing generation, to pre-Inquisition Spain!

I am still attempting to obtain a book about the Jews of Saint Eustatius. It is listed in the Library of Congress computer, but is so new that it has not been assigned a call number. My next stop will be a nearby Mormon library because they have microfilmed American Jewish Archives information about the Jews of Saint Eustatius. There is also a book listing Sephardic *ketubot* recently published by the Dutch Jewish Genealogical Society. Finally, and most important, I shall write to Charles Rubin in England and ask for the references in his article.

Given the damp, unprotected conditions in my mother's basement, it was difficult to believe that the diary actually had been written more than 200 years ago. Perhaps these events were set down sometime later. I presented the book to a librarian to estimate the age of the diary. A portly gentleman, seated in front of the librarian's desk, asked to see the watermark. He could not find one, but recognized the type of paper and said it probably was 200 years old, but certainly at least 100 years. After he walked away, I inquired about the gentleman with the British crest sewn on his jacket and was told that he is an appraiser and past president of a state historical society. As I said, "*beshert*."

Gail Greenberg spent 25 years in corporate America and now is semi-retired. She lives in Reston, Virginia.

Grandma with the Funny Name
by Rosanne Leeson

Winter 1994

When I was a little girl of perhaps five or six, my special time was a Sunday morning walk with my father. No sooner had we exited our apartment building then I would slip my hand into his and demand, "Papa, tell me a story." My father was a marvelous storyteller, and he particularly loved to tell me stories about his family. Of course, I soon knew them all by heart, but I loved to hear them, over and over again. And I had a favorite. He would talk about his paternal grandmother, who had never come to the United States, but whose picture was in a locket my father's father had given to his mother when they became engaged. What I loved so about this story was his grandma's funny name. He would let it roll off his tongue: Mamele HEMMERDINGER!!![1] This would reduce me to fits of hysterical giggles. As I grew older, and the genealogical flame, first lighted by my father's tales, grew into a wildfire, I would declare, "What a ridiculous name! There couldn't possibly be anyone else in the world with such a funny name." Not so—and seriously not so.

At this moment, after 25 years of research, I have close to 3,000 names [now 5,000 names] in my Hemmerdinger database. In July 1999, we had a family reunion of 110 persons, all of them descendants of Hemmerdingers, in the small town of Scherwiller in Alsace, France, where our earliest identified common ancestor lived and was the rabbi in the last quarter of the 17th century. This represented just a small percentage of descendants whom I have located, but not all were able to join us.

My husband and I had prepared name tags for all of the family in the shape of small family trees showing each individual's line of ascendancy back to the original rabbi and his wife. Each was also color-coded, so that the descendants of each of the six children of this couple could easily be identified. The highlight of our reunion was the dedication of a plaque in honor of our ancestors which was placed on the wall of the small oratory in the nearby old cemetery where they and many other family members have been buried over the centuries. This cemetery, in the town of Sélestat, about five kilometers from Scherwiller, dates back to the late 16th century.

In the days preceding the reunion, family members began to arrive—from the U.S., Israel, Germany, Martinique and many places in France. The last Jew in Scherwiller, after 300 years, is a family member. We all gathered at the cemetery

---

[1] *A Dictionary of German-Jewish Surnames* suggests the origin of the name is the town of Heimertingen, Germany.

for a moving service of dedication. One of our presiding rabbis was a six-times great-grandson of the original rabbi; he had come from Jerusalem for this historic event. All were deeply moved, and many were in tears from the emotions of the day—and I wore the locket with my great-grandmother's picture.

On the final evening of our reunion, we joined all the townspeople of Scherwiller in their annual Grand Bal on the eve of the celebration of Bastille Day (July 14). By this time, we had gotten to know one another well. We danced together, sang together and ate together. Everyone had a joyful and riotous time as we took up the traditional torches and marched through the entire town, following the band of the local fire department. What would our ancestors have thought of all this!

The reunion itself ended with hugs and kisses, exchanges of addresses, e-mail addresses, fax numbers and promises to meet again "in Paris," "in New York," elsewhere. Perhaps the most enthusiastic group of all were the younger family members who swore never to forget this event and to pass on the tradition to their children, whenever they had any. What greater success than this?

After all had departed from Scherwiller, my husband and I took advantage of the relative calm to drive across the Rhine to the small town in Baden, Germany, where my great-grandmother had married, lived and died. We visited her grave in the cemetery, and as I stood before the tombstone of Mamele Hemmerdinger, I opened the locket and told her all about the wonderful reunion of the many de-

scendants of her great-grandparents.

We had exemplified life in the Diaspora. We were now Jews, Catholics, Protestants, agnostics, black and white, and from all over the world. We had come together to give honor to the memory of our common ancestors, and we had departed a family, reunited again after 300 years—all because Grandma had such a funny name.

Rosanne Leeson was born in New York City. She attended the High School of Music & Art, has a BA from Barnard College and an MLS from Columbia University School of Library Science. She is currently co-coordinator for both ROM-SIG and FrenchSIG of JewishGen, and vice-president of the San Francisco Bay Area JGS. She is a member of the JGSNY, Texas Jewish Historical Society and Cercle de Généalogie Juive of Paris. Together with her husband, Dan, she is an IAJGS award winner for the 2-volume index to the volume of 5000 marriage contracts deposited with notaries in Alsace from 1701–1791.

Reunion of Hemmerdingers in Scherwiller, Alsace, France, in 1999.

Our Family's Link to the Civil War
by Stephanie Wroblewski Isaacs

Winter 1990

Row after row of little tombstones stood in front of us in the bright sunlight of a south Georgia morning. Little tombstones so small that an eight-year-old child could easily climb over them.

The history of past events that had laid these men to rest suddenly came alive. Andersonville National Cemetery was the site of one of the largest Confederate prisons during the Civil War (1860–65). Within about 26 acres, more than 25,000 men were confined; during the 14 months of its existence, 45,000 Union soldiers passed through the prison's gates. In total, 13,000 men were reported to have died there of disease, malnutrition, exposure, overcrowding, execution or poor sanitation.

One of the Union soldiers who died there, Sergeant Julius Baywood, Company I, First New York Cavalry, may be more than just a name on a tombstone; he may be our family's link to the Civil War. It was purely by chance that we found Sergeant Baywood's grave at all.

As history buffs living in Atlanta, Georgia, my husband and I are naturally interested in the Civil War. A book on Andersonville Prison with a preface by Clara Barton, founder of the American Red Cross, caught our eyes one day. Included was a listing of all the Union soldiers who had died at the prison. Men are listed state by state along with their rank, company, date and cause of death. If Dorance Atwater, a young member of the Second New York Cavalry, had not had the foresight to make a copy of the death books in his charge, most of these Union soldiers would have ended up as unknowns. Atwater's lists enabled Clara Barton to mark the graves of the dead when she was asked by President Abraham Lincoln to determine the whereabouts of prisoners so that their families could be notified.

Reading the lists gave me a welcome distraction. I eyed each page for family names and was startled when I saw Sergeant Baywood's name. In many years of genealogical research, a member of the Baywood side of the family had never come to light through either telephone books or periodicals. J. Baywood could have been my husband's paternal great-great-grandfather who had come from England about 1860 with his wife and young son, Albert (Abraham). John Baywood was in the textile trade and immigrated to America presumably to find a better life.

Family stories about the Baywood family mentioned Civil War involvement, but no definite facts were known. John Baywood was not buried in the family plot in New York with his wife Harriet, son Albert, and Albert's wife and children. In fact, Albert seemed to be the only child born to John Baywood and Harriet Harris Baywood. We wondered if John Baywood had died shortly after coming to America.

Andersonville National Cemetery

The J. Baywood in the Andersonville lists seemed a possibility. New York was full of war fever in the 1860s and many young men enlisted in the Union Army to fight for Lincoln and country. As a new immigrant, this would have been a way to earn a salary and to exhibit newly found patriotism.

A newspaper article in the *Atlanta Constitution* in February 1989 discussed the 125th anniversary of the Andersonville National Historic Site the week we bought the book. The story included an interview with a park ranger (Andersonville is part of the U.S. National Park Service) and gave his name and address. I decided that writing to Andersonville directly would be a good starting point.

The ranger soon answered my letter, verifying the information in the Atwater lists, as well as supplying a few new facts. Baywood also was known as Boywood in some records. The family name was originally Bieholtz and changed in England to Bywood. Since John Baywood was born presumably in Germany and could have had a mixed German/English accent, Baywood might have come out as Boywood. The gravestone, #9380, was carved Boywood, but the records showed Baywood.

A confusing bit of information was this Baywood's first name on official papers—Julius. Yet, our John Baywood had a granddaughter Julia and a grandson Julius. Perhaps John was a middle name or a name assumed in England; perhaps this relative was a great-uncle—perhaps, perhaps, perhaps.

Due to the circumstances of death, many records had not been turned over to the federal government, but to cover all bases, I wrote for military records to both the U.S. National Archives in Washington and to the State Archives in Albany, New York. Answers were received within a few weeks. The National Archives had no military or pension records for our Union soldier, but the New York Archives sent back a gold mine of information. Julius Baywood's muster papers covered his military service from beginning to end. Unfortunately, only a few personal facts were mentioned; nothing was noted about personal family connections.

Julius Baywood had been born in Ostrow, Prussia, in about 1823. He was 5 feet 7 inches tall with dark hair and dark eyes. He enlisted for three years as a corporal in the First New York Cavalry, Lincoln Brigade on August 1, 1861. The First New York Cavalry was formed in New York City where the Baywood family had lived. In January 1864, Julius Baywood re-enlisted and became a sergeant. Sergeant Baywood was taken prisoner near New Market, Virginia, May 13, 1864. He was sent to Andersonville where he died of scurvy on September 20, 1864.

Curiosity about this man and his life grew until searching out information about the Lincoln Brigade became almost an obsession. A book by Bertram Hawthrone Groene, *Tracing Your Civil War Ancestor*, provided definite direction and led to many other publications. General information about the Brigade was gleaned from the Official Records of the Union and Confederate Armies in the War of the Rebellion, commonly known as the OR. A complete set of the 128-volume collection may be found in various libraries. (For naval unit information, see the 31 volumes of the Official Records of the Union and Confederate Navies in the War of the Rebellion, also known as the ORN.) The OR contains information based on daily reports written by officers about engagements and casualties. Although usually slanted to sit well with superiors, these reports provide excellent descriptions of daily life.

Military Bibliography of the Civil War, by Charles Dornbusch, should be consulted by anyone researching the Civil War. It reports mustering in and out dates, as well as other details for each military group. Lists of publications done by individuals or regimental organizations are also included. Many are tributes and memorials. The books are listed by state and contain a complete index to military units and individuals. Because he was not an officer, there was no listing for Baywood, but there were listings for the First New York Lincoln Cavalry, about which I am now searching for books published by a fellow officer.

Civil War Books, by Alan Nevins, James I. Robertson, Jr. and Bell I. Wiley, is a critical bibliography of all books published on the Civil War. In two volumes, it lists valuable books that give depth to the daily life of the soldiers.

One young soldier made it his life's work to record every Union military group along with its engagements and basic history. This valuable collection, *A Compendium of the War of the Rebellion*, by Frederick H. Dyer, is usually available only in reference sections of libraries. Note that when the Civil War was written about, the Union side called it "The War of the Rebellion," while the Confederates called it "The War Between the States." Unfortunately, a collection similar to

Dyer's was never compiled for the Confederate forces.

Even after consulting all of these collections, I still have no absolute proof that Julius Baywood was my husband's great-great-grandfather, or even a great-great-uncle. Still, the available facts make it seem very believable. Even if in the future I will be proven wrong, our family has decided to adopt Julius Baywood as our own.

No one can take away the rush of excitement when, after searching aisle after aisle for the right tombstone, our two sons, ages eight and five, found tombstone #9380 for Julius Baywood. Their laughter pierced the silence of that somber place with the joy of their discovery. After explaining to the boys the significance of the event, my husband took a few moments to himself, just pondering and looking over the spot. When he rejoined us and we started walking away, I asked, "Even though we are not sure if he was your great-great-grandfather, maybe you should say *Kaddish* (prayer for the dead)?" Turning to me with a smile, he answered, "I already have."

Welcome, Sergeant Baywood. Welcome to our family.

Stephanie Wroblewski Isaacs is a New Yorker now living and working in the north Georgia mountains. She has been researching her family history since the late 1970s, and currently she corresponds with family, friends and researchers all over the world. She continues to write about various branches of family and the society they lived in, especially pertaining to the Sephardim, the Holocaust and other topics. Her two sons, referred to in this article, have both graduated from college and still enjoy learning about and helping their mother chase down genealogy leads.

A Jewish Civil War Veteran
Finally Receives a Visitor
by Alexander Woodle

Winter 2005

S imon Woodle was one of thousands of German-speaking immigrants who arrived in the United States between 1840 and 1880 to seek a better way of life. His story is not of an extraordinary man who cured a disease, wrote a famous novel or created a new technology to improve society. He was a common man who found employment, married, provided food and shelter to his family and served his country during wartime.

Simon barely registered on the genealogical radar screen when I began my family research, but as I delved into the vital records, census, city directories and other records, a clearer image of him began to emerge. His paper trail led me to the home village of my ancestors in Bohemia,[1] and along the way, I was able to flesh out the bones of this man and his life in America during the last half of the 19th century.

Simon Woodle, an older brother of my great-grandfather, David Woodle, was born in Ckyne, Bohemia, on April 7, 1841. He embarked for New York City from Hamburg in May 1856, listing his occupation as farmer. The trail ran cold until he appeared in the New York City directories in the 1870s. During this period, his occupation was listed as hat maker, the same profession of his brothers, Moritz and David.

Confusion arose when the 1880 U.S. census revealed a Charles Woodle, hat maker, living in New York City, born in Bohemia around 1840. The two sisters living with Charles during this time previously had been confirmed from the archives in Prague, Czech Republic, as Simon Woodle's siblings. The birth register for Simon's family found in the central archives in Prague revealed a stillborn baby on October 29, 1839. Simon's birth in April 1841 left no room for Charles Woodle to fit into my great-great-grandmother's pregnancy schedule. Who was Charles? Could Charles and Simon be one and the same person?

I began to track the wife and children of Charles Woodle to see if I could solve this mystery. I finally breached the brick wall when I found marriage records for two of his children listing Simon as the father in one and Charles in the other, but both married to the same woman. I concluded that Charles and Simon must have been one and the same person. When I combined their records in my family da-

---

[1] "A Journey of Discovery," AVOTAYNU, Vol. XVIII, No. 4 (Winter 2002).

tabase they meshed perfectly. I do not know why both names were used.

The most important find, however, came from Ancestry.com, a commercial website, that listed a Civil War pension record for a Simon Woodle. I ordered and received from the U.S. National Archives a voluminous record of Simon's complete military history. The file included information on his enlistment and discharge and an extraordinary number of medical reports in support of his pension application, including doctor's examinations and anatomical sketches denoting his wounds received in combat. His unit, the 15th New York Heavy Artillery, had been in a number of significant engagements in Virginia during the years 1863–65.

In 1920, Simon's daughter Mary, crippled by an unknown malady and institutionalized, attempted to secure his pension. Letters from her relatives and sponsors pleaded her case, but to no avail. Her request was denied because her father's death in 1898 was deemed not due to war injuries.

Hidden within this pension file were other important genealogical facts: the early death date of his wife, the birth of a previously unknown daughter and his address in New York City in 1890. With this address, I was able to examine the 1890 Manhattan Police Census to determine who was living with him at that time.

Finally, this massive file also revealed his place of burial: the Civil War East Cemetery on the grounds of the Government Hospital for the Insane (since 1916 called St. Elizabeths Hospital) in Washington, DC. The federal government had established a number of hospitals across the country to treat the thousands of soldiers wounded physically and mentally during this horrific conflict.

In the National Archives Northeast Branch, in Waltham, Massachusetts, I found a microfilm showing the record of Simon Woodle's admittance into the eastern branch of the National Home for Disabled Volunteer Soldiers in Togus, Maine, in 1893, because of defective vision attributed to his service at the siege of Petersburg (Virginia). The following year, he was transferred to Washington, DC, where he died in July 1898 from "organic brain disease."

I contacted the National Archives in Washington and spoke with the curator for St. Elizabeths' records. He said there was a small file on Simon Woodle, and he would send me copies by mail. The file included a letter written in 1896 by a woman representing Simon's daughters asking if he were alive or dead, as he had left home without informing his family! She wrote, "Hoping you will be kind enough and let me know something about him, as his children are anxious to know about him."

A second letter from the then-superintendent of St. Elizabeths notified Simon's next-of-kin of his death. Another letter written by Simon's daughter, Henrietta Woodle, following the death of her father states in part:

We are very sorry we could not come on to see him as we are not in circumstances just at present. We are very thankful to you for notifying us as we are very happy to think that he was well taken care of in his last moments and to think we know where he is buried now.

This flood of information filled in many blanks in the life of this man, but I now wanted to find his tombstone and establish closure for the family. I spent an entire day researching everything I could find on the Internet about St. Elizabeths Hospital and telephoning various governmental bureaucracies to find out more about the Civil War cemetery located there. My persistence paid off, and I received the first of many e-mails from an employee of the Government Services Administration (GSA) whose job included property administration over a portion of St. Elizabeth's. He became my genealogical guardian angel, writing to me every day.

I learned that two Civil War cemeteries are on the grounds of St. Elizabeths, the "east" and the "west," but they are not well documented. My guardian angel was able, however, to establish that Simon was buried in the east cemetery. He contacted a local cemetery historian who promised to look for the grave. The cemetery is located just outside St Elizabeths' security wall (the current home of the would-be assassin of President Reagan).

I received an e-mail from my guardian angel that evening stating:

I wish I could tell you I scanned the 1000s of gravestones that are out on the East Campus, but we were there only about 5 or 10 minutes. There were four of us wandering through the cemetery, just talking and I turned, and damn if Sgt. Woodle's gravestone wasn't right in front of me!

It was one of those miraculous moments all genealogists live for! In this vast sea of graves, they had accidentally stumbled onto Simon's marker. My GSA contact told me that St. Elizabeths was celebrating its 150th anniversary in June and that I should come at that time. I contacted the organizers of the birthday celebration and was invited to lay a wreath at the memorial service. I purchased an official Grand Army of the Republic (GAR) grave marker to bring with me to mark Simon's grave.

In June, I flew to Washington and spent the weekend listening to speakers talk of the work of the hospital, the horrific accounts of casualties including thousands and thousands of soldiers who suffered from what we now call post traumatic stress disorder (PTSD). Simon's illness, classified as "brain disease" and "chronic dementia," may very well have been PTSD. We will never know for sure. What I do know is my visit to Simon's gravesite probably was the first by a member of my family. I proudly placed the grave marker next to his tombstone and stood for a moment of silence.

Alexander Woodle is a member of the Jewish Genealogical Society of Greater Boston and former Director of the New England Historic Genealogical Society's (NEHGS) circulating library. He has published articles on Jewish genealogy in AVOTAYNU, Mass-Pocha and NEHGS' newsletter. He has spoken to many genealogical groups and forums on his research including the annual conference of the International Association of Jewish Genealogical Societies and the New England Regional Genealogical Conference. Now retired, Woodle is a freelance genealogical researcher.

On the Trail of Uncle Herschel, The Jewish Gaucho

by Scott D. Seligman

How an improbable, two-continent search for a family black sheep and a generous dose of fate and coincidence united a family that didn't know it had been separated.

The real challenge in genealogy lies beyond the mere accumulation of names, begats, dates and places. Having dabbled in family history for several years and having amassed records of nearly 3,000 souls, living and dead, with whom I can claim a familial relationship of some sort, I have found that the process offers up two true rewards. First is the *mitzvah* (good deed) of honoring an ancestor through faithfully reconstructing his or her life and time. The second is the connection you establish with the people you meet along the way.

This is the story of my hunt for my great-uncle Herschel Rudbart—or rather, for information about him, since he died in Argentina when I was ten years old. I had never met him. Herschel was the black sheep of the family that begat my *bubbe* (grandmother), my father's mother. His parents, Esther Milsky and Israel Meyer Rudbart, lived in a *shtetl* on the border of Poland and Byelorussia called Porozów.

My grandmother, Gussie, was the second child in the family. Her elder brother, Lazar, had been the first to immigrate to the United States in 1906. His siblings followed in succession with great-aunt Mary, the youngest, the last to arrive. After their father died in 1920, she came with her mother, my great-grandmother Esther. All settled in or around Newark, New Jersey, and we were a fairly close-knit family, seeing each other frequently at weddings, bar mitzvahs and funerals.

Herschel was Bubbe's only sibling who never made it to the States. For some reason we will probably never know (although there has never been a shortage of theories), he was unable to get a visa, despite the presence in the United States of his entire family. Dad had understood vaguely that his *persona non grata* status stemmed from trouble with the authorities in the Old Country. Others, less cynical, cited his irrepressible wanderlust and sense of adventure.

Since staying in Poland was not a viable option, Herschel took another route. Several years after Mary and his mother had left, Herschel sold the house in Porozów and followed an aunt and uncle to Argentina, where he lived, toiled, married and eventually died, childless.

I found it curious to find such a nonconformist on the family tree and decided to learn more about Herschel. Dad remembered meeting him during his one visit to the U.S. in the late 1940s. He also knew that earlier, Uncle Lazar had gone to Argentina to see Herschel, but that was about it. Aunt Frieda, Dad's sister, knew a bit more, and what she didn't know, Herschel's sister, my great-aunt Mary, was able to fill in. According to the two of them, Herschel had married in the Old Country, but that marriage had not worked out. When he immigrated to Argentina with his mother's sister, his destination was a small, experimental Jewish agricultural settlement called Moisesville more than 500 kilometers northeast of Buenos Aires. There he met and married Frumka, a Russian-born widow with two young daughters. Aunt Mary, who never met Frumka, remembered her from photographs as "the cross-eyed one." Indeed, the one picture I was able to find of her bore out this description.

Aunt Frieda even remembered the name of Herschel's aunt; it was Chaska, née Milsky—and Aunt Mary supplied the uncle's name—Moishe Schwartz. After my grandmother's death in 1960 and Hershel's death two years after that, it all became ancient history as far as our family was concerned. But I was curious about the story of Herschel's life.

Researching Herschel's Life

My first step was to read about Moisesville. I learned that Eastern European Jews had begun immigrating to Argentina in the late 1800s at about the same time as they set off for America in record numbers. Moiseville was Argentina's first all-Jewish colony, founded in 1889 by 800 or so Jewish immigrants, mostly from the Ukraine. Sponsored by the German-Jewish philanthropist, Baron Maurice de Hirsch, they formed large farms and cooperatives and helped set the pattern for Argentina's agricultural economy. Moisesville was also said to have begotten the famed "Jewish Gaucho," a concept I found incongruous to say the least and a sight I hoped one day to behold.

The only way to get information about Herschel himself, of course, was to write to Argentina, but the question was where to write. From the Jewish Genealogical Society in New York, I got an address for the *Federacion de Comunidades Israelitas Argentinas* (Argentine Federation of Jewish Communities). I was told that the Federation (whose building was destroyed in a horrendous terrorist attack in 1994) held most of the burial records for the Argentine Jewish community. As in the U.S., immigrant Jews to Argentina had formed cooperative societies to share the burden of funeral costs, and these organizations had generally kept pretty complete records.

I wrote to the Federation telling them all that I knew about Herschel, his aunt and uncle. Then I waited, not so patiently, for about four months. About the time I was beginning to give up hope of ever getting a reply, fretting because I had chosen to write in English instead of having the letter translated into Spanish, a registered letter arrived from Buenos Aires. Written on the Federation's letterhead in creditable English, it was signed by the director. It began like this:

I received your letter sent to the burial department of the Argentine Jewish Community in Buenos Aires in which you request information about your Argentine relatives.

As you describe it well, Jasha Milsky and her husband Moises Szwarc were both buried in the Jewish Cemetery of Moisesville, Province of Santa Fe, Argentina. As regards Herschel Rudberg (sic), he also died but was buried in the Jewish Cemetery of La Tablada, pertaining to the Jewish Community of Buenos Aires.

It was a great surprise for me because, as the director of the Federation of the Argentine Jewish Communities, one of my tasks is to reunite families; therefore, your request about my grandparents deeply moved me.

I had to reread the letter a couple of times, wade through the variant spellings and study the signature—that of one Professor Alberto Abraham Szwarc—before the real thrust hit me. What the director was telling me was that Uncle Herschel's aunt and uncle were his own grandparents. This would make him my father's second cousin! All sorts of thoughts went through my head. Could this be some sort of scam? It didn't seem so. I replied at once with a long letter introducing myself and my family and enclosing a complete family tree, as well as copies of some photographs.

One of my second cousins, the son of Uncle Lazar's youngest daughter, had inherited several boxes of photographs when his mother died, and he had had the good sense to preserve them. In his attic archive, we found half a dozen photographs that clearly had been taken in Argentina, including several shots in Moisesville during Uncle Lazar's trip. I sent copies to Alberto for identification.

Alberto replied quickly, naming the individuals shown. One even turned out to be a photograph of his own father. He told me that he had copies of some of the same pictures in his own family album, and he sent a tree of the Argentine branch of the family, including information about several members who had made *aliyah* (immigration) to Israel from Argentina.

By this time, I was no longer suspicious, just stunned by my good fortune. Through coincidence and just plain fate, I had stumbled onto a host of Argentinean relatives that my family had never had the remotest notion even existed.

Even if we had not had photographs or elderly relatives with sharp memories, the family trees themselves would have offered some pretty convincing evidence of the relationship. The clues come from the Ashkenazic custom of naming children after deceased relatives and the penchant on the part of Diaspora Jews to give their children two names, an everyday name in the vernacular of the country in which they live and a Jewish name in Hebrew or Yiddish that memorializes a deceased relative. When a close relative dies, the general practice in our family has always been to name the next child born into the family for the deceased. In a large family like ours, that means children in several branches are likely to be

Uncle Herschel Rudbart, center, with four of the "gaucho" drinking buddies in Moisesville, Argentina. Far from being Jewish cowboys, these "gauchos" were peace-loving men who made their living through farming and animal husbandry.

named for the same individual.

In our case, although the children of Alberto's grandmother, Chashka, had been given typically Spanish names like Luiz, Adolfo and Ernesto, these told only part of the story. Their Yiddish names—Lazar, Velvel and Herschel—are extremely common in the eight branches of our family. Each individual who bears one is a namesake of some forgotten common ancestor. My grandmother had brothers named Lazar and Herschel, and—no coincidence—Velvel is my father's Jewish name.

I corresponded with these newfound relatives for nearly two years. When Alberto invited me to visit Argentina in October for the wedding of his daughter, Clarisa, I decided to seize the moment. I had never been south of the (U.S.) border and speak not a word of Spanish, but I figured that this was just too good an opportunity to miss.

Trip to Argentina

I arrived several days before the wedding. At the Buenos Aires airport, I was met by an attractive young woman of 19. She introduced herself in flawless English as Clarisa's cousin, Leila, the daughter of Alberto's identical twin brother, Arnoldo. She was with her uncle Alberto, and we greeted each other like the long-lost cousins we are.

Despite the fact that we had never met, Alberto really was a fairly close relative, my father's second cousin. I had grown up knowing lots of my own second cousins and had seen them frequently as a child. But here was one who had been living a fruitful and productive life totally undetected by our radar screens—and in such an odd part of the world.

Our first stop was La Tablada Jewish Cemetery where Uncle Herschel is buried. Alberto knew his way around this cemetery, and he led Leila and me first to the graves of several relatives and then to that of Uncle Herschel's third wife, Ida. (Frumka the second wife had died in Moisesville about six months after marrying Herschel; shortly afterwards, he had moved to Buenos Aires and married for a third time.)

Finally, we came to Herschel's grave. As is common in Europe, many gravestones in the cemetery had photographs of the deceased set into them. Herschel's photograph had been taken late in life, later than any picture we in North America had ever seen of him. Without being overly melodramatic, I must say that looking at it was like staring into my dad's eyes. Of his four hereditary lines, this is apparently the one that proved dominant in my father—at least as far as appearance is concerned. Herschel at age 70 was the image of my dad, now 76.

That first night Alberto took out a box of photographs to prove that he did, indeed, have some copies of some of the same pictures I had sent to him. We sorted through formal portraits taken in Europe more than three-quarters of a century earlier and together deciphered the Yiddish inscriptions on the back of many. Here was Aunt Leah who had lived in Newark. There was my great-uncle Lazar on his visit to Moisesville. At the bottom of the stack was one they couldn't identify but I could. It was a formal portrait of my own grandmother that had been taken in Newark—and here it was 90 years later and half a world away.

On the night before Clarisa's wedding, a large family gathering was held in my honor. There I met great-uncle Adolfo—himself a Velvel—the patriarch of the family. He was an expansive sort who was visibly delighted at the encounter. At 83, Adolfo was clearly beloved by all, and one look at him revealed beyond any doubt the side of the family from which my father had inherited his ears. There was simply no mistaking their size or angle; I had been looking at Milsky ears all my life without knowing it.

Adolfo remembered my great-aunt Mary clearly and asked me for her photograph. He told me to remind her of the time that he had brought her a goat from Volkovysk, where he had lived, to her home in Porozów so that her ailing father might benefit from its milk. This, I calculated, would have been in 1919. Together—with no common language—we named his mother's seven brothers and sister and their spouses. And on the back of a napkin, with the help of his nephew, Arnoldo, he sketched out a map of greater Volkovysk as he remembered it, identifying key sites of interest and even naming the street on which our families had lived. He had not been there, of course, since 1929.

Adolfo also knew a few things about Uncle Herschel, whom he described as a simple man of simple pleasures, among which were an occasional hot cup of *mate*, a local, tea-like infusion drunk from a gourd, as well as a more-than-occasional *schnapps*. A cheerful sort who worked hard in Moisesville as an agricultural laborer before moving to the city, my great-uncle was known fondly as "Herschel the *Schvartzer*" or Herschel the dark one, because of his olive complexion.

Also at the gathering was cousin Juana Feldman, the only child of the only daughter of Aunt Chashka. At age four, Juana had posed for a studio photograph that had made its way to my second cousin's attic in New Jersey. It was one of the pictures that Alberto had identified. Herschel, who had had no children of his own, had been especially fond of Juana, known in the family by her Jewish name,

Herschel Rudbart later in life.

Chana Reisele. Nearly half a century ago, he had proudly sent the picture to his brother Lazar.

Juana, now 51, invited me to spend the next day with her family. A school teacher, she had some limited English, and we were able to communicate fairly well. I met her family and interviewed her about Herschel, as well. A clock he had once owned—one of the few possessions he left behind at his death—decorated her living room wall.

She remembered Herschel with great fondness. She had known him only in Buenos Aires, where he had come to work after his second wife died. He had worked as a laborer in a meat factory on the outskirts of town and, as a result, had been able to keep meat on the table for Juana and her mother. Juana's parents had divorced when the child was quite young, and Herschel had functioned as her surrogate father.

To be closer to the meat factory, he and Ida had moved from a one room flat in town to a suburb called Tigre, not far from the house on Garibaldi Street from which Israeli agents kidnapped the Nazi Adolf Eichmann in 1960. There Herschel and Ida lived in an isolated shack, accessible only by dirt roads. It consisted of one room and a kitchen, with an outhouse and a garden in the back.

Times were tough, and the wretched conditions in factories such as Herschel's were giving rise to a labor movement in Argentina. After some prodding, Juana told me that Herschel had been a union organizer and probably a communist as well, a fact that suggested the most plausible theory I have yet heard about why he had been denied an immigrant visa to the U.S. so many years before. Herschel had probably been deemed undesirable because of his leftist tendencies.

Juana's shoebox of photographs was a gold mine. Among its treasures were a photograph of my great-grandmother, Esther; several pictures of Aunt Chashka and her children; and a shot of Herschel with some of his drinking buddies. We also found Herschel's pensioner identification card—which revealed that he was illiterate—and his death certificate. Even his passport, issued by the Polish embassy in Buenos Aires in 1947, was there. He had used this passport to visit his siblings in the United States. It provided no insight into the man, although it did pinpoint his date of birth. I was just excited, after so much searching, to hold something of Herschel's in my hands.

Moiseville

After Clarisa's wedding, Alberto and I hopped an overnight bus to Moisesville. This pilgrimage to the town for which he had left his home in Europe was to be the final stop on my search for Uncle Herschel. The whole concept of Jewish colonization in Argentina had been something of an experiment, consisting in large part of a wholesale transplant of European *shtetl* life into the Western Hemisphere. There were, however, a few important differences, including self-government and the self-imposed charge to become a model community not only for Argentinean Jews, but for others in this land dominated by European immigrants.

Touted in song as a *Yiddishe Medina* (Yiddish country), Moisesville was a farming community devoted primarily to animal husbandry. At its peak in the late 1930s, it was home to about 7,000 European refugee Jews. It also served as a cultural center for several other Jewish settlements in the area, boasting a thriving Yiddish theater, two Jewish libraries and a Hebrew teacher's seminary. It once had four synagogues, three of which still stand. They now take turns hosting Sabbath worship, since the number of Jews has dwindled to only about 500, mostly elderly colonists.

Alberto not only knew his way around Moisesville, he might as well have owned the place. He had served there for three years as director of the Hebrew Teacher's Seminary and knew virtually everyone. One of the first places he showed me was the site where the fourth synagogue, the *Litvaker Shul* (Lithuanian synagogue), had stood. His grandparents and parents had worshipped there, as had Uncle Herschel—when he went to synagogue, that is, which I gathered was not terribly often. Although the structure had been destroyed, Alberto had contributed money to build a park on the site. In the middle of a grove of trees was a simple monument to his grandparents and the other early settlers who had helped to build the community.

Alberto persuaded the president of the Jewish community to take us to the cemetery on the outskirts of town (he was the one with the key). There we found the graves of Alberto's grandparents, Chashka and Moises Szwarc. The only plot that eluded us was that of Frumka, Herschel's second wife and the mother of his two stepdaughters.

We asked several older residents if they remembered Herschel the *Schvartzer*, without much success; apparently he had not been all that memorable a character. Several people suggested that we consult Yankel the barber, an elderly resident with the reputation of knowing everyone. Yankel not only remembered Herschel, but when prompted about Frumka, he recalled that she had been a relative of a woman who still lived a few doors from his barber shop. We hurried to see if Rosa Trumper was at home and willing to receive us.

Rosa was a charming lady who turned out to be a ready source of information. Frumka, whose official name was Frieda, had been her mother's sister. Rosa explained that we had not found her grave, because she had been buried under the surname of her previous husband—and she knew exactly where Frumka's two daughters, Herschel's stepdaughters, could be found. One lives in Israel, the other a few hundred kilometers away in the city of Rosario. She happily gave me addresses for both so that I might follow up with them.

I asked for Rosa's impressions of Herschel; what she had to say was no surprise. An illiterate common laborer, Herschel was a hulking sort of guy beloved by pretty much everyone who knew him. He was, indeed, a gaucho, but that did not, I learned, imply the lasso-throwing, Judeo-Hispanic cowboy *kvitching* (screaming) at his dogies in Yiddish that I had allowed myself to imagine. To an Argentinean, a gaucho is simply a peace-loving man who makes his living either off the land or through animal husbandry. No Jewish Gene Autry (an American movie actor of the 1940s famous for cowboy roles) alas, but from all I had learned, it seemed a fairly apt description of my great-uncle.

During my week in Argentina, I found out most everything there was to know about my great-uncle, but the story of humble Herschel turned out to have been only counterpoint to the real significance of the trip.

I learned that *shtetl* life, whether in Europe or in South America, was probably doomed to extinction. I learned that living on the bottom of the world for so long has caused Argentineans to stay up at night and sleep during the day. I learned that *mate* has an exceedingly unpleasant flavor, and I learned where my father's ears came from. Most of all, I learned that family is family no matter what language they speak or how long you have been out of touch with them. I am far richer for being reunited with a delightful group of relatives with whom I fully intend to stay in touch. Thanks to Uncle Herschel, we will now forever share a good deal more than simply a common set of ancestors.

Scott Seligman is a recently retired corporate executive living in Washington, DC. He is the author of several books on China and designer of several genealogical- and Jewish-interest websites, including www.porozow.com, a site about the shtetl (village) in which his paternal grandmother and his great-uncle Herschel, the subject of this article, were born.

Lost and Found
by Roslyn Sherman Greenberg

Winter 2006

I become so angry when I hear that some supposedly intelligent person claims that the Holocaust never happened. How can they say such a thing when there are people still alive who witnessed the massacre with their own eyes?

Then there are those, like me, who know they have lost relatives to the Holocaust. I know that two uncles, two aunts and at least 15 of my cousins all died on March 8, 1942. Eyewitness reports state that they were taken out to the woods near the ghetto of Lida, where they had been forced to live. There they were all shot, along with the other residents of the ghetto, and thrown into a mass grave.

Recently, I came into possession of letters my aunt and uncle had written to my father and his brothers during the years between 1923 and 1937. The letters are in Yiddish, and I remember as a child how the family would gather each time a letter arrived. My father would read the letter aloud, and everyone would listen attentively. After the reading, everyone would comment, and plans would be made to help the family remaining in Russia. Yiddish is a very expressive language, and I remember thinking that whoever wrote the letter was a wonderful writer.

The letters were extremely moving, because the writers' lives were so difficult. My uncle Noah had tuberculosis, and he didn't have enough money to go to the doctor in the big city. The family lived in a small *shtetl*. My aunt Minna's husband was a shoemaker who was not well, and they always had a hard time making ends meet. They had six children, but one had died of tuberculosis. Their son was married and had gone to Lida to teach school. He and his wife had two babies. I know that one of my aunt Minna's daughters was married and had a child, but she had a very hard life. She had been blinded in one eye when she was a child.

My uncle Avrom, my father's youngest brother, was a tailor. He was married to a very beautiful woman, and they had five children. The youngest was four years old when they were all killed, except for the eldest girl, Riva. She was 17 and worked in a bank in a neighboring town. When the bombing started in 1939, one of the employees of the bank who had a car told her that they should flee to the Russian border. They drove as far as they could before the car ran out of gas, and then they started running on foot. The bombing followed their route. Pretty soon Riva found herself running alone. She kept running until her hunger was so great that she felt she was dying. She lay down under a tree. A girl came along who had two partial loaves of bread. Riva asked her for a bite, but the girl didn't want to share. Riva pleaded with her and told her that she was dying, but the girl still refused. Then Riva said that she would give the girl food someday if the girl needed any, and somehow the girl allowed her to have a bite. This bit of food revived

Riva, and she was able to continue on her way to the border. Along the way, she worked on a farm, so she was well fed, and—of all strange events—one day she was able to return the favor of a bite of bread to the same girl who, starving, arrived at the farm.

Riva left the farm and came to Leningrad, where workers were needed to clear the streets after the bombing. This skinny young woman picked up the rubble of Leningrad. Later she worked in a factory making machinery. She said that she was covered in oil every day. She only had one blouse, but she washed it every night and tried to keep clean. She received an award for being the best worker.

When the war ended, she was sent to a displaced persons camp in Germany. There she married a young man, and her daughter, Minna, was born. Riva contacted the family in New York, and they arranged for Riva, her husband and baby to go to Montreal, Canada, since the quota would not allow them to come to the United States. After five years, they were allowed to enter the U.S., and the family rejoiced. Although we had lost so many, we were able to rescue one.

When Yad Vashem, the Jerusalem memorial to the six million Jews killed in the Holocaust, asked for Pages of Testimony about friends and relatives who had perished, I felt that I had to memorialize my relatives. I knew that Riva suffered deeply from survivor's guilt and couldn't talk about her parents, brothers, sister and cousins, so I entered Pages of Testimony for them. Years later, she did so as well.

I felt very strongly that I could not let these people be forgotten. They had hopes and desires just as we all do. Why should their lives have been cut short? There but for the grace of God, go I. If my father hadn't left home and come to the U.S. in 1921, where would I be now?

Among the old photographs I inherited from my mother's father, my grandfather Kalman, I found a photo of a family dated 1937 in Voronovo, the town where my mother was born. On the back was an inscription in Yiddish reading:

> To my dear uncle Kalman. This is a picture taken on the occasion of my brother Barnett's visit from London. In it are my wife Rivka and my two sons. Your loving nephew, Zalman.

If the family had been in Voronovo in 1937, I was afraid they also had perished in the Holocaust.

In many instances, the surviving residents of Jewish communities that had been destroyed wrote books years later memorializing the town they lived in. These are called *yizkor* (memorial) books, and there is one for Voronovo. These books usually give a history of the town and tell about the prominent personalities of the town, the Jewish organizations, the teachers, etc., and they all have a list at the back of those who died in the Holocaust. I looked at the Voronovo *yizkor* book and found that Zalman and Rivka Levin and their son were killed. I didn't know the names of the sons, who both looked as if they were in their twenties at the time the photo was taken, so I didn't know if the other son had also been killed, but I thought the entire family had probably been destroyed. Who would be able to memorialize them with Pages of Testimony at Yad Vashem? I decided that I should fill out Pages of Testimony for Zalman and Rivka.

Last winter, when I was in Carpinteria, California, I was awakened early in the morning by a phone call. The caller was obviously someone who didn't know me. He kept asking if I was Roslyn Greenberg, and he told me he was calling from Israel. He had been referred to this number when he called my phone in the Chicago area. When I finally convinced him that I was really Roslyn Greenberg, he told me that his wife had accessed the Yad Vashem database, which had recently been placed on the Internet. She had found that I had entered Pages of Testimony for her grandparents, and he wanted to know who I was.

Still groggy from sleep, I asked him for the name of her grandparents. When he told me Zalman and Rivka Levin, I figured that one of the sons had survived—but no, both sons had perished. I hadn't known that in 1933, before the picture in my possession had been taken, their daughter Chaya (whom I had no idea existed) had left for Palestine. This was the husband of Chaya's daughter, Carmela, who was calling me.

We exchanged e-mail addresses, and we agreed to send each other pictures of the family. When the picture arrived, I knew that there could be no mistake. These were definitely cousins. It turned out that Carmela and her husband, Schmuel, planned to come to the U.S. in April. Schmuel had a daughter in New York and a son in San Francisco. I asked if they could make a stop in Chicago, and they changed their itinerary to include a few days in my city.

I picked them up at O'Hare wearing a bright pink raincoat, and Carmela told me she would be wearing a red hat and scarf. We spotted each other immediately and had a joyful meeting. Carmela turned out to be a beautiful woman of 68. Her husband was a nice-looking man of 75. His English was very good, and although Carmela was shy because she felt her English was poor, it really was not bad. These Israelis turned out to be world travelers. Schmuel was professor emeritus of Sub-tropical Horticulture at Hebrew University and consulted all over the world in his specialty.

I am so grateful to know that there are survivors in my family, and I am thrilled to know that they have children, grandchildren and great-grandchildren. Because I could not forget the lost, I found cousins I would never have known existed.

Roslyn Sherman Greenberg is a past president and co-founder of the Illiana Jewish Genealogical Society and now serves as the society's newsletter editor. She has been researching her family for 35 years.

How I Learned That Rashi Was My Ancestor
by Asher Bar-Zev

Winter 1990

Like most children born into families with a famous ancestor, I learned very early that I was descended from the Hasidic Rebbe Elimeleh of Lezajsk. Although we were Orthodox Jews, we were not Hasidim. Nevertheless, my mother never missed an opportunity to instill in me a sense of pride because of my heritage of Hasidic rabbinical aristocracy. She was not alone. Every one of my cousins, no matter how estranged from his or her Jewish roots, was well aware of being the Rebbe Elimeleh's *ainikle* (literally, grandchild). This was a function of being told the fact hundreds of times in the process of growing up.

Rebbe Elimeleh is most recognizable by the humorous folksong about how, in moments of joy, he would send for various musicians to play for him. He was actually a historical person. He lived at the end of the 18th century in what is now southeastern Poland, then the province of the Austro-Hungarian Empire known as Galicia. He was one of the five disciples of Dov Ber of Mezeritch, who in turn was the disciple of the Baal Shem Tov, the founder of the Hasidic movement.

As such, the Rebbe Elimeleh was one of the prime movers in the development of Hasidism in its early years. Legends, some rooted in historical fact, have been collected and published about how he was drawn to Hasidism, how he wandered through Galicia together with his brother, Rabbi Zusya of Anipol, preaching Hasidic thought and how he lived a life of great asceticism. He originated the idea of the Hasidic rabbi or *tzaddik* as an intercessor or mediator between the ordinary Jew and God. The logical outcome of this teaching was the establishment of the procedure whereby Hasidim would come to the rabbi and present him with petitions asking him to pray for them in the hope of having their personal requests answered by God. He implemented this policy in his rabbinical court in Lezajsk.

One of the many depictions of Rashi—Rabbi Shlomo ben Yitzhak, (1040–1105)

As an adult, I attempted to trace the actual generations from my famous ancestor to me. My mother knew and gave me the names of specific individuals who linked the Rebbe Elimeleh to both my maternal grandparents. However, my mother was not entirely clear on all of the lines of descent and suggested that I speak to a cousin who was a Hasid and who, she felt, would know all the details of our genealogy. As a result of information gleaned from this cousin, I learned that my descent was more complex than I had thought.

In a custom not at all unusual among Hasidic rabbinic families, two first cousins, grandchildren of the Rebbe Elimeleh, had married. Their descendants had given rise to my grandfather, Asher Alter Gewirtz, while my grandmother, Haya Sheindel Weissblum, was the descendant of still another grandchild. My grandparents were fourth cousins. Both were the sixth generation from the Rebbe Elimeleh. That made my cousins and me the eighth generation from our famous ancestor. Since most people can trace their ancestry back only three or four generations, I felt that I was well ahead of the game and let the matter rest there for several decades.

Over the years, I collected materials on the Rebbe Elimeleh including encyclopedia articles and other biographical information. I also acquired magazine articles and photographs of a well-known Hasidic rabbi of our time, Rabbi Moshe Yitzhak Gewirtzman, the famous Reb Itzikle of Antwerp, who happened to be my grandfather's half brother, and hence my granduncle. Reading the biographies fleshed out somewhat the origins of the Rebbe Elimeleh and taught me something about his family and siblings. All of the foregoing was done on a casual, hit or miss basis.

With the advent of personal computers, I acquired a genealogy program that allowed me to enter my information in a logical fashion and, more importantly, to generate descendant and predecessor charts of any individual in the database. My reading heightened my curiosity about the Rebbe Elimeleh's predecessors. I, therefore, took the opportunity when in Israel two years ago to visit the genealogy section of the Jewish National and University Library at Hebrew University in Jerusalem. There I struck gold! In retrospect, it was one of the turning points of my life.

In an adventure too long to describe here, I came across the biographical encyclopedia *Meorei Galicia* (Galician Rabbis and Scholars), by Rabbi Meir Wunder. It included the biographies of numerous predecessors and descendants of the Rebbe Elimeleh under his family name, Weissblum. I photocopied the relevant passages and brought them home to be worked on at leisure.

In numerous late night sessions at home, the biographical material from Israel was integrated with the genealogy I already had. When completed, I was able to extend my ancestry back an additional five generations. I could now trace ancestors back 13 generations to the early 17th century.

"They Were All Rabbis"

While I was growing up, my mother had repeated to me many times, "They were all rabbis!" I had always taken this as the natural exaggeration of a parent trying to instill a sense of pride in ancestry in her children, but it turned out that she was correct. The proportion of rabbis across the generations was very high. It may be that non-rabbinical individuals were not deemed worthy of remembrance, so that the sample of ancestors about whom I had information was skewed to emphasize the rabbis. Nevertheless, to have multiple rabbis in each generation was surely a legitimate source of pride.

By this time, I had become enthusiastic about genealogy in general, not to speak of my own ancestry. I read books about Jewish genealogy and subscribed to AVOTAYNU, whose articles were extremely helpful in establishing links with others interested in the subject. I learned of a book by Dr. Neil Rosenstein entitled *The Unbroken Chain*, which claimed to trace the genealogy of many famous rabbinic and non-rabbinic families. The book was long out of print and unavailable for purchase even secondhand. Apparently, those who had copies were not selling them. Finally, I managed to obtain a copy via interlibrary loan from the University of Florida library. Rosenstein had done a phenomenal job.

The central figure of his research was Rabbi Meir Katzenellenbogen, the MaHaRaM of Padua, who lived from 1482 to 1565. Rosenstein showed that this pivotal figure was the ancestor of many famous medieval and modern Jewish families, including a number of Hasidic rabbinical dynasties. Although he could not show that the Rebbe Elimeleh was a descendant of the MaHaRaM, he did include a section on him because of the general interest in Hasidic dynasties. However, much to my dismay, my own research on my illustrious ancestor was more detailed and accurate than Rosenstein's.

Nevertheless, the main body of Rosenstein's book was an inspiration. Seven hundred pages of text and extensive genealogical charts provided some of the most interesting connections among the most disparate of individuals. Who would have dreamed that the philosopher, Moses Mendelssohn; the composer, Felix Mendelssohn-Bartholdy; Helena Rubinstein; Martin Buber and Karl Marx all had the same ancestor? In wonder, I spent hours browsing through the listings of the descendants of the MaHaRaM.

During one of these excursions, I noted that a great-great-great-granddaughter of the MaHaRaM was married to Rabbi Eliezer Lipmann Heilperin, the *Av Bet Din* (senior rabbi) of Tarnogrod. Both the name and the place triggered a memory. This very individual was the great-grandfather of the Rebbe Elimeleh. I had made a connection!

With renewed vigor, I proceeded to chart the genealogical tree showing the ties between the MaHaRaM and the Rebbe Elimeleh. Through Rosenstein's research, I was able to demonstrate the relationships of my family with such giants of Jewish life as Rabbi Shlomo Luria, known as the MaHaRSHaL, and Rabbi Moshe Isserles, known as the ReMa. While articles in AVOTAYNU by Rosenstein and others showed that some genealogical lines were in dispute, the connection between my ancestors and the MaHaRaM was never in question.

Descent from Rashi

One of the traditions that existed in Jewish genealogy was that the MaHaRaM was descended from Rabbi Shlomo Yitzhaki, or Rashi, who lived in Troyes, France, from 1040 to 1105. Rashi's commentary on the Bible is known to every Jewish school child, while his commentary on the *Talmud* is credited with opening up that frequently abstruse body of literature to anyone willing to take the time to study it. He was one of the greatest, if not the greatest, rabbis of the Middle Ages. To have him as an ancestor would be a real thrill!

The problem was that the genealogists doing the research could not make a clear and undisputed connection between the MaHaRaM and Rashi. A number of speculative and tentative lines were drawn, but with no real assurance that they were historically accurate.

The definitive connection between the MaHaRaM and Rashi has now been made. The task was completed by one of the foremost Jewish genealogists, Dr. Paul J. Jacobi, in an AVOTAYNU article[1] that arrived on Passover this year, the season par excellence when Jews look to their ancestors and the events of the past. The clear lineages shown by Jacobi, though still disputed in some details by Rosenstein, convinced me that there was, indeed, an unbroken line from Rashi through his daughter, Yoheved, and grandson, Rabbi Yitzhak ben Meir, known as the RiBaM, to the MaHaRaM.

I confess to more than a little pride in the knowledge that I am the 31st generation from Rashi and that I have, through no merit of my own, passed on this lineage to my granddaughter, Ariel, into the 33rd generation. There are actually descendants of Rashi within my family (first cousins thrice-removed) into the 34th generation.

One of the unforeseen dividends of this odyssey has been the connections that I have discovered between many of my ancestors and many prominent figures in Jewish history. While I am not a direct descendant of these individuals too numerous to list here, it engenders a wonderful feeling of oneness with the events of Jewish history over the last 1,000 years to know that so many of my ancestral cousins were prime movers in these events. For me, these are no longer mere descriptions of occurrences in history books, nor even happenings to which I can relate in an abstract way as part of the history of my people. Rather, they have become very real personal incidents in the lifetimes of my extended family in the past. It is almost as if I had been there and had these experiences myself.

Still another dividend has been the growing number of connections that I have made with other amateur and professional genealogists, some of whom are dis-

---

[1] "The Historicity of the Rashi Descent," by Paul J. Jacobi. AVOTAYNU Vol. VI, No. 1, Spring 1990.

tant cousins, since they and I have common ancestors. The mind boggles at the diversity of personalities and occupations of the individuals living today who are descended from common progenitors.

One last possible dividend may still accrue as a result of my being descended from Rashi. According to Jewish tradition, although unsubstantiated by modern genealogical criteria, Rashi was descended from the great Talmudic sage, Hillel, who was, again according to tradition, descended from King David and his wife Avital. If some day, this connection could be verified by modern genealogical techniques, my friends would have to address my cousins and me as "Your Majesty!"

Asher Bar-Zev, received his Bachelor of Science degree from the City College of New York, and a Master of Hebrew Literature and rabbinical ordination from the Jewish Theological Seminary. Rabbi Bar-Zev holds a Master of Science degree and a PhD in Molecular Biology from the University of Massachusetts. He recently retired as a vice-president/financial advisor after 22 years in a major brokerage firm. His articles have been published in journals of science, religion and genealogy, including AVOTAYNU.

Back to the Old Country

An Incident in L'viv
by Victor Armony
Winter 2005

Boryslaw, Lutsk, Kowel...I still remember the profound effect these strange-sounding names had on me when I was 10 or 11 years old. When they where uttered by my grandparents, they were much more than references to places and memories. I could tell that those names conveyed an incredible sense of sorrow and loss, but they also fascinated and intrigued me. I somehow felt that the horror they represented could not touch me, as they were as far in space and time as the mythical places I read about in my adventure books.

Last year, a work-related opportunity to travel to Ukraine occurred. I had been doing genealogical research for more than a decade, but still could not quite imagine myself actually walking on the streets of those cities. I think that, in a way, I needed them to remain remote and abstract, as they were to me during my childhood, so they could do me no harm. But, after much hesitation, I finally decided to go. What follows is an incident on my trip that was particularly meaningful to me.

The Incident

In October 2005, I was sitting in a conference room at the Hetman Hotel in L'viv, participating on a panel on "Intellectuals and Government" convened by an American-funded organization. The few foreigners who attended the conference had been assigned interpreters. Two young college students were seated with me, one on each side, taking turns translating from Ukrainian into English.

Five speakers were scheduled to talk. I was the fourth on the list. The third speaker was Mr. S., a high-ranking officer from the L'viv City Council Department of Culture. By the time his turn arrived, I was bored and sleepy. This gentleman walked solemnly to the podium and started his talk on "Morals and Politics" by expressing some platitudes about his department's policies. I didn't expect to learn much from him.

At one point, Mr. S. became quite agitated and his tone rose sharply. From what I understood (my interpreters could hardly keep up with him), he apparently was ranting about the central government in Kyyiv. I guessed that he was venturing into some controversial policy issues. I could see that some people in the audience became restless, and two of them shouted something. This definitely was becoming interesting.

One of the interpreters told me vaguely that Mr. S. was referring to the bad "influence" of a particular "millionaire." I asked her to be more precise, but she was evasive. "They're discussing politics." Immediately I sensed that there was something more to it. "What is he saying right now?" I insisted. "Well, he's saying that the purity of the Ukrainian culture should be protected from non-Ukrainian elements."

Someone in the audience interrupted the speaker. I don't know any Ukrainian, but I clearly heard the word *zhydivs'kyy* (Jewish) which someone had taught me to recognize the previous day. "Are they talking about Jews?" Both students clearly were embarrassed. They kept smiling nervously, "Well yes, it's about the influence of the Jews on the current government."

I couldn't believe my ears! I was witnessing an act of public, quasi-official anti-Semitism in the very city to which I had come to reconnect with my family's past. After all the killing and destruction, they still blame the Jews!

My Turn To Speak

My heart was pounding as the speaker stepped down and the panel chair called me to the podium. I had planned to start my talk by referring to my personal attachment to L'viv. Now I was not sure what to do. I hadn't fully grasped how the previous debate had unfolded. Were the people in the audience protesting or supporting the bureaucrat's tirade? Should I just stick to reading my paper on Latin America's civil society?

I stood silent for a moment. Then I began, "I'm thrilled to be in L'viv, this beautiful city where my grandmother was born and raised." I hesitated for a few seconds. I went on, "She was Jewish, by the way. That seems to be relevant to some people here."

What followed was one of the most poignant events I've ever experienced. The audience burst into applause. I felt that a tiny bit of historical justice had been restored. A group of Ukrainians in L'viv spontaneously vindicated the memory of my grandmother whose entire family was exterminated here because they were Jewish.

This experience gave me a new perspective on this country and its troubled relationship with its Jewish minority. Anti-Semitism obviously is still alive in Ukraine, but many people—at least among the intellectuals—do not condone its explicit manifestations. Cynics may contend that this group reacted the way they did because Westerners were present in the room, and that they expressed their sympathy to me rather than to Jews in general, or that they were just rebuking some right-wing lunatic.

I prefer to take this as an example of an attitude change. I must point out, however, that I was puzzled by one little thing. Even though several people came to congratulate me on my talk, to leave me their business cards or even to raise a glass of wine to my health at the conference dinner, no one made any allusion whatever to the "incident" itself. No one, that is, except one philosophy professor from Kyyiv. We discussed Judaism and anti-Semitism. I was happy to find a Ukrainian who wouldn't act as if nothing had happened that afternoon. It was only after a while that she confided in me (in French, a language no one else at the table understood) that her son had immigrated to Israel a few years ago.

Victor Armony lives in Montreal, Canada. His father, Paul Armony, is AVOTAYNU contributing editor for Argentina and president of Asociación de Genealogía Judía de Argentina.

A Trip to the Shtetl of My Ancestors
by Roseanna Tendler Worth

Winter 1987

It sat on a shelf for 42 years. Fifty pages of typing paper, yellowing around the edges, plus a hand-drawn map. A birth of Louis Medow, born Lazar Medvedovsky, in 1885 in the village of Goroshina, in the district of Poltava in the southern Ukraine. Fifty pages of the story my grandfather had begun to write in 1943. He wrote it for his grandchildren whom he saw growing up in Detroit, having no idea what his life had been like as a boy growing up in Czarist Russia.

He died before he could finish the story. My father, the late Lou Tendler of the Editorial Staff of the *Detroit News*, had helped him and done the writing after my mother, Mollie, had translated the original from Yiddish. They planned on a great deal more than the fifty finished pages, but ill health had sidetracked this project along with others. I'm sure they always thought there would be plenty of time to go back and finish the job. My grandfather died in 1953; my father in 1956.

So it sat on my shelf after my mother died in 1976. She had passed it along to me, knowing that I had an interest in family history. However, my interest had confined itself to collecting old family pictures in a display which threatened to overwhelm an entire wall in the family room. When the genealogy bug bit, and it bit hard, there was the story, waiting for me.

I decided to carry out my grandfather's wishes, to recopy the story and distribute it to all his grandchildren and to the great-grandchildren who had come along in the intervening years.

In the course of retyping the story, I became fascinated with Goroshina. My grandfather said that there were only 18 Jewish families in the entire village, population of 3500, and that they lived scattered among the rest of the peasant population. Even stranger still, they got along well with the peasants. However, after all my advertising in various Jewish genealogy journals, it seemed that the Medvedovskys had been the only one of the 18 Jewish families of Goroshina to leave for America.

Because my grandfather was a carpenter and cabinetmaker, he was very interested in how things were made. He was interested in physical things rather than relationships, and he spent a great deal of time describing just how the peasant constructed his house. He went into detail as to where the Jewish cemetery was located, the home of the rich man in town, the synagogue location and spent loving detail on his map.

By the time I had finished retyping the story, I was burning with two questions. Did Goroshina still exist? Could I visit it?

It took almost a year of careful research in map libraries at the University of

Michigan and by mail with the Library of Congress, to ascertain that there was still a Goroshina on current maps and that it was not under water due to the construction of the Kremenchug Reservoir on the Dnieper River. Armed with this information, I contacted a travel agent in New York City approved by Intourist. They stunned me with the information that it was not possible to get the approval of Intourist to travel to Goroshina without actually going to the Soviet Union. Once there, you would travel to the nearest city with an Intourist office and then ask permission.

For almost a year, I tried to figure out what to do. I did not feel that I could afford, either financially or emotionally, to go all the way to the Soviet Union, make my way to the city of Cherkassy in the Ukraine, and once there find out that I could not have permission to continue the relatively short distance to Goroshina.

Then one of those strange events occurred that come up in life now and then. I was invited to a social event about which I was not very enthusiastic. My husband Don urged me to go. We went and met an old friend whom we hadn't seen in years. In the course of a catching-up conversation, I told her of my desire to go to Goroshina and the problems involved with Intourist. She, in turn, told me of hearing from a friend of a friend about a man in Virginia who had done just that two years ago. I got his address and began a detailed correspondence with him. He had been successful in getting to his ancestral village, also in the Ukraine. I finally decided that I had to try. I would take the risk.

I made all of my travel arrangements with an Intourist-approved travel agency in New York City. My agent was very discouraging about my chances of getting permission in Cherkassy to go to Goroshina. I shut her out and kept on with my planning. Part of that planning included trying to imagine what it would feel like if I made my way to Cherkassy and was told "No."

Author at age 14 with her grandfather, Louis Medow (born Lazar Medvedovsky) at age 62 taken on Passover in 1948.

I left for the Soviet Union on September 30, 1985. After a quick visit to Moscow, I flew to Kiev and had an equally brief tour of the city. I was then provided with a car, driver and guide/translator for the three-hour drive south of Cherkassy, in the heart of the lower Ukraine.

It was interesting to see the similarities and differences in the landscape. The major crops, wheat and corn, had been harvested. In many places winter wheat was coming up. The root crops, such as turnips and cabbage, were in the process of being harvested—by hand. Groups of old women were working, bent over in the fields, digging up or cutting off. At one point, I saw a school bus parked in a field and a group of children helping with the harvest.

The other thing which struck me about the landscape was more personal. When I was a child, my parents had bought a summer home in Canada on the shore of Lake Erie near Harrow. I had a sudden flash of intuition about why my grandparents had loved the cottage so much. The landscape was just the same in Canada as where they had come from in the Ukraine. In both cases, lines of Lombardy poplars marked the edges of fields.

My guide and translator, Eugene, was a charming young man of 24. He was on a vacation break from his studies in English, French and Spanish. He asked if I had any tee shirts with me. Tipping for services is not legal in the Soviet Union,

Stable which, according to the Goroshina people, was once owned by the author's great-grandfather.

but tourists are encouraged to bring along such small items as pantyhose, felt tipped pens, candy, gum, postcards, eye makeup and postage stamps as gifts. Since I was concerned about the cumulative weight of all these things in a suitcase which I had to carry myself, I had brought only small things. Eugene, however, collected tee shirts, so I promised to send him one from the University of Michigan. His concern was that it would cost me in the vicinity of $20, and my fear was whether or not he would receive it. His concern has proven false, as I have purchased a shirt for $6.75, and only time will tell whether my fears were well founded.

I shared with Eugene my anxiety about getting permission to travel to Goroshina. He was very interested in my story and promised to explain to the Intourist people in Cherkassy that Goroshina was the focus of my entire trip to the Soviet Union.

While Eugene was my guide and translator, it was Andre who was our driver. Intourist provides you with a car, a driver who does not speak English and a guide who does not drive. This was just one of the many aspects of full employment which I was to encounter while on this trip. At one point, I was roundly chastised because I had brought my own bags down from my hotel room to the lobby. This was the porter's job, and I was taking away his work.

Cherkassy

We arrived in Cherkassy and met with my guide for the three-day stay. Her name was Svetlana. I was taken to the hotel in Cherkassy which is for foreign tourists. It was like no hotel I've ever been in. Situated at the end of a long road which snaked through a grove of trees, it stood alone, without all of those things which mark a building as "hotel" in the West. No signs...brass and chrome...lights...carpeting...drapes...potted plants. It might have been an abandoned school. Very low light level; very shabby in appearance; hard, echoing floors. After a conference in the lobby with Eugene, Svetlana showed me to my room on the third floor. Eugene went back to Kiev, and Svetlana left to make arrangements with her Chief at the Intourist Office, promising to call me in about an hour.

In my room I decided to reread my grandfather's story. I cried from relief of apprehension, since Svetlana had seemed confident that the trip to Goroshina could be arranged without difficulty, and I cautioned myself not to be hopeful until I actually had permission from the Chief of Intourist.

Gradually I became aware that time was passing and that Svetlana had not called me. There seemed, however, to be a phone ringing persistently in another room down the hall. I finally figured out that Svetlana was probably calling the wrong room and that there wasn't anything I could do about it! I was the only person in the whole building who spoke English. I was trapped, at that point, by language, or the lack of it.

For four hours, while I read, napped, knitted and looked out of the window, the phone rang down the hall. Finally at 6 p.m., with hunger driving me from my room, I proceeded downstairs and switched from English to charades and limited language. I approached the young woman at the desk and asked her, "Svetlana? Intourist? Telephone?" with appropriate accompanying gestures. It worked! She attempted to call Svetlana, but I could hear that the line was busy. Having exhausted my ability to communicate, I was saved from further difficulties by the sight of Svetlana hurrying through the front door. She, of course, was worried that I had wandered off since I was her responsibility. It wasn't until later that I discovered that I was her very first guide job!

After sorting out the wrong-number problem, we got to the heart of my worries. What had her chief said when told of my request? No problem, according to Svetlana, but it would cost me $131 in American currency to make the trip tomorrow. I easily concealed a great silent shout of relief and joy! Since I had no idea at all what Intourist would charge me for this venture, I'd been told by my travel agent to have one thousand dollars in American cash with me to cover all eventualities. I thought that it would be somewhere between $200 and $500, so her figure of $131 seemed like a major bargain to me. To Svetlana, however, who earns about $240 a month, I am sure it seemed like a fortune.

Svetlana went home to have dinner with her family, and I had mine in the hotel dining room. For each meal in that dining room I was assigned to the same seat, alone at a table for six. The food was tasty, if uninspired, and seemed a great bargain to me at no more than three rubles per meal. However, to a Soviet citizen earning between 150 and 200 rubles per month, it would have seemed very expensive. The exchange rate, while I was there, was one ruble to $1.20 US.

That night I did not sleep very much. I experienced great mood swings between elation and despair. Elation that it seemed likely that I would finally get to Goroshina, and despair in case some unforseen obstacle would rear up at the very last moment. I spent some time wondering if I needed my sanity tested. After all, I had journeyed halfway around the world on the strength of a letter from the Map Division of the Library of Congress telling me that a tiny, unnamed dot on a 1982 map was indeed Goroshina, the 'Horoshin' of my grandfather's story. I willed myself not to think negative thoughts.

The morning finally arrived, as did Svetlana. This time she joined me in the dining room and had some tea. After breakfast, we met our driver, a man named Ivanovitch, who did not speak English, and who drove a shiny, black Lada car. We headed downtown to the offices of Intourist and the fateful meeting with her chief.

The building was old, with high ceilings and wood paneling. Svetlana and I went in to meet her chief, who also did not speak English. He seemed cordial, but I was so nervous that I probably didn't realize it at the time. I sat across from his desk in a low chair, and Svetlana sat between the two of us to translate.

The very first question from the chief caused my heart to sink down to and out of my shoes! "What made you think that you had to come to Cherkassy to get permission to go to Goroshina? Goroshina is not in Cherkassy district; it is in Poltava district!!" I was sure that this was the end of my quest. I showed nothing of my inner fear.

I knew that Goroshina was in the *oblast* (district) of Poltava, because my grandfather had said so in his story. However, when I had compared the list of cities permitted to Westerners with the map, the city of Cherkassy was much closer than the city of Poltava which was so far away as to be off the map entirely. My map did not show district boundaries, and I did not know that they were relevant. With the city of Poltava so far away, it would have been more than a one-day round trip journey, and as such, forbidden to me. My travel agent had double checked my conclusion that Cherkassy ought to be my destination with the Intourist office in New York City. So I calmly told the chief, "Intourist in New York told me to come here." He seemed satisfied, and I relaxed a little bit.

Next Svetlana translated for me, "My chief wants to know exactly why you want to go to Goroshina, and I am to translate exactly." I told him that I had promised my grandfather that I would attempt to go back and visit his village and find the family burial plot. He accepted this and cautioned me that it would be a difficult, ten-hour round trip. I assured him that I could handle it, and if it were going to be that long, we should get going.

The chief called in his secretary for the necessary papers to be signed, and we again ran into a snag. In my wallet was $500 in American cash. I needed to pay the $131 for the trip to Goroshina. To my dismay, I found that while I had fifties, twenties and a one, I did not have a ten.

I asked if there were a money exchange office where I could break a twenty. Of course, there was no American money in Cherkassy other than that which was in my own wallet. They asked if they could give me ten dollars worth of rubles in change. That solution would not work; I needed a voucher for each currency exchange I made and knew that I would have difficulty with customs when I left the country.

Finally, I came upon an ingenious solution to this problem. I convinced them to charge me $141. Beaming smiles all around. Problem solved. We were on our way. Even at $141, I knew it was a bargain.

Off to Goroshina

Svetlana, Ivanovitch and I set off in our shiny black Lada. We crossed north over the causeway, which spans the Kremenchug Reservoir at its north end, and then turned east towards Goroshina. Ivanovitch and Svetlana, it was soon apparent, had never been in this direction before. Ivanovitch stopped in each village we passed through, asking directions. Each time he asked I was sure that we would either be turned back or that someone would tell us that there was no such place as Goroshina. Each village had its official to whom we had to show our papers, allowing us to pass through. I was in such a state of total disbelief about the whole journey that I could not accept the evidence of my eyes and ears. Each villager stopped, pointed down the road and gave directions which always included the word "Goroshina." My grandfather was apparently wrong when he said in his story, "This place no longer exists."

We rapidly left good roads and along with them, the 20th century. The roads were so badly rotten with deep, black mud that Ivanovitch had to drive off the road, between trees, around boulders, through fields and brush to stay out of that mud. If we had attempted the roads, in some places, we would have been mired up over our hubcaps. I'm sure that my grandfather, had he returned from the grave, would have found nothing changed since his departure in 1905. The only addition to the landscape which he would not have placed in his 1905 picture was electricity. Lenin's dream of electrification of the countryside had happened after my grandfather had left.

After much bumping along on these roads, we came to a river. The Sula River was shown on my grandfather's map as winding all around the village of Goroshina. There was no bridge across this river. Instead there was what they called a ferry but what I would call a raft. We got out of the car and waited for three tug boats, towing barges loaded with crushed rock, to pass so that the ferry could be pulled, hand over hand, to our side of the river. There was a man with a bicycle also waiting to cross the river, and Ivanovitch struck up a conversation with him. There was a flock of geese wandering around unattended.

The land near the river was marshy, low lying and flat. There were many clumps of reeds growing in and near the river. My grandfather had gone into great detail about the construction of a peasant's house at the turn of the century. Because of the shortage of logs to build houses, the peasant used what was available, the reeds. They were woven around a framework of upright logs set into holes in the ground. At this point the house resembled a large, rectangular basket, with holes for door and windows. Then a mixture made of manure and mud was flung by the handful at the basket framework. The mixture would stick to the woven reeds and would be built up in this manner to a thickness of about a foot. After this "insulation" material had dried out over a period of several days, it was "whitewashed" with a special white clay found on the banks of the Sula. The building was then thatched again with bundles of the ubiquitous reeds.

We did not see any homes which looked as though they had been built in this manner. I suppose that over the course of time they eventually would have melted in the rain. However, we did see women, standing in the mud, bundling the reeds together to be used for thatch. Many of the homes of Goroshina, built mostly of whitewashed brick, were thatched with bundles of reeds. Otherwise, they had roofs of corrugated metal sheeting.

We finally crossed the river with Ivanovitch, the man with the bicycle and the ferry man pulling us hand over hand on a wire which stretched shore to shore. It was a totally silent, totally calm and smooth ride. On the other side was a small toll house. I was concerned lest this be yet another official deterrent to our trip. However, it seemed that it was merely the place where Ivanovitch had to pay the toll, unlike the man on the bicycle, since he was a member of a collective farm and rode toll free.

Not too far down the road, Ivanovitch came to a stop in front of a road sign. Just one word on a simple sign, much like many we had passed on our trip. Unreadable to me, it spoke just one word to him and to Svetlana…"Goroshina." We were there. An unremarkable country road, trees on one side and open fields on the other, but my quest had ended. We had entered the village of my grandfather's birth.

Arrival in Goroshina

As a disclaimer for what is to follow in the way of descriptive material about Goroshina, I must state here that I was in a state of totally stunned disbelief the entire time I was in the village. This trip, and its possible conclusion, had occupied my fantasies for so long that to actually be standing in this place, a very real place, wiped out most of my ability to function for several hours. I've been asked how long I was in the village, and I have to answer truthfully that I have no idea! I know that we left Cherkassy at 9:30 a.m. and returned there at 5:30 p.m., but that's all I know. I think the trip was about 2 1/2-3 hours each way.

We drove down the road, beyond the sign and found an area of small homes. Most of them were whitewashed brick, with painted wood trim of either light blue or dark green. A very few of the homes were built entirely of wood. Each yard was fenced, mostly with picket fences, with a woven reed fence here and there. We turned left and recrossed the river. This time there was a bridge, which was in the process of being repaired. There were several people at work on the repairs, most of them women.

There were a few wagons on the road pulled by heavy farm horses and a few farm trucks, but no other cars, except ours. We pulled up in front of a building which Svetlana identified as the town hall. It was a very modest one story building of perhaps three or four rooms. She asked me to wait outside with Ivanovitch while she went in. Shortly she came back out with

Entrance to one of the few houses that survived the Holocaust. The author's grandfather was a carpenter, and the ornate lintel may have been his creation.

another woman whom she identified as Valla, the secretary of the village council. Svetlana had a very large smile on her face.

"You are very lucky," she told me. "I told Valla your family name, Medvedovsky, and she told me that he had been a butcher and that she could show us where the house had been!!" Off we went together in the car. Valla was forty years old and had been born right after World War II. However, she seemed well versed in the history of the village, which was in the midst of a three-year celebration of its 900th birthday.

Ninety percent of the village had been destroyed by the Nazis. Of the ten percent left standing, the oldest structure was the barn or stable on the Medvedovsky land!

Svetlana had asked me on our trip to Goroshina what I wanted to do or see when we got there. I had listed four things: see the family property, see the synagogue, see the Jewish cemetery and talk with the oldest person in the village.

Valla directed Ivanovitch to the home of the oldest man in the village, born in 1902. He wasn't at home, and others were dispatched to find him. In this manner, I'm sure that many other persons in Goroshina became aware that an American descendant of a Goroshiner was in the village. That would account for the people who came to stare at us as we proceeded around the village. I'm sure that the sight of our car was also cause for comment.

While the oldest man was being found, we proceeded to the site of the Jewish cemetery. Valla recalled playing there as a child. My grandfather had said, in his story, that the Jewish cemetery was on the road to Cherkassy. Since we had come in on that road and not seen a cemetery, I was puzzled. Valla cleared up this puzzlement by saying that the cemetery was on the old road to Cherkassy. With the construction of the dam which formed the Kremenchug Reservoir, parts of the Sula River had also changed course over the years, causing the rerouting of certain roads.

Goroshina Cemetery

We drove along a road which bordered a field of newly emerging winter wheat. The intense black of the Ukrainian soil contrasted beautifully with the bright green of the shoots. I looked for any evidence of gravestones. I was prepared to find destruction, desecration, desolation. After all, there were only 18 Jewish families in the village at the time of my grandfather's story. The Nazis had destroyed the village and in addition had a concentration camp just ten miles away at Khoral. I was sure a Jewish cemetery would not have escaped their attention to detail in their drive to obliterate Jews and any records of Jews. I was right.

We came to an area, about 100 feet by 300 feet of very dense thicket, what you would call "second growth" of trees. They were about 15 feet tall and growing so close together that, try as I might, I could not force myself in amongst them. In trying, I saw an empty paint can and two beer or wine bottles but no grave stones.

Valla, Ivanovitch, Svetlana and I circled around this grove to the side bordering the field, and there we found a very old woman who was tending a nearby orchard. She told us several interesting facts. She told us that no one had been buried in this cemetery since 1915. She said that the local peasants knew that it had been a Jewish cemetery and, respecting this, had not plowed the ground for planting. She also pointed out one old gravestone turned up by a tractor at the edge of the field, with markings on it too worn to read. However, it was possible to tell that the chiseled letters were of the Cyrillic alphabet rather than Hebrew.

When I questioned whether this stone could actually be a Jewish stone, Svetlana asked me whether it was a Jewish custom to put stones on graves. It seems that Ukrainians, at least in that part of the Ukraine, put metal crosses on their graves. So, if it was a gravestone, it was a Jewish one.

One sticking point in regard to all of the information about the cemetery did not occur to me until we had left the village. If no one had been buried there since 1915, why were all the trees so small? They were certainly not 70 year old trees. They weren't even 40 year old trees, assuming that the Nazis had plowed under or otherwise destroyed all that had been on the surface of this small cemetery. As yet I have no answers to this puzzle.

I did question Valla about Jews in Goroshina. She told me that they were all gone before the war. She also said that one Jewish couple had returned after the war. They were teachers named Rabinovitch. They had two sons; the parents died and the sons moved on, one to Kiev and one to Kharkov.

We left the site of the cemetery, after I tossed a pebble into the midst of the trees. Surely, I thought, there was an ancestor buried somewhere in all that tangle, and I could only honor his or her resting place in a general sort of way. We drove down a few more roads, all unpaved and most very muddy, and suddenly we were there.

Homes of Goroshina

A large area of unkept grass was where the Medvedovsky home had been and a barn was next to the grass. I got out of the car, wandered around the barn taking pictures and crying at the same time. While standing back and taking a picture of one end of the barn, I suddenly realized that the material clinging to the entire side, stuck there for the past 85 years, was the manure/mud mixture that my grandfather had described in his story! Nothing moved me more, since it had been so carefully described.

There were two outbuildings near the barn. One was the privy and one was a low brick shed, with sloping roof, high in front and lower in back. This turned out to be the entrance to the *ludnick*, a cold storage cellar. While my grandfather had described the building as a 200-foot-long *ludnick* for the entire community, I presumed that at some later date, the idea of individual *ludnicks* must have evolved, since I saw these cellars in almost every yard in the village.

Valla pointed out to us that there was a house next door, now abandoned, which had also been built in 1900. It was the typical whitewashed brick, with light blue, wooden gingerbread trim around the windows and doors. Since my grandfather was already a carpenter by 1900, I would like to believe that he had done the trim. I questioned Valla about records, asking her, "If you know that these two buildings were built in 1900, do you also have records of people?" Her answer was that they had all been destroyed in the war.

We went to find the oldest man and spoke with him and his wife. Although I showed him pictures of both my grandparents and great-grandparents, he did not seem to remember either of them. It was again, only after I got home, that I realized that I should have asked him, "When you were a child, to whom did your mother go when she wanted to buy meat?" She probably would have gone to my great-grandfather. His wife and I exchanged a long, smiling stare, and somehow despite our lack of ability to speak directly to one another, I knew that she knew all about me and my journey. It was one of the most meaningful moments of my time in Goroshina.

We drove off to the site of the former synagogue. It, too, had been destroyed in the war. We stopped in front of another small brick home in Goroshina. Valla pointed out that this home sat up on a mound of land about four feet higher than that of the surrounding area. The reason, Valla said, was that this was where the foundation of the synagogue was. There seemed to be a communications gap when I expressed a desire to get out of the car and take a picture. Off we drove!

Dinner in Goroshina

Svetlana told me then that Valla had invited us to her home for lunch. Svetlana seemed as pleased and surprised as I was. She had fortified herself for the day with two small apples in her purse, and I had a small, pop-top can of tuna in mine. While the invitation seemed, at the time, to be spontaneous, I have had second thoughts since returning home. When a Russian friend of mine viewed my slides of the lunch table in Valla's home, she told me in no uncertain terms that Valla had been prepared for us. The one item on the table which gave my friend this clue was a bottle of Pepsi! There was no way, my friend stated, that a Ukrainian peasant, this far from sources of supply, would have a bottle of Pepsi just sitting around awaiting the visit of a wandering American guest. My friend is certain that Valla had received a phone call from the Chief of Intourist in Cherkassy.

We drove to her home. It was the typical small brick home, with chickens scratching in the yard, a privy and well at the back of the yard and electricity. Valla had been baking bread and the large, round loaves were still warm from the brick, wood-fired wall oven in her kitchen. She also had a pot of chicken soup in the oven.

Svetlana helped to set the table in the living room while I wandered about looking at things. There was a great deal of beautiful embroidery and pulled-thread work which Valla had done herself. Two walls were hung with large, room-sized rugs. There were several old family pictures on the walls. There were two large storage cabinets against the walls. One was full of books, in sets. The other had a large collection of crystal ware. In the corner sat two TV sets, one on top of the other. On an adjacent table sat a third TV set and a stereo cassette recorder! Not one surface was free of knickknacks.

Although supplied with electricity, Valla's home did not have running water. The kitchen was very simple. There was the wood-fired wall oven, a table, a couple of shelves for storage and a large bed built into one corner.

On the table was a bottle of vodka and one of Pepsi. Although a Coke drinker at home, I welcomed the sight of Pepsi, which was available everywhere I had been in the Soviet Union. I told Svetlana that I did not drink alcohol, and she said to me, under her breath, "Here, you drink. It is the custom." So I made a toast to friendship and tossed off a sip of vodka. We had an animated discussion about a plate of something which I didn't recognize. I finally decided that it was some sort of preserved eggplant. I told Svetlana that we called it "eggplant," and she said that here it was called "blue." I described the shape of an eggplant with my hands and Ivanovitch immediately joined in enthusiastically! Mystery solved.

As we were leaving Valla's home for the return to Cherkassy, Svetlana said to me, "The hearts of our simple peasant folk are so good!" I assured her that they were that way everywhere.

Conclusion

Upon my return home, I found I had a sense of unreality about the whole trip. Not only was I disbelieving about finding myself in Goroshina after all this time and effort, but I had little nagging doubts about the validity of everything that I had been shown. Could the whole thing have been a setup? Could one phone call from the Director of Intourist in Cherkassy to Valla in Goroshina arranged for her to "remember" Medvedovsky, the butcher, caused her to bake bread, prepare chicken soup from one of the chickens scratching in her yard, show me a vacant plot of land and an empty barn passed off as belonging to my family? Since I will never truly know the answers to these questions, I have chosen to believe that what I saw was real, valid, true, uncompromised by deceit and Soviet desire to give me what I so obviously wanted.

I know that my trip to Goroshina will enter the body of oral family history, along with the trip in 1935 of my mother's sister Sylvie Medow, to Moscow, where she visited her paternal aunts. The aunts later vanished in the maelstrom of

World War II. I visited the place in Moscow where one of them had lived in 1935. Where my Aunt Sylvie found her Aunt Baila, I found only a vacant lot where an apartment house had stood. I wondered why my Aunt Sylvie had not visited Goroshina on her trip through the Soviet Union. Was it because my grandfather, who had not yet written his story, believed there was no Goroshina left to visit?

Later I found out my great-aunt, Baila M. Tovbin, had actually died in 1982 at the age of 90. She apparently cut off contact with her two brothers in America, perhaps thinking that it would endanger her to write to America. How sad that my grandfather had died thinking his younger sister had been dead all of those years.

I feel a connection to him that I didn't feel before reading his story and undertaking this trip. Wouldn't he be vastly surprised to hear where I went on Friday, October 4, 1985, because of his words on yellowing paper?

Roseanna Tendler Worth has been researching her family history for nearly 25 years. She states she is doing it for grandchildren and their grandchildren. "Tracking down names and dates is just the tip of the iceberg for me. Learning about how our family lived at other times and in other places is what is really interesting."

Dedication of the Fragments from Roudnice
by Carol Davidson Baird

Winter 1989

This year we celebrated the seventh anniversary of our synagogue by reading every word of the Torah at the Kiryat Hatorah. We gave life to the words of our ancestors by remembering. Torahs are not just pieces of parchment wrapped in velvet. Aside from the words they contain, they have a history and a story to tell. Certainly our Holocaust Torah could tell us of Shabbath mornings in Roudnice, Czechoslovakia, when congregants fondly kissed it and of bar mitzvah boys who read their *maftir*[1] from it. The Torah could also tell us of its vicious abduction by the Nazis and its loneliness sitting catalogued in a dark warehouse in Prague until the end of World War II. Then it was transferred to Westminster Synagogue to be restored and later sent to a new home for its rebirth at my synagogue, Congregation Beth Am in Solana Beach, California. Like the phoenix, rising from its ashes, our Torah lives again and will endure.

As a genealogist, I bring ancestors to life by remembering and recording their personal histories and stories and by caring for their heirlooms and old photographs. But having notebooks filled with documents of rites of passage, having antique jewelry or religious artifacts, and possessing volumes of old pictures was not enough. I needed to return to the land of my ancestors to feel their presence, to make memories come to life.

Two months ago, my mother and father, Eva and Ernie Davidson, my husband, Steve, and two sons, Danny and Geoffrey, generously made this strenuous and emotional journey with me to our family's past as we drove in two cars through Germany, Poland, Hungary and Czechoslovakia. We went as three generations; my parents as German survivors of the Holocaust, myself as the first child born in America, and my sons, the future of my family and our Judaic heritage. Hearing the stories from their grandparents' mouths in a land where those stories happened, gave life to those words. It was truly *l'dor v'dor*, from generation to generation.

In Germany and Poland, we visited all those places associated with the life of my family. In Auschwitz, we said *Kaddish* (prayer for the dead) for those family members who perished there. Afterwards, walking back to our cars, the skies clouded overhead, the rains came and the thunder roared.

After going through Hungary as my ancestors did 600 years ago on their way to Germany, we went to Czechoslovakia to see Prague and Theresienstadt. Be-

---

[1] Last portion read from the Torah on Sabbath mornings as well as the additional portion read from the Prophets.

cause of a large student demonstration in the main square in Prague accompanied by military and police intervention, we opted to avoid seeing Prague and instead went to Terezin (Theresienstadt) a day early. Fate works in strange ways, for we had more time to visit the countryside outside of Prague, and that time proved to be the most remarkable part of the trip.

We drove to the Terezin concentration camp memorial and wandered through this fortress until we came to the women's barracks. All alone, except for the wandering souls of those who perished there, including my ancestors, we gathered close together to say *Kaddish* again. Walking to our cars, as in Auschwitz, the skies blackened and the thunder boomed

About ten kilometers south of Terezin we noticed a sign—Roudnice nad Labem. Since we now had time to explore, we got off the main road and headed for this town we had heard so much about at every bar and bat mitzvah in our synagogue—a town in north central Bohemia where our Holocaust Torah came from. We set out to find the synagogue which once housed our Torah.

First we drove to the old center of town, parked, and looked around the square for the oldest person who might remember where the synagogue was. Mom quickly drew a primitive picture of a building with a Star of David on top and set out for an old lady waiting for a bus. After looking at the picture, she replied in German that she did indeed know where it was and directed us around the corner and down the middle of the next street. Not believing our luck, we raced around the corner and scoured the street for any sign of an old synagogue. We saw an old abandoned church that Steve thought might have once been a synagogue. We saw another building which could have been it, and we took many pictures of an overgrown vacant lot where it could have stood long ago. We kept trying to make something out of nothing.

Not giving up, we continued down the street asking people if they spoke English or German, and as we showed them our drawing, we asked if they knew where the old synagogue was. We got one "no" after another and a lot of shoulder shrugging. Dangerous as it was, Mom, Dad and Steve finally entered a police station and asked if they knew about the synagogue. The young policeman shrugged his shoulders and got an older officer from the back who only offered, "Synagogue *kaput.*" Figuring that the vacant lot is what he was referring to, we dejectedly headed back to our cars in the city square. I suggested we approach the old lady again, but she had gone. Geoff wanted to ask more people, but Steve was ready to leave after so many false hopes. As we got to our cars, a young couple was looking into them, obviously impressed by the lovely new German cars. Mom went through her routine again with the lady who, to our surprise, spoke a little German. The lady took the piece of paper with the drawing and went off across the street to a beauty parlor where she asked another woman our questions. That woman, in turn, called another lady out of the place and she, too, called another lady out. Together, they all came over to us and one who spoke German told us that this young woman would go in our car and show us the way to the old Jewish cemetery which should be near the synagogue.

Off we went, out of the center of town, onto a dirt road. Half way down the road, Mom stopped her car in front of a Catholic cemetery and church. Used to dashed hopes by now, we all figured she had misunderstood what we were searching for. Finally, a man got her attention and pointed further down the dirt road. Again, hopes renewed, we followed my parent's car down to the very end of the road where we saw them turn around and stop. We also stopped, got out, and expressed our disappointment, until the lady pointed to a clump of trees enclosed by a crumbling wall.

We all slowly bent down to look under the branches of the trees and, there in the overgrowth, was a little synagogue in ruins—the synagogue of Roudnice. Parts of the walls were gone; it was overgrown with weeds, bushes and trees, and what was probably the tiny sanctuary where the Torah was housed, was a pile of burnt debris. The synagogue had been gutted by fire, and the roof had fallen in. It looked as if no one had touched it

Abandoned ceremonial burial hall in front of the cemetery in Roudnice, Czech Republic. The inscription above the star reads "...and you shall rest and you shall arise to your destiny at the end of days." Daniel 12:13

since the day in the 1940s when the Torah had been taken and its home destroyed. After catching our breath, we roamed the building taking pictures, climbing over the burned wood and tumbled blocks of the wall. We all had the incredible feeling of how much meaning and life the Torah in Solana Beach now had.

Rabbi Dosick tells each bar or bat mitzvah that by using this Holocaust Torah they stand for the little children of Roudnice who could not have their bar or bat mitzvah because their lives ended in a puff of smoke from a crematorium chimney. Our sons, Danny and Geoffrey, stood on our *bimah*[2] a few years ago so that

---

[2] The raised platform in front of the sanctuary that holds the ark in which the Torah is kept.

those children would be reborn and given new life through them. How ironic that they had just been to Terezin where those little boys and girls probably perished and only 15 minutes away stood upon the ashes of their synagogue. Danny and Geoffrey gave life to their memories by returning to proclaim, *Am Yisroel Chai*, the people of Israel live.

So this is the story our Torah would tell. It had a life long ago, was lost and then found, to be reborn in our synagogue. We give life to the Torah and it, in turn, gives us words to live by. The Rabbi told me that the inscription over the decaying wire Star of David is a part of the last words of the Book of Daniel which says, "...and you shall rest and you shall arise to your destiny at the end of days." This probably referred to those who lay in the cemetery there which we never found, but I prefer to think that Congregation Beth Am was the destiny of that tiny synagogue in Roudnice and that their community lives because we remember.

Remembering and making stories come to life means tangible mementos to this congregation. Toward this end, we brought back to our congregation fragments of our Torah's first home. Danny and Geoff collected a broken stone from the Roudnice synagogue wall and a charred timber from the sanctuary.

This is the story of the abandoned little synagogue of Roudnice, Czechoslovakia.

As we walked back to our cars, the skies darkened, a slight drizzle came down and the thunder rumbled. We had the feeling that God was following us all along the way. When we remember our heritage, He remembers us.

Carol Davidson Baird is the only child of German Holocaust survivors. She is past president of the San Diego Jewish Genealogical Society and the North San Diego County Genealogical Society. She published the JGS Presidents' Forum newsletter and wrote the manual for International Association of Jewish Genealogical Societies on how to start a Jewish genealogical society. She teaches and lectures to genealogical societies and Jewish organizations. She co-edited Stammbaum– The Journal of German-Jewish Genealogical Research, was a columnist for Family Tree, and was newsletter editor for both the SDJGS and NSDCGS.

Epilogue

On a subsequent visit to Roudnice, it was determined that the place visited was not the synagogue of Roudnice but the ceremonial burial hall in front of the cemetery. The main room that was thought to be the sanctuary was where the family prayed for the deceased, and the side rooms were for the *chevra kadisha* (burial society) to guard the body and to prepare the body for burial.

Genealogical Adventure
by Melody Amsel-Arieli

Winter 1997

My surname is Amsel—named for a songbird known throughout eastern Slovakia. In 1787, Emperor Joseph II of the Austro-Hungarian Empire decreed that each Jewish family adopt a surname in order to facilitate the Empire's growing order and bureaucracy. It is said that the head of my family, too modest to choose a name for himself, was named by the recording clerk who said, "You sing so beautifully that I will call you *amsel*." So, in those rural villages the amsels sang, and the Amsels sang—orthodox Jews who were often as not, cantors and readers in the synagogues.

Even today, among the rolling hills and cornfields, it is easy to imagine life as it once was. Numerous tiny clusters of cottages here and there, seemingly unchanged over many years, sit amid glorious late summer gardens. Some are so tiny that, in the blink of an eye, the driver on a through road may miss seeing them at all. Larger villages spread out in the fields, typically with small stores, a church or two, a village square and maybe a hotel with an adjacent restaurant. There are very few tourists. Slovakian and German are spoken; Czech is understood, maybe even Russian, learned in the recent Russian occupation of Czechoslovakia.

The religion here is obviously Christian Orthodox from the look of the onion-shaped domes on the churches. Statues of Jesus languishing on the cross guard both the entrance and exit of the villages.

The Jews are long gone.

As a child in America, my grandfather told me that he came from a town in Slovakia called Stropkov, but he never added another word. He didn't tell me about his father and grandfather and great-grandfather, his sisters and brothers, his nieces and nephews. I knew only my American Amsels. When I was much older, I was told, "We are the only ones left; all were killed in the Holocaust."

Many years later, after I had immigrated to Israel, I chanced to see the name Amsel mentioned in an article in the *Jerusalem Post*. Another Amsel! And so my journey began. I contacted all the Amsels that I could locate in Israel and around the world. I began to gather whatever information they could offer about their small families. Each person said, "All Amsels are related."

I found Amsels whose origins were from all over eastern Slovakia, from Bardejov, Hertnik, Huncovce, Michalovce, Stropkov, Vranov and other towns and villages. Once this area teemed with Amsels, intertwined, intermarried. Today, any synagogues that survived the German destruction stand empty; the *mikvahs* (ritual baths) are destroyed. There is very little to remind the villagers of the Jews who were deported, but the cemeteries remain.

Just outside Stropkov is a tiny village called Tisinec; it was here that the Jews of Stropkov and the surrounding settlements were allowed to bury their dead. The cemetery is not in the town itself, but out in the fields, removed from sight, but not removed from mind. When we asked the elderly ladies who were walking home from church about the cemetery, they were happy to direct us there. They asked my name and exclaimed, "Hamselova, Hamselova!" It made their day—not much happens in a tiny village like this on a Sunday afternoon. We drove out into the fields, out past where the road turns into a two-rut tractor path, so overgrown with weeds that I feared for the rented car. Seeing only field and forest, we turned back to the village. The ladies were still there, and they would not give up.

They sent for the only teenager in Tisinec who studied English and for the caretaker of the cemetery. After this kind man had finished his Sunday dinner and arrived from Stropkov, we all assembled in the car and drove out again over the path. This time when the going got rough, we walked. It was no wonder that we had not seen the cemetery the first time! It was nearly invisible in the wild unchecked overgrowth and undergrowth, nearly returned to nature. Only upon entering the area, sensing rather than seeing the fence, could we see that it was really a cemetery—hundreds of tombstones askew, overturned, mossed over, Hebrew inscriptions barely legible. There was one small building within the enclosure, built to protect the grave of one of the noted Hassidic rabbis who had lived in Stropkov. It had been defiled: *Juden raus* (Jews, get out!) was scrawled on the walls. My son,

Author in front of an ohel (mausoleum) of a Hasidic rabbi in Tisinec. Graffiti on the structure says "Juden raus" (Jews, get out).

a proud Israeli, stood shocked. Yet, on this humid afternoon in August, it was nearly impossible to conjure up the image of skinheads, young neo-Nazis, arriving in the dead of night, laughing, singing, defiling. This abandoned, neglected cemetery, final resting place of Jews from c1400 until c1890, was peaceful in the sunlight, lovely with scattered wildflowers and sweet with wild strawberries underneath.

The Jews of Stropkov accompanied their dead on carts to the cemetery in Tisinec; they ritually cleansed the bodies in the house where we received directions.

In the late 1800s, they were given permission to establish a cemetery on the outskirts of Stropkov. By the time we visited, it had long been enveloped by newer residential areas and stood within the town itself. Indeed, even after we entered the cemetery through a hole in the fence, next door neighbors were sitting in their adjacent yard on the ground, sorting potatoes. I wondered if it felt strange to them to live so near an abandoned, overgrown Jewish cemetery, but they didn't even look up.

We wandered around with sketches of the family tree in hand, hoping to locate graves of our great-great-grandparents, great-grandparents or anyone of ours who had died before 1942. We found nothing familiar because the names were written, according to the Jewish tradition in Hebrew, "the son of," "the daughter of." There were no family names on these tombstones, and most were illegible anyway, half-hidden by the wild grasses and flowers and bushes. I walked around slowly, very conscious that here, literally under my feet, were my roots.

One grave stood out, different from the others, impressive, fully upright, marble, clearly marked "Here lies Jakub Grunfeld." Jakub Grunfeld, the last Jew of Stropkov, caretaker of this cemetery, with whom I had corresponded. Now he, too, was dead. Some kind soul had buried him among his ancestors. The circle had closed.

Most of our family actually hailed from Sitnik, a tiny hamlet just outside Stropkov. It was from here that my grandfather, Shaya Amsel, and two of his brothers had immigrated to America, leaving behind their father, Yosef, three sisters—Ida, Rivka and Chaya—and their youngest brother, Peretz. It was here that two of their families lived—Chaya Ritter with her husband and eight children and Peretz with his family and his elderly father. And it was from here that they were deported in the spring of 1942.

As we entered Sitnik, I impulsively stopped the car near several older women talking by the side of the road and told them in a combination of broken Russian and gestures that I am an Amsel. They answered in Slovakian, talking among themselves, obviously understanding, obviously excited. They called their husbands and neighbors to come hear the news. They cried.

A tall man in an embroidered skullcap paused, seeing the crowd of people who had gathered around us. He introduced himself—Adolf Vateho—a priest who had grown up in Sitnik and had once lived in Canada. He remembered the Amsels very well. He had been a boy then. The grandfather was called Yossel, not Yosef, but he didn't know why. He remembered that Peretz was a wonderful person. He recalled the Ritter children by name—Manya, who had married Grossman and had immigrated to Palestine only to return home because life was so difficult there; Sima; Shaya; Rachel; Sara; Meyer, called Miklosc; Avram, who was Arpad whom the children called "Boom;" and the littlest, Lea, who was called Laura. For a few moments, he made them all live again.

The neighbors knew who had survived—just Laura Ritter and Peretz's daughter, Roshinka Amsel. "Look," they said, pointing across the road to an abandoned cottage. "That's the Ritter house." The doors were smashed, the windows were gone, debris was everywhere, but we were touched by what we saw inside. The walls and even the ceilings had been decorated with stencils as was the custom many years ago, preserved as if it had been painted yesterday. The original heating stove stood in the middle of the living room, eastern European style, dark brown, tall, nearly up to the ceiling. The original cooking stove, tiled light blue, stood in the kitchen. True, it was crumbling now, crumbling enough to see that beneath the tiles lay an insulation of clay, but around the perimeter of the stove was a ceramic blue and white flowered border, still beautiful today.

We visited Laura Ritter Spanikova and her family in Bratislava. Laura doesn't speak about her past, and, in fact, Darina, her daughter, was told of her Jewish roots only when she was an adult. Andrea, Laura's granddaughter, was told at an earlier age. Having no common language, we communicated with hugs and kisses. We felt like family.

We left Slovakia with a small piece of the decorative border from Laura's cooking stove. We carry with it our shared memories of a Jewish childhood—of family, of Shabbat meals, of holiday preparations, of all the warmth, love and nourishment that a stove can symbolize. Somehow this destroyed stove touches both our past and present.

Melody Amsel-Arieli, who lives in Maaleh Adumim, Israel, is a professional flutist, teacher, avid genealogist, and freelance writer. She is the author of Between Galicia and Hungary: The Jews of Stropkov (Avotaynu, 2002)

Number 10 Forrasvolgy Street
by Viviana Grosz

Winter 2004

On June 19, 2003, I sat at an outdoor neighborhood cafe in Miskolc, Hungary. It was a sunny mid-afternoon in a quiet residential area of one-story dwellings, some well kept and obviously remodeled, others showing signs of neglect. No one was around except the girl who worked in the cafe and a couple of gypsies carrying buckets of cherries on their way to the market.

A friend had warned me that there were few interesting sites in that industrial city, but I was not interested in tourist attractions in Miskolc. I had flown to Hungary a few days earlier from London, primarily to look up a street address I had previously located on a city map from the Internet. And I had found it. Number 10 Forrasvolgy (Spring Valley, in English) Street was the forwarding address on the envelopes with folded letters that my grandparents and my father's younger brother had written to my father between 1936 and 1941.

I sat across the street from the house where I imagined my grandparents sitting at a kitchen table after a day's work decades before, writing to my father who had left Hungary in 1933 at age 19. Like other young Hungarian Zionists, he was poor, unemployed and with little hope of studying in an institution of higher learning that restricted entrance to Jews. Like many, he immigrated to Palestine to make a life for himself and, as he recounted years later, to help build the streets of Tel Aviv.

In my possession are 11 letters from each of my grandparents and two from my uncle, and five postcards, none of them from the short time my father spent in Palestine. I have only some black and white photographs that attest to the time he was there. In the snapshots, I easily recognize a handsome, tall and slim man with blue eyes in a tanned face standing among other young men at various construction sites.

I found the pile of letters and postcards neatly kept and stashed away in the drawer of my father's night table in his apartment in Mexico City. He arrived there at the end of 1936, having left Palestine a year before. During 1935, he lived with family friends in Antwerp while he waited for his visa to Mexico; only two letters date from his stay in Belgium. After he left Hungary, my father never saw his family again. His only contact with them was through the letters he received and those he wrote, the frequency of which would have been subject to the irregularities in mail delivery during wartime.

The letters are written on both sides of one sheet of paper. Sometimes, my grandparents shared equal space, but often my grandmother wrote more extensively, leaving my grandfather a quarter of a page or less at the end. Their distinct cursive strokes are easily recognizable. My grandmother's are round and clean characters on straight lines with symmetrical spaces between words, while my grandfather's look like scribbles difficult to read.

I know little about my father's family. He didn't talk about his parents or his younger brother, and I didn't question him. Once I asked him to read the letters to me in the hope he would talk about his parents and brother, but he never could

find the appropriate time for it. Although I suspected that he might have avoided evoking events from another time and the sorrow that they would cause him, it was only after he died that I had someone translate the letters and I learned of their sad contents. It then became clear to me that my father had not wanted to bring back memories of this painful period of his youth.

In the absence of relatives who could fill in the gaps of the family history, the letters and postcards my father saved enabled me to reconstruct a personal history of my grandparents and uncle. The letters became the only source of information that would help me attempt to answer questions about what my grandparents and uncle were like, what they thought, how they lived and why they didn't leave Hungary to join my father in Mexico.

While I drank a glass of mineral water in the outdoor cafe across the street, I thought of another day in June when my grandparents were forced to leave their one-story house on 10 Forrasvolgy and ordered to move to the ghetto in the center of the city. Between June 11 and 16, 1944, they were deported to Auschwitz and most likely, by June 19, nearly 60 years before I sat across from the house that had been their modest home, they already had been gassed. My uncle had been spared the crematorium. In October 1941, he went to serve for what were supposed to be two years of military service in a labor battalion. What took place between October 1941 and the time he was taken to Auschwitz is unknown to me. I only know what my father learned of his brother's fate from a survivor who said my uncle died of food poisoning when the Russians liberated the camp.[1]

---

[1] In 2007, I met twice with the man who was the last person to see my uncle, Bandi, alive. I had gone to see him with the hope of finding out more about Bandi's life and death in the concentration

I took with me to Miskolc copies of the letters and postcards and two black and white photographs I found in a box of family pictures. In one of the photographs, there is a boy of about 12 years old with a big smile. He is in short pants standing next to a tall and bold man with a moustache in a suit and tie who, I am certain, is my grandfather. I have scrutinized the image to find the resemblance to my father, to me or to my son who bears his Hebrew name, but I find none. Nevertheless, I want to believe there is some likeness in the way my son and my grandfather stand up, letting their body come forward. The inscription on the back of the photograph revealed the name of my uncle and the term of endearment the family used for my father. It read:

To Emlikul: From your little brother, Bandi. November 2, 1933

At age 22, my father was working in Mexico City, striving to learn the language and to adapt to his new surroundings. He needed to secure a better job with higher pay to help his family. In 1937, my grandparents were overjoyed to learn that my father had arrived safely at his final destination and that he was already earning a living. They placed their hopes on him to help them alleviate the economic distress caused by the anti-Semitic policies of the Hungarian government. On March 3, 1937, my grandmother wrote:

There is nothing new to write about. We work hard to make ends meet and to pay our taxes. The economic situation worsened a lot in our place since a young Christian moved nearby and competes and harms our business. Besides, the rent is very high and the apartment and the store are very costly. Not far, there is a house and a shop, in the Forrasvolgy Street, which is for sale. Its price is five thousand pengő but, unfortunately, we cannot afford it.

I thought we would be able to pay off the house with your help, and that our future would not be so hopeless in our old age. I didn't want to write all this to you because you can't help us anyway, at least for a while, but I wanted to ease my heart.

> *Your loving mother,*
> *Ilka*

My grandparents moved to the Forrasvolgy house on November 7, 1937, but the pressure to repay their debts overshadowed the joy of finally owning a home. Scarcely six months after my father had arrived in Mexico, my grandmother

---

camp. In my first short visit in May, Mr. Reisman said, without me prompting him, "Your uncle was a very good and intelligent man." I had promised to return later in the summer and spend more time. Mr. Reisman, in return, said he had photos he would show me. When I went back in July, Mr. Reisman looked frail and weaker than previously. It was hard to understand his words, and he didn't volunteer much information. He again said Bandi was a very good man and that they had both spent many years together, sharing the same barracks. I then asked for the name of the place where they had been together, and Mr. Reisman mumbled a couple of times, "Gunskirchen." So my uncle apparently died in Gunskirchen, not Auschwitz.

wrote sternly on June 17:

> *Try to go ahead in your work so you can make more money, for we really have to work hard to cope with the upkeep of the house expenses. Uncle Henrik is asking for the money he lent us to pay for your ship's passage to Mexico. Don't take it lightly and send him as much money as you can. Don't spend your time with non-sense, but study and work conscientiously to be able to fulfill your responsibilities. I am very sorry that you didn't come home from Palestine, and that we went along with your request to go to Mexico. Pull yourself together and show me what you can accomplish so we will not be disappointed. I could not survive that we, old people, should pay the debts for someone who is young and strong. I hope that you will accept [this] in good heart because I only want, above all, the best for you.*

I do not know if my grandmother's scolding influenced my father's ability to settle down in Mexico without the emotional and material support of family, but I

Bandi

am certain that my father's willingness to ease his parents' and brother's harsh situation met insurmountable obstacles that only worsened with the threat of war in Europe. To add to their increasingly deteriorating living conditions, my grandparents grew fearful for my uncle's future. He was in his last year of high school when they moved to 10 Forras-volgy. In their desperation, even if it meant to be left alone in their old age, they inquired how Bandi could get emigration papers to join my father in Mexico, and what trade he should learn in the meantime so he could find employment after his immigration. But the persons who could have helped them never replied.

In Hungary and elsewhere, relatives were concerned for each one's future, and my grandparents had no one to turn to except my father. Most certain, it will remain unknown whether at age 24 he was still unable to send sufficient money to pay off his debt or if the money he dutifully mailed to his family was lost or stolen along the way. In their letters, however, my grandparents did not hesitate to write about their increasing sorrow and frustration and continued to urge my father not to send empty envelopes and to work hard. In an undated letter probably written before November 1937, my grandfather wrote:

> *My dear son, if you could borrow a bigger amount from the acquaintances there [in Mexico] we would be more helped in our worries because we really have a big burden on us—without capital it is impossible to keep up with the store. All our hopes are in you, and we don't want to be disappointed, don't take lightly this request [you] are our last resort. S.O.S Forgive my disorganized, sloppy letter, but I am very nervous.*

Your loving father,

Jenő

In a letter of July 31, 1938, my grandmother explained that her reprimands were not to insult him, "But whom can I tell our problems if not to my child? Write us about your life, and don't make us worry with your silence."

For a short time, the small grocery business adjacent to their new living quarters prospered on Forrasvolgy Street. Nonetheless, they worked harder than before to pay the tax collector and their bank loans. A few years earlier, they had feared for my father's future. Now they were anxious about my uncle's future. In a letter written on April 10, 1938, Bandi described the distressing situation with the new anti-Jewish laws:

> We were happy to receive your letter of March 13 in which you wrote that you have a good job. You also wrote if you save some money you will come home. I can only tell you not even to think of it. It is better to live in the free Mexico than home with gangs of anti-Semites. [They are discussing] the solution of the Jewish problem. They already worked out some laws to introduce in Parliament in which there will only be 20 percent of Jews in factories, the press, the film industry; and only 5 percent will be able to get a job in the next 5 years. Furthermore, there will be no ritual slaughtering of animals, because these are only for non-Jews. You can imagine, with these kinds of laws, how I look forward to my high school graduation. I really don't know how I will get a job.
>
> I would go to Abyssinia [Ethiopia], but mom doesn't want to hear about it. We wouldn't even need money for this trip; the embassy [referring to the Italian embassy, perhaps] would help us with a contract for work and a permit too. What do you think of this?

Like my father before him, increasing unemployment and economic uncertainty and more restrictions on Jews impelled my uncle to seek a way out. My grandparents knew that while they waited for permits, young people were learning languages and training in skills that could facilitate employment in the countries where they wanted to immigrate. They probably preferred that their younger son join my father in Mexico rather than have him embark on a North African adventure, but they knew that "to stay here is impossible," as my grandmother wrote in the only letter found from January 15, 1939, albeit they would be left alone when they were getting old and frail.

My grandmother added:

> Bandi studies engine construction and English and Spanish. Where will the fate throw us is the secret of our future. We have faith in God who won't abandon his people. Maybe His help will come in the twelfth hour. Yes, it hurts us terribly that we could be left alone in our old age, but I will stop complaining. Let's see what happens. The youth here is learning skills in industry and languages, and they are

impatiently expecting to depart from here. Considering the circumstances, we are well, we don't let anything bother us, all little problems are small compared to our big worry.

On the same date, my grandfather wrote:

Dear Imi, we are happy that you encourage us with hopes. God should help us make this a reality. It would be about time! How can we endure this?

And he ended his desperate note sharing their biggest concern. "I don't know what will happen to Bandi."

There is only one postcard from June 24, 1940, and although my grandmother wrote, "It is not necessary to describe our situation [because] I am sure you are informed of everything," she was unable to conceal their grief when she added:

Unfortunately, the time is getting closer when according to the law every single civil right will be taken away from us. Our future is very dark. We will somehow live the little time we have, but what will be of the young people? Bandi works conscientiously and he really progresses in learning his new skill. But it doesn't matter because, unfortunately, he cannot get a license to work on his own. Write to us often, of many letters [you send] maybe we will receive some. Don't forget us whom think of you incessantly day and night from far away.

Hungary stopped all emigration in the fall of 1941. The only letter saved or received that year, dated October 12, gives the news about Bandi's last days on 10 Forrasvolgy Street. In it my grandmother wrote:

We are very tired, we can't endure the fight for existence, and our patience and willingness diminished. In a short time, fate had two blows on us. One year ago, they took away our business, and today Bandi had to go into a forced labor camp for two years. We will miss his earnings immensely. I don't fear for Bandi because he is very smart and skillful, and he will adjust to every situation, but we have remained like a tree without leaves.

The letters and postcards that my father kept by his bedside until he died a few months short of his 85th birthday are the source of what I now know of my grandparents' and uncle's lives. Reading them allowed me to understand the silence that shielded my father from the pain of surviving. I am sure that the tragic fate of his family left an indelible mark on his character. He may have been haunted by guilt for his inability to respond timely to his parents' pleas and for lacking, as a new émigré, the legal resources to sponsor a visa for his brother. Did he feel that his own short experience in Palestine had prevented my uncle from seeking that way out from Europe? Or did he blame himself for living in free Mexico while his family was subject to vexation that ultimately led to annihilation? I don't know, except that he loved and cared for his parents and brother and kept them as close as an arm's reach until his end.

I felt as if almost a lifetime had gone by in front of my eyes the few hours I spent on Forrasvolgy Street. I debated whether to knock at the door, identify myself and be invited inside, or not. But my intentions were not to trouble the new owners with fear that I may want to claim my grandparents' property. Instead, I just wanted the contentment to flaunt the new leaves of the family tree in front of the house on 10 Farrasvolgy.

Viviana Grosz has a degree in literature from the Universidad Nacional Autónoma de México and an M.A. in English As a Second Language from Kean University, New Jersey, where she teaches part time. The discovery of correspondence from Hungary and relatives' oral histories raised her interest in the Holocaust and led her to independent research in genealogy.

Searching for Roots and Finding Much More
by Howard Margol
Winter 1994

A s roads in that part of the world go, the one we were on was not bad. The traffic was light and our driver managed to avoid most of the potholes and rough spots. My wife, Esther, and I were on our way from Riga, Latvia, to Jakobpils, one hour and forty minutes away. Esther's father, Ben Landey, had left there in 1898, and his cousin, Rose Druck, had followed in 1907. They had lived in Kreitzburg, a small *shtetl* across the river from Jakobpils. In later years, Jakobpils and Kreitzburg both grew and became the one city of Jakobpils. In 1910, Ben and Rose were married in Chicago. In 1920, they moved to Valdosta, Georgia, where Esther was later born.

Upon arrival in Jakobpils, we stopped at a small outdoor bazaar. Our Latvian interpreter, Indra Dagile, got out and made inquiries among the women in the various booths. Indra, a tall, shapely blond wearing a very fashionable—and very short—skirt, presented quite a contrast to her surroundings. Indra was from Riga, a large cosmopolitan city, while Jakobpils was in the "boonies." Most of Jakobpils probably had changed very little since Ben and Rose had left. Indra asked a number of people in the area if any Jews by the name of Ludkin lived in Jakobpils—the name I thought was the Latvian version of Landey. As Indra returned to our car, the disappointment of not finding a Ludkin showed on her face.

We were driving away from the bazaar area when a woman came running over and stopped us. She explained that a Jewish photographer was in his studio on the second floor of a building only 50 feet from where we were. Quite excited, we got out of the car and hurriedly went up to his studio. Between Esther's Yiddish and Indra's Latvian, communication was no problem. After an exchange of pleasantries, the photographer insisted on closing his studio in order to show us the Jewish cemetery in what was once Kreitzburg. I felt badly when he turned several customers away and told them to come back several hours later, but he did not seem to mind. After all, it was not often that he saw Jews from America. In addition, he had a sister in New York, and he hoped we would call her upon our return to Atlanta.

The size and condition of the cemetery was somewhat surprising. There seemed to be between 300 and 400 graves, with almost all of the gravestones in comparatively good condition. Quite a bit of growth and underbrush was around most of the graves, but that was understandable. The few elderly Jews left in Jakobpils had neither the strength nor the resources to care for the cemetery properly. The photographer showed us where his parents were buried. Their graves stood out compared to the surroundings, because he maintained the site with lov-

Kreitzburg, on the east side of the Daugava River from Jakobpils, circa 1910.

ing care. He also showed us a mass grave where 300 Jews were buried. They had been murdered in the nearby woods in late June 1941. He also told us that the Germans put another 300–400 Jews in the synagogue, starved them for 10 days and burned them alive. We looked around, failed to find the graves of my wife's ancestors, and returned to the photographer's studio.

He told us that two other Jews lived in Jakobpils, one named Lotkin. Could Ludkin have actually been Lotkin? I felt that there was a strong possibility, but the odds were not favorable. As far as Esther knew, her parents had no living relatives remaining in Latvia when World War II broke out. Unfortunately, Mr. Lotkin was not at home and could not be located. We stopped by the house where the other Jew lived and paid him a short visit. He appeared to be in his late seventies, but was strong and rugged looking. He told us how, to escape the Germans, he had walked all the way from Jakobpils to Stalingrad, a distance of at least one thousand miles. After the war, he returned to Jakobpils and has lived there ever since. We were two of the few American Jews he had ever met. He told us that there was no life for him anymore in Jakobpils, and in three weeks he was immigrating to Israel. We gave him two pounds of coffee and several other items, bid him *shalom aleichem* (peace be with you) and left. Tears were streaming down both of his cheeks, and, I must admit, our eyes were not exactly dry either.

After returning to Atlanta, Esther decided to write to the Lotkin in Jakobpils who was not at home when we were there. It was a long shot, but worth trying. The reply she received a month later was not only surprising, but exciting. Lotkin said that he had an uncle who had moved from there and was currently living in Berlin, Germany. He recalled that the uncle's father, Leibe, had two brothers, Ben and Sam, who immigrated to America just before the turn of the century. Esther's father was Ben, and he had a brother, Sam!

Esther always knew that her father had a sister by the name of "Leeba"— Americanized to Libby. Over the years, we heard the name as "Leeba" and sometimes as "Layba." Esther, along with her brothers and sister, always assumed that it referred to their Aunt Libby, but with a slight variation in the pronunciation. Was it possible that Ben Landey had a brother Leibe we never knew about? Letters and telephone calls to the Lotkin in Berlin quickly followed. Among other things, he told us about Sam Landey visiting his family in Jakobpils in 1926. He was a small boy at the time, and Sam brought him amazing toys from America. When Esther was growing up in Valdosta, Georgia, one of the family stories was about Uncle Sam's visit to Latvia in 1926. Unbelievable as it sounded, all the pieces fit. The Lotkin in Berlin also informed us that he had a brother living in New York who had emigrated there two years ago from Riga. Telephone calls and additional letters to New York produced further proof of the relationship.

I had gone to Lithuania to visit the *shtetl* where my mother and father were born. Esther, being a loving and caring wife, went with me in spite of the rough conditions and accommodations we knew we would have to endure. Little did she know that she would end up finding two first cousins and a dozen or so second cousins whose existence she never suspected. But, as the accompanying story illustrates, it's not only my wife who has had some amazing genealogical successes lately.

Howard Margol, a retired business executive in Atlanta, Georgia, began tracing his family history in 1990. He served a two-year term as president of the Jewish Genealogical Society of Georgia. He was elected to the board of the International Association of Jewish Genealogical Societies in 1996, and served for a total of nine years during which time he also served a two-year term as president of IAJGS. He is currently president of the LitvakSIG. Since 1993, Margol has taken groups of Jews, primarily genealogists, on trips to Lithuania to visit their ancestral shtetls.

Epilogue

After 1994, Esther and Howard made a trip to Berlin, Germany, and met Moshe Lotkin, Esther's first cousin. They also went to Brooklyn, New York, and met Moshe's brother, Abram Lotkin, and his family. In July 1999, Esther and Howard returned to Jakobpils/Kreitzburg to meet and visit with the Lotkin second cousins living there. They not only took their children with them but also arranged for Abram Lotkin to meet them there. It was Abram's first return visit since he left years before. Moshe in Berlin was too ill at the time to travel. Several years later, Howard and Esther brought both Moshe and Abram to Atlanta, Georgia, to visit and spend time with their family and to meet other members of the Landey/Lotkin families.

Family Footprints in Lithuania
by Daniel A. Kirschner
(with contributions from Davida Sky)
Winter 1994

"O h! Dan, come here! I think I've found it 'Abba ben rav Shmuel!'" Davida was excited but uncertain. It was late afternoon, the sky had darkened prematurely with storm clouds, and the winds had continued to freshen, joined intermittently by light showers. Here we were, standing in some soon-to-be-drenched, pre-Holocaust cemetery in northwest Lithuania in a former *shtetl* known as Luknik. What were we doing here?

Davida had taken a year off from work to complete writing her family histories and had decided to culminate this year with a trip to Lithuania, Belarus and Ukraine to research her own ancestral shtetls. So what was she doing traipsing about in one of my *shtetl* cemeteries? She and I had met several years ago through the Jewish Genealogical Family Finder, where we discovered that we were putative cousins-by-marriage. We were both researching the Quasser (Kwasser/Kwass) family name associated with the towns of Tryskie and Telshe in northwest Lithuania: Davida's maternal grandfather was a Kwasser, and my great-grandfather, Abba Kirschner's brother, Gershon, had married a Quasser.

When Davida invited me to join her on safari to Lithuania, her cousins-by-blood having already turned her down, I considered the offer for a month. I had always hoped to go some time, but never thought to go so soon, saw that it was indeed feasible, and decided to rationalize it as a 50th birthday present to myself. Davida and I spent July and most of August planning our trip—from visas to vaccinations, from maps to money belts, from guidebooks to gorp, from rolls of film to rolls of toilet paper, from *tsatskes* (trinkets) to *tzedakah* (charitable contributions), from interviewing returning tourists to Internetting potential guides, and so on.

This was our fourth full day in Lithuania, and we were already on energetic overload. In Vilnius, our intrepid guide, Regina Kopilevich, had filled our one day with touring various sites of Jewish interest, and Dina Kopilevich, Regina's sister and our driver, made sure that we got from one place to the next. The sites included the Jewish museum, part of the ghetto, the Jewish cultural center and its adjoining kosher restaurant, and meeting with Emmanuel Zingeris, a historian and the lone Jewish member of Parliament. We also visited the Vilnius cemetery, where I discovered the grave of my father's first cousin, Aryeh, son of Joseph Katzav, who died 22 Shevat 1959. We recited *Kaddish*, the traditional Jewish prayer for the dead, and took photographs of the grave.

In the evening, we attended a Japanese theatrical production honoring Chiune

Sugihara, the Japanese consul to Lithuania, who saved more than 6,000 Jews in the summer of 1940 by issuing visas to them—against the explicit orders of his government. At the reception following the play, Davida was honored by being asked to speak about her cousin, Aaron Kalman, who was one of the fortunate persons saved by Sugihara.

During the following days, we traveled to Pumpyan (Pumpenai), Posvol (Pasvalys), Vashkai, Tryskie (Tryskiai) and Luknik (Luoke). At each *shtetl* (in these cases, my ancestral villages), we asked three things: Where is the Jewish cemetery? Where is the Jewish synagogue? Who are the elderly people with whom we might speak? The cemeteries and sites of mass murder were invariably marked with plaques, placed recently by the Lithuanian government owing to the efforts of MP Zingeris. In reality, having but a few remaining tombstones, the cemeteries barely existed, and being located on large tracts of land, they were now used in some cases as short-cuts or grazing pasture for cows. The synagogues, too, had been recycled: in Ponevez (Panevezys) it was a tire company; in Pumpyan, a meeting hall; in Posvol, a brewery.

Dan Kirschner at gravesite of his great-grandfather in Luknik (Luoke), Lithuania.

Regina and I deciphered what tombstones we could find and recorded the information. Having recently examined in Vilnius some of Isaac Zibuts' cemetery and tombstone photographs, we realized the extreme difficulty of reading the inscriptions from photos. We, therefore, put considerable time and effort into reading the Hebrew. In many cases, weathering had nearly obliterated the text, but by using our fingers to trace the letters repeatedly, we made the names and dates eventually come through the mist of time. At each cemetery, Davida and I said *Kaddish* for the departed members of our families.

The first *shtetl*, Pumpyan, yielded no genealogical information, except for a few tombstones, although the local Lithuanians were friendly enough. Davida gently interviewed two of the older residents, and they remembered which had been the Jewish houses, and in some cases who had lived there before the war. In Posvol, the second *shtetl*, we had better luck. We spoke with 82-year old Tsipa Davidovitch, the sole Jew there, who remembered my maternal grandfather's sister,

Esther Eliashevitz and whom she had married (Chaim Rochman), their children's names, their business, and most important, that one of their descendants (Moisey Rochman) was living still in Kirgizija, a former Soviet Central Asian republic northeast of Afghanistan. We also found the Rochman home by the Valevens River and were welcomed warmly by its current owners. We had brought with us a photograph of the main street taken in the early 1930s by my second cousin, Moses Ellis, when he visited Posvol as a bar mitzvah present from his parents. A group of elderly women leaving church were able to point out how the current street pattern was related to the one from 60 years earlier.

Our good luck in establishing my ancestors' footprints in Lithuania extended to the third *shtetl* that we visited. Vashkai was the home of my maternal grandmother's parents, Eliezar and Frayde Siegal. We found the inn that they had owned (now a variety store in one room of the house) and saw the church, built in 1901, that my mother had summoned as perhaps her earliest and only memory from Vashkai. She had immigrated to the United States in 1906 as a toddler. In the Vashkai cemetery, we diligently chased the few inscriptions that we could find. Regina had a sixth sense for locating tombstones. She found two that were protected in a dense copse of lilacs, one for "Ita Leah, daughter of Eliezer, died 1901." My mother's Hebrew middle name is Leah, and so on my return to Boston, I telephoned and asked the origin of her middle name (I knew that her first name, Freda, came from her grandmother Frayde). She replied, "I think that was after my mother's sister, who died as a teenager about the time that my parents married, in Vashkai, which was in 1901." My mother was born two years later, in 1903—so, incredibly, among the few remaining tombstones in the Vashkai cemetery, we had discovered the gravestone belonging to my mother's aunt!

Despite our good fortune, the paucity of tombstones in the pre-Holocaust Jewish cemeteries was appalling and depressing. Where the Nazis had not completed their attempt to erase our presence in Lithuania, the Soviets had nearly succeeded. Thus, standing at the gates of the Tryskie cemetery, a large enclosed tract that was overgrown with grass, brush, shrubs and trees, we were not surprised to observe that there were only a few tombstones toward the back wall. As we approached to inspect them, the weather took a sudden turn for the worse, and cold winds picked up, bent the grasses, and more tombstones appeared. We hunkered down to decipher the inscriptions, as more and more markers seemed to thrust up from the grasses. It was as if our ancestors were collectively sighing, parting the vegetation so that we might witness and record their past presence. The weather worsened, droplets of rain teased and the winds now seemed to be telling us to move on. Time constraints compelled us to head to Luknik, where we hoped at least to establish if there was still a recognizable Jewish cemetery.

Luknik was the ancestral town of my paternal grandfather, Abba Kirschner, after whom I received my middle name. My father, Carl, was born there, and his first cousin, Sam Kacav, grew up there and, as a teenager, escaped just ahead of the Nazis. Sam has related to me and to his grandchildren many warmhearted stories about Luknik, so I was eager to see what, if anything, remained. As we headed to Luknik, little showers danced across the road.

Up ahead, a man with an ox-drawn cart appeared through the muddy windshield. Dina slammed on the brakes of her little Russian Fiat-look-alike, jumped from the car, and ran after the man to make our usual inquiries. He pointed straight ahead and to the left. We drove another hundred meters, and there perched on a little rise of land in a valley behind some farms were scores of tombstones, standing upright and nearly filling up a walled cemetery. We could not believe our eyes! Of the pre-Holocaust cemeteries that we had visited, this was the best preserved. We ran down the path to the cemetery gate, which had the usual plaque affixed to the stonework. I was excited, but felt overwhelmed knowing that this was where some of my ancestors must be buried; but how could we possibly find them before the gathering storm broke. There were just too many tombstones! I ran frantically from one to another, trying to speed-read weathered Hebrew inscriptions. It started to shower again, and Dina headed back up the hill to the car, and then the rains abated. I ran further into the cemetery, hoping for some shelter under the trees, passing but not reading many tombstones. Occasionally, I would notice a familiar given name, but nothing definite registered.

Where was Regina when we most needed her and her sixth sense? Between Tryskie and Luknik, she had hitched a ride back to Vilnius for another commitment and expected to catch up with us in Plunge in two days. And then, just as frustration and disappointment were rising in me, I heard from somewhere up the hill toward the far side of the cemetery: "Oh! Dan, come here! I think I've found it. 'Abba ben rav Shmuel!'" I climbed slowly to Davida, afraid that her rusty Hebrew skills had somehow failed, and I carefully read the inscription. Yes! Davida was absolutely right; the names were correct. It started to rain very hard at this point, and Dina brought an umbrella to us. Still not quite believing, I scrawled down the date of death (15 Tammuz, 1923), and we all ran back to the car, soaked. I quickly looked in my Kirschner family tree for the information I had about Abba and saw immediately that the dates matched! We had discovered my great-grandfather, lying peacefully and undisturbed here in the Luknik cemetery for more than 70 years!

How had this cemetery escaped both the Germans and the Soviets? And why was it in such good condition? A partial answer to the latter question became apparent when moments later Dina made inquiries of a passing elderly woman. Stasen Kwilkostatin remembered the Kirschner and Kacav names, told us where the Kirschner house had been (it had been destroyed by fire) and led Dina and me through a downpour and along muddy roads and paths to the home of the mayor or "principal" of Luknik. Genovaiti Linkuviene, an agronomist by profession, welcomed us into her home, and told us that Rafael Gemys of the Jewish community of Telshe, which is responsible for this district, had insisted that the cemeteries be cleaned up. She apparently took her directive seriously. I thanked her and told her how important it was to us, the descendants of Lithuanian Jews, that the cemeteries continue to be maintained.

The next day, the weather having cleared, we returned to Luknik, said *Kaddish*, took some additional photographs, but had time to record only a fraction of the inscriptions. Davida did a rubbing of Abba's gravestone. Later, in studying my records, I discovered that we had also found the grave of Abba's wife (Sarah, daughter of Zev, died 7 Tevet 1924). Who knows what other family footprints are to be found in the Luknik cemetery? There must be many other discoveries, just waiting. Clearly, it would be a very worthwhile project for some Lithuanian Jewish students, perhaps as part of a youth group project, to visit Luknik and the other pre-Holocaust cemeteries. They could begin the laborious task of deciphering, recording and cataloguing the slowly dissolving tombstones of our ancestors.

Conclusion

For me, the discovery at Luknik was the genealogical highpoint of our trip. In fact, though, we made many discoveries and had many priceless experiences. Other places that we visited included Seda (one of Davida's ancestral shtetls), where we explored the inside of the former synagogue, soon to be torn down, and discovered the imprint of a *mezuzah* on the doorpost; Plungyan (Plunge), where sculptor Jacob Bunka welcomed us into his home and then accompanied us to nearby woods where many of his monumental wood carvings memorialize the

Davida Sky (left) and Daniel Kirschner (right) with Lithuanian sculptor, Jacob Bunka, and his wife.

Holocaust; Salant, my paternal grandmother's *shtetl*, where my father lived until coming to the United States at the age of eight; Kovno, where we visited the Jewish ghetto and the infamous Ninth Fort; Serednik (Seredzius, one of Davida's shtetls), where Davida interviewed at length a robust, elderly Lithuanian man (Antanas Balsys) who spoke Yiddish, remembered names, occupations and houses of the Jews, and recalled helping his father collect *hametz* (leavened bread) from them before Passover. In Belarus, we visited Minsk, where we spent *kabbalat Shabbat* (Sabbath eve) with a youth group at the small, remaining synagogue; and Vasilishki (one of Davida's *shtetls*), where she interviewed several elderly women (Stanislas Slovena, and Stefania and her daughter Regina), and discovered one woman (Yurdvega Yurovsikaya) who remembered Yiddish and actually sang *Oifn Pripitchik* for us! It was an unforgettable trip in more ways than can be described here. I would not hesitate to go back in search of more footprints—all it takes is time and litas (Lithuanian money).

Daniel A. Kirschner, today, is a biology professor at Boston College and founding member of the Boston Klezmer Ensemble. Davida Sky, an occupational therapist for children near Portland, Maine, has taken off a year from work to devote her time to writing her family histories. Davida and Dan met through the Jewish Genealogical Family Finder and believe themselves to be distant cousins-by-marriage.

Making Lemonade Out of Lemons
by Howard Margol

Winter 1998

On a fine summer day in June 1998, I traveled from Vilnius, Lithuania, to Panevezys, the fifth largest city in Lithuania. The previous year I had been told that Jewish vital records, dating back to 1880 for Panevezys and the surrounding area, were stored in the Panevezio Skyrius Civilines Metrikacijos Archyvas (Civil Register Archive) at Respublikos 25. This was extremely important information not previously known. The purpose of my trip was to go to the archive and create an index of all the Jewish records.

Imagine my disappointment when, after arriving at the archive, I was told that all of the Jewish records had been transferred to Vilnius two months before. As I was not returning to Vilnius, this was a severe blow. In an effort to make me feel better, the archivist gave me an extract of ten vital records, none of them ancestors of mine. My next thought was, "How do I change this lemon of a wasted trip into lemonade?" I suddenly remembered my paternal grandmother's death record. She died in Pusalotas and was buried there, but her death was recorded in Pasvalys. I mentioned this to the archivist and suggested that perhaps the archive in Pasvalys held old Jewish records. She picked up her telephone, called the Pasvalys archive and repeated my question to the archivist in charge. My excitement increased when she received a positive response. "Yes, the Pasvalys archive did have some old Jewish records."

Rachel Kostanian, my guide and interpreter, quickly asked our driver to take us to Pasvalys, about 25 miles north of Panevezys. After arriving at the Pasvalys archive, we met with the archivist and explained the reason for our visit. Again, we encountered a disappointing response. She had misunderstood the archivist in Panevezys and was not aware that we were interested only in Jewish records. She had a large quantity of old Catholic records, but no Jewish ones. In 1992, in accordance with a government decree, they had sent all Jewish records to Vilnius. At this point, my lemonade was changing back into a copious quantity of lemons.

Pasvalys held no personal interest for me, but, as long as I was already there, I decided to make the most of it. I asked the archivist if there were a library or museum in Pasvalys. She ushered me to the window and pointed out a white building about a block down the street. She explained that it was a combination library and museum and offered to call and tell them that we were coming.

Two women greeted us warmly when we arrived. On a table in front of us, they had spread out 40 or 50 photographs. These were pictures taken of Jews who had lived in Pasvalys, mainly during the 1920s and 1930s, including some taken a little earlier. On the back of most of the pictures were written the names of the indi-

Mass grave of Jews in woods outside the village of Pusalotas.

viduals in the picture. Two photographs were particularly interesting. One showed a group of students in a Jewish gymnasium (high school). The other, taken in 1995, showed an elderly woman standing in front of a monument being dedicated to the memory of the Jews of Pasvalys who were murdered in the Holocaust. One of the girls in the high school picture and the elderly woman in front of the monument were one and the same. She had somehow survived the war, returned to Pasvalys, and lived there until she died in 1997. These photographs could be a veritable gold mine for anyone who had family living in Pasvalys during the early part of this century.

As we finished looking at the pictures, a man about 45 years of age walked in and joined us. Unknown to us, he had been called and asked to come to the museum and to meet with us. He was introduced as a Lithuanian historian, not Jewish. He told us that he was writing a history of the Jews of that area, mainly Pasvalys, Pumpenai and Pusalotas. When he said Pusalotas I almost fell off my chair. "Why Pusalotas?" I asked. He answered that he was born and raised in Pusalotas after the war, so he could not have known my aunt, uncle and their three small children who were living in Pusalotas in 1941 and were murdered in the Shoah.

I replied that I also was writing a book about the history of the Jews of Pusalotas, the ancestral home of my Margolis family, and we could collaborate and exchange information. He opened his briefcase and gave me a number of handwritten documents. Included was a partial list of the Jews who were living, in 1941, in each of the three places mentioned above before the Germans arrived. He had gleaned these names from the elders in each village, depending on their memories. For Pusalotas, 32 families were listed of a total of 60. My ancestors were among them. There they were, Moishe Zuk and children. But where was Moishe's wife, Chana, my father's youngest sister? Could she have died before 1941? If so, perhaps there is a record of her death. I hope additional research will give me the answer.

The Lithuanian historian gave me some additional information, including names of Jewish families who, in 1941, were living in small settlements in the area consisting of four or five families. I had with me a number of Pusalotas records I had just acquired at the State Historical Archive in Vilnius. The librarian made copies for me, and I presented them to the historian to show my appreciation for the information he had given to me. I also plan to send him additional information I have in my file and he, in turn, promised to send me updates of his written history of the Jews who formerly lived in that area. I have every expectation that our meeting will result in a mutually beneficial relationship.

Howard Margol, a retired business executive in Atlanta, Georgia, began tracing his family history in 1990. He served a two-year term as president of the Jewish Genealogical Society of Georgia. He was elected to the board of the International Association of Jewish Genealogical Societies in 1996, and served for a total of nine years during which time he also served a two-year term as president of IAJGS. He is currently president of the LitvakSIG. Since 1993, Margol has taken groups of Jews, primarily genealogists, on trips to Lithuania to visit their ancestral shtetls.

Crypto-Jews

I Am a Marrano
by Anne Cardoza

Winter 1989

As I sit in a synagogue service and pray, often I wonder what it means to be a Marrano. I know my grandmother told me she was a Marrano. Pauline, my grandmother, would sew Catholic medals and crucifixes in the hems of skirts and pillows. She would light votive candles on Shabbat and go to Mass but never take communion. She would touch her forehead or face or shoulders in various places so that it would look as if she was making the sign of the cross. What she really was doing was whispering *Adonai* (Lord) and making rapid movements that had some secret meaning.

In church, she would pray in Spanish in her native accent from Gerona, Spain. She also spoke Portuguese and knew a few Hebrew words. Grandma sold cloth to the nuns from which they made their habits.

My mother was raised never to speak to anyone about being Jewish. From her earliest years, she was told that "she had the map of Jerusalem printed on her face." Jewish practices had to be performed in total secrecy. There was a connection between the Marranos of Gerona, Spain, and the Marranos of Belmonte, Portugal.

I had been handed down the same practices. On Friday night, the Sabbath candles were little red or blue glass Catholic votive candles—the perfumed kind which I bought in a candle shop. The candles would always be in the bedroom, so as not to embarrass the non-Jewish members of my family. Today, I go to the synagogue alone, and my non-Jewish husband picks me up outside, but I go.

For generations, being a Marrano meant my family absolutely forbade any member to tell an outsider that he or she was Jewish. Even though the Inquisition had been over since the 1820s, the feeling was that it was never really over in most people's beliefs, and under no circumstances was any Jewish practice or mannerism to be shown to strangers.

Everything Jewish was done in the home. The holidays were celebrated by lighting votive candles. Sabbath meals consisted of a porridge of cooked whole rye, wheat, brown rice, millet, lentils, chickpeas, with celery, carrots and parsley.

Mother would take me to Mass at the church. We would sit while the others took communion. Many times I was told to cross myself and kneel in church while saying Jewish prayers in Spanish. Occasionally, a Hebrew word or two was mixed in. The word *baruch* (blessed) and *Adonai* were the only Hebrew words I remember.

In my early teens, my mother told me I was Jewish and to keep quiet about it.

Later, I began to search my roots. Why did my mother tell me I was a Marrano, a secret Jew? I was told that ancestors centuries ago had been tried in the Spanish Inquisition and reconciled to the Catholic Church or sent to the stake; that those who watched the *auto de fes*[1] and who *abjure de vehementi*[2] went home and practiced Judaism in secret. For generations, the only way they preserved their religion was by an agreed-upon family code:

> *Never take communion. Always say Adonai when you cross yourself and touch your closed eyelids. Light the Sabbath lamps in a room where no one can see light escaping. The unsuspected votive candles lit on Friday night were lit in the bedroom, sometimes even in the bathroom, but never on the dining room table, lest someone say you were a Jew.*

> *Wear big crosses, sometimes five inches in diameter. Share the family secret with adult children over age 13, so they could keep a secret. On Passover, outdoor picnics, no indoor Seders or Haggadahs. Eat lentils, honey cakes and greens, no meat, sometimes fish, vegetables and grains.*

When Grandma was young, she left Gerona for Buenos Aires. Later, the family came to the U.S. She had two marriages. On both my mother's and my father's side, cousin marriages had taken place for generations back, for another rule of the code was to stay genetically Jewish by marrying only relatives such as cousins. My father's brother was my maternal grandmother's second husband. My uncle's youngest brother married my mother.

Outside, no one knew of the Jewishness, the secret religion. Inside the home, we were taught how to conceal our Jewishness and why this had to be done. "If anyone finds out you're a Jew, they will bash your face in." I was taught this from early childhood.

People who say there are no more Marranos don't know the real story. There are 500 to 600 Marrano families in Portugal and many in Spain, also. In the New World, some live in South America and some in Mexico. I'm talking about those people who remained genetically Jewish through cousin marriages for the past 300 years; who knew for sure that their families were Jewish; who kept preserved relics like a 300-year-old *kiddish* cup (cup used to bless wine), tear vials, candlesticks, etc.

These people are in the U.S. today and are coming out of their secrecy. The one thing that preserved the Marrano way of life was the profound secrecy of their religion. Today, in Albuquerque, New Mexico, people such as Loggie Carrasco are doing linguistic research in archaic Hebrew language found among the local Hispanic population. For 300 years, Loggie Carrasco's family clung to Marrano practices and secret Jewish rites while outwardly simulating Catholicism in order to keep the family's rights to Mexican land grants. If the Mexican government had discovered that Loggie's family was Jewish, they would have lost their huge prop-

---

[1] Literally, "act of faith." It was the ritual of public penance of condemned heretics and apostates that took place during the Inquisition. The term is usually associated with the act of torturing the condemned or burning at the stake.

[2] Literally, "vehemently denied under false oath." The term used for Jews who denied under oath that they still practiced Judaism but did so in secret.

erty holdings. In a recent court trial, Loggie won her rights to her property and the story was brought to light.

Today, Loggie Carrasco, a Marrano, searches the U.S. Southwest looking for clues to the language and customs of the ancient community which existed in this part of the country when it was part of New Spain—in colonial Mexican days during the 17th century. Now she attends the local synagogue.

Another Marrano, Victor Diaz of San Diego, is the owner of the radio station, Radio Latina in Chula Vista, California. He owns many radio stations throughout Mexico and San Diego. For 300 years his family lived in Guadalahara, Mexico, as Marranos. He remained genetically Jewish by constant cousin marriages for generations. He and his wife are both Marranos. He describes himself as a Catholic Jew, who had been a Catholic man all his life and suddenly became Jewish after contact with a rabbi who specializes in converting Marranos back to Judaism.

Marranos should not be confused with Indian Jews or the descendants of Mestizos who converted to Judaism of late. They are not the descendants of Indian slaves of Jews who adopted their religion, either. Although the recently converted Mestizo Jews of Mexico are devout Jews, the term Marranos applies here to specific families which have remained consciously, genetically Jewish through cousin marriages and selected marriages with other secret Jews from European ancestry in the Iberian peninsula (Spain and Portugal). Many of these people have been living in Mexico for more than 300 years and can be seen as totally different from the general Mestizo Latin American population at large.

For example, without exception, all the Marranos I have met so far have similar coloring: fair skin; green, hazel, golden brown, blue or gray eyes; brown hair; Semitic profiles and Armenid-shaped skulls. They differ slightly from the Sephardic Jews of the eastern Mediterranean since they are lighter in coloring with short, very narrow heads. They are extremely in-bred from generations of marrying close neighbors or cousins, but do not have any genetic diseases peculiar to their people, perhaps because there are so few of them.

Marranos came out of the closet during the 1930s Marrano renaissance in Belmonte, Portugal. At that time, the Jewish Board of Guardians set up the Basil H. Henriquies Portuguese Marranos Committee of London on Commercial Road. In Majorca, for example, after 300 years, the Inquisition still taints the Chuetas. (Chueta comes from the Catalonian word for Jew, *xueta*). All the family names were engraved in a church saying that they were secret Jews. Today, their descendants are still shunned by the local populace.

One Marrano from Majorca, Spain, Nico Aguilo, went to a yeshiva in Israel, formally renewed his conversion to Judaism, returned to Majorca, and proudly wears his skullcap, trying to help other Jews come back.

In the Iberian peninsula, it has become fashionable not to remain secret Jews. In Cordoba, Spain, the Beit Sephardi was established by two local business people who felt that it was time to announce their secret Jewish faith. It is a local center for study and culture of the Jewish history of Cordoba. Since one out of ten Spaniards reputedly were Jewish prior to the Inquisition, the social stigma that formerly was attached to being a Marrano is diminishing.

The important Marrano holidays are Passover and Quippur (Yom Kippur), also called *El Gran Dia De Pardon*, when all Marranos fast. Among Portuguese Marranos, Quippur is called *Dia Grande* or *Dia Puro* (pure day). The *pascua*, or Passover, was called the day of the lamb. Marranos do not sit down to a *seder*; they sit down to a Haggadah, accent on the last syllable. However, Portuguese Marranos do not have a Haggadah book. They use the Bible and read from Exodus.

Matzoh was made by mixing water and rye flour or chickpea flour, kneading it, and throwing it into the fire or oven. Matzoh was round, tasteless, undercooked dough. No tasty crackers for Marranos on this day of bitter bread. Portuguese Marranos in Belmonte call their matzoh, *pao santo* (holy bread). They pray in Portuguese and use the word *Adonai*, instead of *Cristos*. Out of 4,000 residents, 600 are Marranos who will tell you that they are Jewish, but they still go to Mass and say their Jewish prayers at home. (See "When Marrano Descendants Met Their Israeli Landsleit," *Jewish Digest*, 6/67, pp. 61–67).

Holidays were always scheduled a week before or after the real dates. This is still done today in the largest cities: Braganca, Rebordello, Oporto and Belmonte, where most Portuguese Marranos live. Gerona is the center of Spain, although many, including some of my relatives, moved to Malaga.

In South America today and in Mexico, there are still Marranos with their quaint customs. They are slowly coming forward, but only when searched out by rabbis wishing to take them into the fold. One of the best sources for information about Marranos is Dan Ross, a St. Martin's Press author, who wrote *Acts of Faith*, examining Marranos on the fringes of Jewish identity who are starting to come back. Amilcar Paulo of Oporto, Portugal, is the world's foremost authority on the Portuguese Marranos living in Belmonte today.

Marranos are just beginning to make themselves known as crypto-Judios in Gerona. In Rebordello, Portugal, the 1930s Marrano renaissance caused local Marrano Moses Abraham Gaspar's father to carve a giant star of David on his doorpost. In Braganca, the local man of wisdom today is Joao Baptista dos Santos. But Belmonte, Portugal, today is the only place where old and new Christians remain a central fact of life. In 1979, the Oporto Synagogue was defaced with swastikas and slogans of "death to the Jews," and a Portuguese Marrano's clothing factory was defaced and burned down.

Anti-Jewishness against Marranos who declare themselves is rampant in northeastern Portugal today. In Spain, in Gerona, and in the whole of Catalonia, Marranos and other Jews are treated very fairly, but freedom to worship openly as a Jew in Spain has only been legal since 1968.

Anne Cardoza is a freelance writer and literary agent who lives in California.

Additional Stories of Crypto-Jews

Winter 1989

Hidden Mezzuzah

My two elderly aunts are Catholic and practice all precepts of their religion; however, they have a peculiar habit. Whenever they leave or return to their home, they use their right hand to tap the doorway's stone arch two or three times. They never explained the gesture to me.

Years later, I learned that the Portuguese word *mesura* (making many compliments with one's hands) may have been derived from the Hebrew word *mezuzah* (doorpost). I had a stonemason remove the right side stone of my aunts' door which was at eye level. Behind the stone, I found a parchment scroll written in Hebrew. It had been there for some centuries.

Cutting of a Male Child's Hair

I am a Cuban Catholic by birth. Two years ago I married my wife, who is Jewish, and I converted to Judaism. There have always been stories in my family that we were descended from Jews. For example, my great-grandmother, whose family name was Mora (teacher in Hebrew), reportedly came from the Canary Islands and was Jewish.

We have a family tradition that we allow the hair of our male children to go uncut until they are three years old. Then, we throw a big party and with great fanfare cut his hair. No one in my family knows the origin of the custom, and I have been unable to trace it to any Cuban or Catholic ritual. I have since found out it is a Jewish ritual.

"Hay Adonai"

I was born a Cuban Catholic. I never had any Jewish influence or heard much about Jews except from the Bible. As I grew older, driven by some subconscious force, I started reading about things Jewish: the formation of the State of Israel, books about Jews, even items such as the formation of a Havana branch of B'nai Birth.

Years passed. I had to leave Cuba and decided to settle in the United States. One day, reading about the Marranos of Spain, I discovered certain religious practices which were similar to practices at my grandparents' house. We would light candles on Friday evenings, always in a concealed place; we washed and salted meat, and I would hear my father and grandfather say a phrase that was meaningless gibberish to me: "Hay Adonai." I remembered that I was told as a child that we were not like other people; that I should not mingle outside of our circle of family. I have inferred from all my findings that my family is of Marrano stock. [This person's ancestry was also from the Canary Islands—Ed.]

Key Leads to Family History

We are not Jewish, but my husband's grandmother once showed me a *Pentateuch* (Five Books of Moses—Torah) handed down to her from her Jewish ancestors. They were in-laws of the de Mendes. A Spanish friend of mine, who is Christian, told us of an exiled Sephardic Jew in Poland who traveled to Madrid, knocked on the gate of a house there and showed the owner of the house (who knew my friend's father) an ancient key. The owner let the Jew try the key in the gate lock and it worked! Then he asked if he could be allowed to excavate a little hole in the patio; his ancestors had buried something there. He was permitted to do so and dug up a leather pouch with some parchments in it! His family had kept that key since about 1492, when they fled their home, now occupied by the Spanish gentleman, and had kept the memory of the parchments!

Remembering Destruction of the Temple

My wife, Sara, is a practicing Marrano Jew, and we were married in Cordoba, Spain. Your mention of the nuns who light candles under the table reminds me of similar ways of evoking an obscure past in Spain. The passing from mother to daughter of a key to some unknown lock or door and keeping a part of the cellar unfinished as a remembrance of the destruction of the Temple are just two examples. There is much more.

We have a collection of excellent recent studies in Spanish, some with reprints of Inquisition records. One author attempted to compose a formula with which the ancient remains of a town synagogue in Spain may with some certainty be found.

A Painful Portuguese Odyssey
by Rufina Bernardetti Silva Mausenbaum

Winter 1997

For me, with my Portuguese background, *Pesach* (Passover) is an especially poignant time. Five hundred years ago, on the first day of *Pesach* 1497, the Jewish children of Portugal were forcibly baptized, *en masse*, and 700 of them were shipped to the island of Sao Tome (Saint Thomas) on the west coast of Africa. Most of them died. When the Inquisition was instituted in Portugal on September 20, 1540, Jews were not given a choice, as they had been given earlier in Spain to be expelled or to convert. Portuguese Jews were compelled to be baptized; very few Jews managed to escape.

Historians often write about this period in Portuguese history as flourishing and romantic. For me, it is painful and tragic. My own origins, history and culture have been effectively obliterated, and it is, for me, a continuing and haunting loss. My grandmother, whose name I bear, was thought to be odd in the village where she found secrecy and anonymity—odd, because once a year (on Yom Kippur) she used to disappear for a whole day and night. Her granddaughter, my cousin, who died recently, was a very devout Catholic, but had requested a plain, not decorated box, for her burial. There was to be no adornment, no jewelry or rosary. Her children are devout Catholics who, on Friday nights, light candles and fill a decanter with wine.

Author's grandmother, Rufina, practiced as a crypto-Jew on the Portuguese island of Madeira.

A feeling of *deja vu* overcomes me whenever I visit Portugal; remnants remain of the period when Jews dominated life in that country. Saturday is called *Sabado* (Sabbath), and Sunday (*Domingo*) is the first day of the week. Policemen wear a badge featuring the six-pointed star—a *Magen David*. Stores in Sintra, a town outside Lisbon, sell pastries packed in blue and white paper decorated with a *Magen David*. In Madeira, arts and crafts shops also feature this emblem.

This beautiful island of Madeira also knew fear. It became a hiding place for many Jews, but unlike places in Portugal, notably Belmonte, the Madeira Jews did not manage to sustain their religious identity beyond the beginnings of this century and all embraced Catholicism.

Jewish History in Portugal

Although the origin of a Jewish presence is obscure, but certainly most ancient, the Jews as a people had been in Portugal and Spain long before those who expelled and persecuted them.

When looking at a map of Portugal, it is easy to see that the main centers of the Inquisition were in the heart of the country—in Lisbon, Evora and Coimbra. Yet the miracle of Portuguese Judaism continues, especially in the town of Belmonte in northeastern Portugal. Previously known as crypto-Jews, they have recently and proudly rejoined mainstream Orthodox Judaism after 500 years of secrecy and fear. Living and hiding in this charming town, high in the Sierra Estrela mountain range, they have managed with faith and perseverance to maintain their religion all this time. As often stated, they were Jews in all but name and Christians in nothing but form. A prayer said by crypto-Jews upon entering a church featured the secret words, "I come here to worship neither wood nor stone. I come only to worship you, Highest Lord, who it is that governs us" (from the 1990 book *Crypto-Jews of Portugal*, 2d ed. by David Augusto).

Crypto-Jews have been very prominent in Portugal. Scarcely an aristocratic family was free of Jewish (tainted) blood. Important positions were occupied by *conversos* (secret Jews): physicians, lawyers, writers, humanitarians, cartographers, mathematicians, shippers, navigators and explorers in the Americas and Africa, financiers and army personnel. Much of the financing of Europe and the New World was controlled by Portuguese *conversos*. Spaniards were known to complain that you could not do business unless you had a "Portuguese" partner; the word "Portuguese" was synonymous with Jewish.

On March 17, 1989, Mario Soares, president of Portugal, publicly asked for forgiveness from the worldwide Jewish community for Portugal's past misdeeds and linked the degradation and downfall of Portugal to the "expulsion" (sic) of the Jews. In reality, there had been no expulsion—only a forcible conversion of Jews to *conversos*. Among the names by which these Jewish unfortunates from Spain and Portugal were known were:

- *Nuevos Christianos.* New Christians
- *Anusim.* Hebrew for "compelled, forced ones"
- *Muraim.* Arabic for "hypocrites"
- *Meshumadim.* Hebrew for "apostates from Judaism"
- *Avaryonim.* Hebrew for "those who have gone over to the other side"
- Crypto-Jews. Secret Jews
- *Marranos* "swine"—a Spanish name never used in Portugal

Many books in English, Spanish and Portuguese have been written about these *conversos* and the cultures in which they lived. After the expulsion from Spain in 1492, Jews who came to Portugal settled primarily in the northern half of the country. There they were known for avoiding pig meat and for using bird flesh in a sausage called the *alheira*.

Portuguese babies often sport a dark grey or blue birthmark on the lower or upper back and sometimes even on the legs. These stains remain some months, and often some years, before fading. Such markings are common in Oriental and Sephardic Jews to this day and, if seen on a Portuguese baby, hint at *converso* origins. The marks are called Mongolian spots, but are better labeled Semitic or sacral spots.

Some names are of suspiciously Jewish origin. In Spanish, the name De Sanctis hints that several centuries ago a Jew was sanctified by baptism. The equivalent in Portuguese is Dos Santos. Other names featuring agricultural themes also were commonly of Jewish origins, for example, Da Silva (forest); Carvalho (oak); Perreira (pear tree); and also names like Mendes, Pinto, Lopes, Hendriques and Rodriques.

Listening to the Portuguese *fado* (folk music), the haunting soulfulness reminds me of *shul* (synagogue), of Pesach, Yom Kippur, Kol Nidre[1] and my *saudade* (nostalgic longing) for the past continues.

Rufina Bernardetti Silva Mausenbaum lives in Johannesburg, South Africa, where her father emigrated in 1936 when Nazism arose in Europe. She attended a predominantly Jewish day school and converted to orthodox Judaism 30 years ago without ever revealing her background as a crypto-Jew.

---

[1] The opening prayer on the eve of Yom Kippur.

The Jews of the Canary Islands
by Gary Mokotoff
Winter 1998

This is the story of how I became an expert on the Jews of the Canary Islands. When I started a computer software business 30 years ago [1968], one of my first employees was a brilliant anti-Castro Cuban refugee named Maria Alemán. She remained with my company for more than 25 years.

In the early years of my genealogical research, I read in the *Encyclopedia Judaica* the entry for the Aleksandrów, Poland, Hasidim and noticed an article on the same page about a man named Mateo Alemán. He was a Spanish-Jewish novelist at the time of the expulsion of the Jews from Spain in 1492 who had fled to Mexico. The next day I walked into the office and jokingly told Maria, "I now know why I think so highly of you. You are Jewish!" Maria laughed as I showed her the article.

Alemán means "German" in Spanish. Why would a Spaniard at the time of the Inquisition have the name "German?" I reasoned that the person might have been a German Jew who had come to Spain and, therefore, was known as "the German."

The matter remained dormant for a number of months until I read in an issue of *Search* a letter to the editor from a Catholic Cuban doctor living in Florida, Dr. Manuel Carta, who stated that he had determined that he was of Spanish-Jewish ancestry.[1] His family had a tradition of going into the basement every Friday night to light candles secretly and another of washing and salting meat. His father and grandfather had an exclamation, *Haj-Adonai* ("Oh God," in Hebrew). He had been told that he was Irish, but an inquiry to an aunt produced the admission they were of Jewish ancestry. In his letter, Dr. Carta noted:

> I later discovered that there was a small group of Spanish Jews that had settled in Dublin in the early 17th century. This information fit perfectly and helped me put everything together. I can trace my name to the Canary Islands in 1604 when the first Carta appears there. I should mention that a significant number of converted Jews (or New Christians as they were called) settled in the Canary Islands as far back as the latter part of the 15th and the early part of the 16th centuries.

I showed the letter to Maria who read it and exclaimed, "My family's ancestry was from the Canary Islands!" Now I really became curious about whether I could trace Maria's ancestry back to the Jews of Inquisition Spain.

History of the Jews of the Canary Islands

Only one book has been written about the Jews of the Canary Islands. It was written by the noted Anglo-Jewish historian Lucien Wolf and published in 1926 by the Jewish Historical Society of England.[2] I live in a small town in New Jersey, but I was able to acquire the book on interlibrary loan. The clerk at my library had never heard of the process, but the head librarian gleefully offered to order the book for me. It was unlikely she had received interlibrary loan requests more than once every few years. She called a few days later and told me that she had located a copy at the Fordham University Library in New York and that the copy would be available to me in about a week.

When the book arrived at my town library, I was amazed to discover that I was only the third person to have borrowed it from the Fordham University Library—and the last patron had borrowed it more than 40 years earlier! The book was not about the Jews of the Canary Islands, but, as the subtitle stated, was "a calendar of Jewish cases extracted from the records of the Canariote Inquisition." The book had an index of names, and it included the surname Alemán. A typical entry stated:

> 11 November 1505. Deponent gives further evidence as to the number of converts seen entering the house of Luis Alvarez where it is commonly supposed Jewish ceremonies are held. Deponent's house overlooks the said house and he has seen many converts entering there at night, among others Martin Alemán and his brother Francisco and Diego de Carmona.

I asked Maria if her family had any traditions, such as unusual songs, the lighting of candles, or the shunning of certain foods. She knew of none, but when she told her father of my discovery, he replied that it was true; the family had a tradition that they were descended from Jews.

Canary Islanders of Louisiana

One of the best sources of information when starting on a genealogy project is the Locality Catalog of the LDS (Mormon) Family History Library. Since the library has millions of microfilms that cover virtually every country, it can generate ideas as to where to search for additional information. Needless to say, its collection of Canary Island records is limited. It consists of some vital records and a handwritten manuscript about a group of Canary Islanders who went to Louisiana in 1778–83. The manuscript has been published since I started my research.[3]

I visit Salt Lake City at least twice a year, so on my next trip I examined the book. It consisted primarily of a list of passengers on the ships; one passenger was a Juan Alemán. Upon returning to my office I jokingly informed Maria, who has never become a U.S. citizen, that I could get her deported back to Cuba. I had evidence that one of her ancestors fought for the Spanish in Louisiana against the United States.

Did the Alemán name survive the early days in Louisiana? It does not appear so. The 1810 and 1820 censuses do not show the surname, although Alemand does appear. Of course, there is the possibility that the Spanish Louisianans avoided being counted in the census.

Research into the culture of the Spanish Louisianan people showed no evidence of Jews or Jewish traditions. The directory of the Association of Professional Genealogists indicates that a professional certified genealogist, Shirley Chaisson Bourquard, specializes in the Canary Islanders of Louisiana. She has written a book that documents the Canary Islanders.[4] She gave me the address of the president of the Los Isleños Heritage and Cultural Society located in Louisiana consisting of the descendants of the Canary Islanders. In 1996, its president, Joan Nuñez Phillips, wrote to me that she had no knowledge of Jewish heritage in her family. It should be noted, however, that Nuñez frequently is a Marrano surname; it appears in the Wolf book about the Jews of the Canary Islands. In her letter, Ms. Bourquard wrote:

> *I know of no Jewish customs in the Canarian families, except for one. Historian Bill Hyland tells me the Campo family stated to him they kept the tradition of lighting candles on Friday nights.*

Bourquard also noted that she was descended from the Solís and Ronquillas families, neither of which she could demonstrate were Jewish (see comment about the Solís surname below).

In his book *The Early Jews of New Orleans*, Bertram Wallace Korn, notes:

> *For decades, the statement has been repeated that two Jews named Mendez and Solis were pioneers in the development of the sugar cane industry in Louisiana during the 1790s...there is no evidence that members of the Joseph Solis family considered themselves Jews or they were Marranos. The lineage of this family is known in some detail; they had come to New Orleans by 1771, after successive residence in Ireland...Boston...and Santiago de Cuba.[5]*

The book goes on to mention that the other party, Antonio Méndez, was born in Havana where his family had lived for generations. Is it a coincidence that the first Jews of Ireland were Canary Islanders? That the Carta and Solís families have roots in Ireland? That the Carta, Solís and Méndez families have roots in Cuba?

At the National Genealogical Society conference in Nashville, Tennessee, in 1996, a lecture entitled "Las Islas Canarias" was presented by Paul Newfield III of Metairie, Louisiana. During the lecture, he disclosed that he was interested in this group because he descends from one of the first Spanish settlers: Juan Alemán. Paul told me he was not aware of any Jewish ancestry through his Alemán line. He provided the attendees with an extensive bibliography, which included articles published in magazines about the lore and customs of these people. Investigation of some of these articles demonstrated no Jewish aspect of these customs.[6]

Origins of Irish Jewry

Jews came to Irish shores as early as 613 C.E., but, according to Asher Benson, a correspondent for the *London Jewish Chronicle*, the first synagogue in Ireland was established as follows:

> *Tradition has it that in about 1660, a handful of Canary Island Marrano sea-merchants, and perhaps one or two Ashkenazi Jews founded the little congregation in Crane Lan, Dublin, five years after the Cromwellian regime permitted Jewish re-entry to Britain.*[7]

Miscellany

A genealogist from South America once told me that *canarios*, a derogatory term for Jews, is used in South America.

History books state that the first permanent Jewish presence in the U.S. began with the arrival of 23 Jews from Recife, Brazil, in New Amsterdam (later New York) in 1654. It is likely, however, that there was a permanent Jewish presence as early as 1566. In that year, a group of Spaniards, under the leadership of Captain Juan Pardo, established a colony named Santa Elena on the shores of South Carolina. Some of the residents had the surnames Braganza, Castillo, Chávez, Gallegos, Gómez, López, Martín, Molina, Moreno, Navarro, Perés, Rivera and Zamora—all Marrano surnames. Oh, yes, Pardo is also a Spanish-Jewish name; AVOTAYNU's first contributing editor for Argentina was Oscar Pardo. One theory holds that after the site was abandoned, many of the residents co-mingled with the indigenous native population, and their descendants today are known as the Melungeons of Tennessee and Virginia. It is an irony of the Anglo-oriented version of U.S. history that the lost colony of Roanoke is mentioned in texts, but the lost colony of Santa Elena rarely is noted.

Notes

1. "Marrano Roots," *Search* 3:2 (Summer 1983).

2. Lucien Wolf, *Jews of the Canary Islands* (London: Jewish Historical Society of England, 1926).

3. Gilbert C. Din, *The Canary Islanders of Louisiana* (Baton Rouge: Louisiana State University Press).

4. Shirley Chaisson Bourquard, *Early Settlers of the Delta: Families of St. Bernard, Palquemines, and Orleans Parishes, Louisiana.* (Self published, 1987).

5. Bertram Wallace Korn, *The Early Jews of New Orleans* (Waltham, Mass. American Jewish Historical Society, 1969).

6. Raymond R. MacCurdy, "Spanish Folklore from St. Bernard Parish, Louisiana," *Southern Folklore Quarterly* 13 (1949). Continued in Vol. 16 (1952).

7. Asher Benson, "Jewish Genealogy in Ireland," *Proceedings of the 1st Irish Genealogical Congress* (Dublin: 1st Irish Genealogical Congress Committee, 1991).

8. N. Brent Kennedy, *The Melungeons: An Untold Story of Ethnic Cleansing in America* (Macon, Ga.: Mercer University Press, 1996).

Gary Mokotoff is the publisher of AVOTAYNU.

Luck

Is It Really Luck?
by Sallyann Amdur Sack

Winter1988

S everal authors in this issue speak of luck or fate. Sometimes we say chance. As a psychoanalyst, I know that we do not do things by chance; behavior is motivated and has meaning, although we may not always be conscious of that meaning. Upon receiving the Nobel Prize, Elie Wiesel commented, "We Jews don't believe that there is any such thing as chance."

I can analyze my behavior and eventually figure out why I have done something, but when amazing external events keep happening, is that luck, fate or what? This past summer I finally made time to write a long-in-the-making book about my maternal grandmother's family, the Slomovitzes. Looking back over the data collected this past 10 years, I noticed something eerie. Four times in the research when it appeared I had reached a dead end, something happened to open up the next path until eventually I had the whole story and 2000 previously unknown relatives.

Using standard genealogical techniques, I easily learned my grandmother's maiden name and birthplace—Maramarossziget, Hungary. I knew the names of her two half brothers and two half sisters and both great grandparents, but nothing more. That didn't seem terribly exciting, so one day while considering possible ways to learn more, I reached for my local telephone directory. After all, I had used directories with great success in tracing my paternal grandmother's family, but they had a fairly uncommon name. It didn't seem to me that Slomovitz was as unusual.

Luckily, only one was listed—Bruce—in College Park, Maryland. I wrote, he called, and I learned that Bruce was a married Viet Nam veteran with one child. His parents had divorced when he was five, and his father died when he was ten, so he knew almost nothing about that side of his family. He did think they were Hungarian, and he knew that he had uncles in Wilkes Barre, Pennsylvania. That conversation was the start of the thin thread which eventually led to Elke Knapp, an old lady on a kibbutz in Israel who remembered seeing a family tree on the wall of her grandfather's house back in Akna-Szlatina, a village across the Tisza River from Maramarossziget. She had a remarkable memory and reconstructed the trunk and one main limb of her family tree. It was clear that we must be related, but I still wasn't sure how.

A *halutz* (pioneer) who had left Szlatina in the 1930s named Elke wrote of her grandfather, Chaim Leib, who had four sons and five daughters. She was a descendant of one son and was able to tell me all about that line, as well as something about a couple of the daughters. She also reported that all of the Slomovitzes from Szlatina were related.

A few months later I attended the first Summer Seminar on Jewish Genealogy in New York City where I met Arthur Kurzweil. When he heard that my grandmother had been born in Maramarossziget, he suggested I write to his teacher, Elie Wiesel, who also comes from Maramarossziget. At first I was diffident about writing to this busy and famous man. It took a full year and a second, harder push from Arthur, but eventually I did write. In short order the following note arrived: "In haste—Yes, I do know the Slomovitz family. Write to my cousin, Elieser Slomovic, Professor of Talmud, University of Judaism, Los Angeles, California, and he will tell you all about your family."

It was my turn for haste. I wrote to Elieser, got my second key telephone call and once more illuminated another whole trunk of the tree. Elieser, Elie Wiesel's first cousin, was descended from another of Chaim Leib's sons. He was a survivor of Auschwitz and the eldest son of the last head of the *kehilla* (Jewish community). Not only did he tell me all about his branch, but also about the last days of the Jewish community of Szlatina.

The following year the Gathering of Holocaust Survivors was held in Washington where I live. Elieser couldn't make it, but his brother Jack did. We had a wonderful meeting, exchanged stories and shared bits of information. He, too, had heard that all the Slomovitzes from Szlatina are related. A few minutes later, while describing the events of the Gathering, Jack mused, "I guess they must have seated us alphabetically. There was another Slomovitz sitting next to me at the Capitol Center. He's from Szlatina too, but we aren't related." I stared blankly at Jack for a long moment and then bolted upright in my chair. "Wait a minute," I protested. "Didn't you just tell me that all the Slomovitzes from Szlatina are related?" Now it was Jack's turn to stare. "I guess you're right," he acknowledged, "but we didn't know each other, and I don't know how he is related. His name is Steve, and he's from Cleveland." Cleveland! My hometown where my parents still live? A quick look in another telephone book! Off went another letter, and I got my third call. A few weeks later, I took an airplane to Cleveland where I met Steve and Alex Pearl, another pair of first cousins who survived Auschwitz and are descendants of the third of Chaim Leib's four sons. Soon there was more information and many more cousins.

Then came the fourth call. This one, unsolicited and not in any way initiated by me, was recorded by my answering machine. It was from Emily of Information on Demand in Los Angeles. She said, "Laura Klein tells me that you are an expert on the town of Solotvina. Would you call me back collect, please?" Would I? Did I? Emily worked for someone named Robert Maxwell, head of Pergamon Press and a publishing magnate in England. He was born in Solotvina (it's now part of the USSR, hence the current spelling), and his wife was writing his biography. She had asked Emily to find out everything she could about Solotvina. (I still don't know how Emily happened to call Laura, who at that time was president of the Jewish Genealogical Society of Los Angeles.) That night, Elizabeth Maxwell telephoned transatlantic from Oxford. She told me that her husband's name at birth had been Lejby Hoch. When I told her that my grandmother was Sure Hanna Slomovitz, she paused and said, "My mother-in-law was Chansa Slomovitz." "Then we are related," I responded, explaining again that all the Slomovitzes from Szlatina are related. Elizabeth, who also feels the value of family history, already had considerable information. We pooled our knowledge, and she, with the vast resources of her publishing magnate husband, amassed a wealth of detail.

Along the way, I finally learned conclusively that I am descended from the fourth and oldest of Chaim Leib's four sons. If I had not happened to look in my telephone book during one of the four years that Bruce Slomovitz was at the University of Maryland in College Park, and if he had not happened to be related, and if Arthur Kurzweil had not happened to urge me to write to Elie Wiesel, and if Elie Wiesel had not happened to be related to the Slomovitzes, and if Jack Slomovic had not happened to mention Steve, and if Emily in Los Angeles had not happened to call Laura Klein who in turn happened to know and remember that I was researching Szlatina (a different spelling than the one she was given), then I never would have been able to learn all about my more than two thousand cousins who lived in Transylvania from the end of the 18th century.

Of course, some of this luck can be traced rather directly to our organized and pooled genealogical efforts, such as Laura Klein's contribution, but how do you explain the other bits? Is this usual? Have other researchers had similar experiences?

Sallyann Amdur Sack is editor of AVOTAYNU.

On Coincidence and Luck
by René Loeb

Winter 1988

M ost genealogists can report fortunate coincidences which allowed them to continue doing their research. It is not easy for me to select something extraordinary from my many years of research, but I would like to describe some of my experiences in the past three years doing research in genealogy.

It started with my asking an aunt about our family. I got elaborate answers about the close relatives, but as soon as I wanted more information about the distant relatives, the answers were shallow. The most interesting detail was the information that the family had brought forth an inventor, Siegfried Marcus. Siegfried was born in Malchin/Mecklenburg and lived in Vienna, Austria, for more than a half century. My aunt knew very few details about him, but she was certain that he was to be found in practically all the known encyclopedias. There is a decades-old discussion among experts which always flairs up. This is whether it was really Karl Benz who invented the car, as the Germans continue to claim, or whether it was Siegfried Marcus.

Consequently, I looked into the literature and wrote to several institutions in Vienna. After a short time, I had more information about the inventor from these sources than my aunt ever knew about him even though he was a first cousin of my aunt's great-grandmother.

Siegfried Marcus

The will of Siegfried Marcus stated that he had two brothers. One had immigrated to the United States, settled in Greencastle, Indiana, and changed his family name to Marquis. The other lived in Hamburg, and one of his children was a daughter named Minna.

I wrote to Greencastle attempting to find out more about this brother. Unfortunately, all the answers were negative; however, the clerk wrote to tell me that almost at the same time that I had sent my inquiries, a person from Israel had also inquired about Mr. Marcus, alias Marquis. They sent me his address, and the Israeli got my address. A few days later, a letter arrived from Mordechai Rimon of Israel asking about my connection with that family. As it turned out, Rimon was a grandson of the above-mentioned Minna. From this source came all the necessary information for my family tree as well as additional addresses. I learned also that a nephew of Minna was still alive and very interested in the family history. Between the three of us, we were able to find information about the brother who had emigrated. He had three children, one of whom had died very young. The path of the other two we could follow until the First World War. After that, this trace was lost, and we haven't been able to get any further information. My aunt gave me the address of a second cousin. With all this correspondence, information in books, newspapers and archives, I found out that part of the family had immigrated to Sweden at the end of the 18th and beginning of the 19th century and had helped to found the Jewish communities of Karlskrona, Goteborg and Stockholm. Now I faced the problem of contacting the Swedish family descendants.

In this case also, luck played a part. We have a casual acquaintance with a Jewish-Swedish couple living in Switzerland, so I went to them for help. The wife asked me what family names I was researching. I mentioned a few, and the woman said she thought she had seen one of these names on a family tree. It so happened that she had a girlfriend in Stockholm whose father had a huge Jewish family tree hanging on the wall of their home. My friend thought she had seen these names on that tree.

Immediately, I wrote to the address she gave me and included all the information that I had accumulated so far. It was a bullseye. An intensive correspondence started. Names and addresses were exchanged, and the gentleman I had written to in Stockholm visited me at my home. On that occasion, I also received some handwritten material. This information came from a period before World War I and had belonged to an uncle of my contact person. The uncle had involved himself with genealogy when he was a boy and had died very young in the early 1920s. In 1912, he had the family tree on his father's side printed up. Later, I received that family tree on loan from a third party in order to have it copied onto microfilm. I could copy all the handwritten material and in this way could look through everything at my leisure, put it in the right order, and time sift it to get the important information I wanted to incorporate into my work. However, it looks like only a trip of several weeks to Sweden will make it possible to get all the information that is still missing.

In the library of the local Jewish community, I found useful information from the family tree of an early Frankfurt family. The producer of the family tree listed the names of the parents of the marital partners as well as their addresses. In this way, I located that branch of the family that had emigrated from Hamburg to England thus bringing my information up to date.

I want to mention a further coincidence. My sister-in-law spent some time in Canada, in Toronto, attending a benefit concert. As usual, the program contained some ads of benefactors. I noticed one family name which was also in a family tree I had been working on. In my research, this person had married into the family, and there was no further information available. Encouraged by my earlier successes, I played blind man's bluff, so to speak. I reasoned that although there might not be a direct family connection between the person mentioned in the concert program and the person I was seeking, I still might get some data. Extraordinary as it seems, the person I wrote to was a first cousin of the one I was looking for.

Many more incidents could be related, and I am sure there are many more surprises in store for me. This story shows that one should not adhere strictly to conventional ways of gaining information but should also take advantage of the seemingly almost impossible opportunities in order to reach success.

René Loeb was born in Basel, Switzerland, and educated in Luxembourg. He is the founding president of the Schweizerische Vereinigung für jüdische Genealogie (Swiss Society for Jewish Genealogy) and its quarterly publication MAAJAN–Die Quelle. Since 1986, he was been AVOTAYNU's contributing editor for Switzerland. He began researching his family history in 1980, creating twenty different family trees of his ancestors, who were originally from Alsace and Poland.

Is It Really Luck?

by Gary Mokotoff

Summer 1989

What active genealogist has not come across instances of luck in researching family history? Who has not had something happen that was so improbable that fate seemed to play a role? Have you ever stared at a file of unindexed information containing thousands of names and pondered whether to peruse the information because of the low probability of finding a relative among the morass of data? You glance at a few pages, and suddenly there it is. By luck, you just happened to open to the page where your relative is mentioned.

In a recent issue of AVOTAYNU (Vol. IV, No. 4), Sallyann Sack relates a sequence of seven "if it had not happened" events that led to her discovery of 2,000 relatives. She wonders if she should attribute them to luck. Rene Loeb wrote of lucky events that took him around the globe searching for relatives.

My own experience in family history research is full of examples of probability and luck. What is the chance a relative of yours is named in *The Shtetl Finder*? There are no more than 2,000 names mentioned from a population of 10,000,000. Would you believe there are two members of my family mentioned? How lucky I am!

At the main exhibit of the Holocaust at Yad Vashem, no more than 100 of the 6,000,000 are named. One is a relative of mine, Tobiasz Mokotowski.

Why do these events occur? Why does the statistically improbable happen? Is there such a thing as luck? I think not. My personal experience is that luck is the product of trying. If you try a lot of things often enough, you will get lucky. An active genealogist tries often; thousands of times. Most tries are not successful; the few that do succeed are attributed to luck.

How is it statistically probable that there are two Mokotows in *The Shtetl Finder*? The answer is, how many books did I look through where there were no Mokotows? How is it possible there is a Mokotowski at the Yad Vashem exhibit? The reality is that I have never found a Mokotow listed in any other book or document about the Holocaust (other than Pages of Testimony and yizkor books). It was, in truth, one success and hundreds of failures. But we never mention our failures; we tell people only about our lucky successes.

Gary Mokotoff is publisher of AVOTAYNU.

Genealogy

Yippee!
by Mort Rumberg

Winter 2006

When I began my genealogy quest about ten years ago, I lived in Washington, DC, and had easy access to the National Archives. I spent many hours in the microfilm library searching for hints of my ancestors. The large microfilm room has about a hundred microfilm/microfiche readers. In front of each, a person would sit, bent over, reading the faded script as the film slowly wound from reel to reel. The room was quiet, the air disturbed only by the soft hum of the machines.

Suddenly, I found my grandfather's census card, Louis Rumberg, with the names of his children. I had struck my first vein of gold. I stood up and let out a shriek of joy. "I found him," I yelled, forgetting for a second where I was. Then I heard the wonderful sound of the other researchers applauding me. I was so pleased and so embarrassed. Finally, I was well on my way to documenting my family history.

Mort Rumberg, now retired, is a USAF veteran, an information technology business systems designer, and an adjunct professor of computer sciences. He began his genealogical research in 1996 and has so far discovered 14 heretofore unknown first cousins living across the U.S. His hobbies include writing, painting, magic, genealogy and travel.

How Does a Genealogist Know When He's Found Ms. Right?

by Mark W. Gordon

Winter 1991

This short article provides insight to the single reader on how to determine if one has found a suitable mate. Perhaps an unexpected genealogical sign helps to lead one on the right path. It worked for me; maybe it will work for you.

Our story goes back to March 1981. I had just moved from Washington, DC, to Springfield, Illinois, to accept a new job. I knew no one in town other than several work colleagues, so I sought out friends at a newly forming Jewish singles group (which folded after one additional meeting). I met Robin Heilbrunn, and we went on our first date one month later. This date involved an excursion to Bloomington and Peoria, including a first-time visit to a distant relative of mine—a designer of merry-go-round horses and carnival games—and a twilight stop at a snow-covered Jewish cemetery.

Robin passed the first test; she survived the above activities (plus my ancillary interest in synagogue architecture), although I did include a romantic dinner as part of the festivities. The next test would come two months later. At this point, her parents from Chicago came to visit Springfield for the weekend. While we strolled through the city's noted rose garden, I noticed that Robin's mother had a monogrammed purse. I asked Mrs. Heilbrunn, "What name does the middle letter of your monogram represent?" She replied that the "Y" designated Yarmo, her maiden name.

I stated that I, too, had relatives by the name of Yarmo from Chicago. After a short conversation, it became clear that her Yarmos and my Yarmos were the same family. In fact, we determined that Robin's grandfather's first cousin had married my grandfather's half-sister.

While the relationship with Robin had been progressing well up to this point, the surprising discovery of common relatives added confirming evidence that I had found my life mate. Two years later, Robin and I were married in Los Angeles County and have lived happily ever after.

Sometimes, when you least expect it, genealogy can add a special dimension to your life which goes beyond verification of one's ancestry.

(Note on name origin: Yarmo appears to be a constructed name based on Robin's ancestor's Hebrew name. Yermiya Leizer Gomler disliked his surname, so he rearranged his first two names to become Lester Yarmo.)

Genealogical wedded bliss: Mark and Robin Gordon posing with the death certificate of Robin's great-great-grandfather, Lester Yarmo.

Mark W. Gordon of Maplewood, New Jersey, currently serves as a principal of Urbana Consulting, LLC, which specializes in transit-oriented development and public/private partnerships. He has been constructing his family's ancestry since 1975, with a focus on northeastern Poland (Białystok, Bielsk Podlaski); Latvia (Jelgava, Riga); Lithuania (Kalvarija, Krekenava, Šiauliai, Vilnius, Žagarė); and the Nordhessen region of Germany (Guxhagen, Obervorschütz, Sontra, Wichmannshausen). Family tree branches reach back to c.1600. Mark can read genealogical documents in German, Hebrew, Polish and Russian and has successfully obtained family records from ten different countries. He has completed three ancestral trips to Europe since 2003.

The Genealogist as "Hit Man": Kaddish for Jakob

by Peter Lande

Winter 1992

When I became a genealogist, I realized that the work would sometimes be tedious or difficult, as well as interesting and rewarding, but I underestimated the range of possibilities until Mrs. X turned up a few months ago. Her request was clear and unemotional, "I want my grandfather dead." Seeing that I was somewhat startled by this approach, she added an explanation. She had nothing against her grandfather; in fact, she had never met him due to a divorce and remarriage. Why was she interested? With the unification of Germany, her grandfather's East Berlin real estate holdings suddenly had become very valuable, and people wanted to buy them. Where was grandfather, the only person who stood in her way? As the only grandchild, she would inherit everything if she could prove that he was dead. Without such proof, she would inherit nothing.

As I read her grandfather's old letters (the last in 1957), the sad, but not unusual, story became clear. Jakob had been a successful real estate investor and manager in Berlin until 1938, when he fled to Holland. From there he managed to escape to Cuba and, after World War II, to the United States. He and his wife eked out their existence in Brooklyn, but he dreamed about the lifestyle he once had. Since, by chance, all of his properties were in East (rather than West) Berlin, he could not get restitution. Unlike West Germany, the communist East German government never accepted any responsibility for Nazi aggression against its Jewish citizens.

Jakob's wife had died in the 1970s and was listed on her death certificate as a widow. Jakob, if alive, would be an unlikely 110 years old. None of this, however, definitively established his death to the satisfaction of the German courts. Mrs. X had hired an expensive New York lawyer who assured her, with his bill, that there was no trace of Jakob, no will, no telephone, no death certificate, etc. Jakob had simply vanished. Yet his letters showed where he had lived, and he didn't sound like a vanishing man.

How to "kill" someone who was almost certainly dead, someone for whom I had no date or place of birth? I turned to the "hit man's" guide to New York, Estelle Guzik's *Genealogical Resources in the New York Metropolitan Area*, after first checking the obvious. He was not listed in the Social Security Death Index. He did, however, show up in the 1950s Brooklyn telephone books. So he had existed.

My first break came through re-reading his letters. In one he mentioned that the next day would be his birthday and said how old he would be. It was nice to know when he had been born, but it was his death that interested me. My first stops in New York were the nursing home where Jakob's widow had lived and the funeral parlor listed on her death certificate. The nursing home reported that they destroy all records after five years, but the funeral parlor still had old records. They checked, but Jakob was not buried in the same cemetery as his wife. They suggested checking cemeteries in Brooklyn, but there was no certainty that he had died there, and with no date of death and a common name, this would have been an enormous task. I considered checking with nearby synagogues, but there is no shortage of synagogues in Brooklyn, and Jakob's letters did not indicate that he was actively religious.

The lawyer had been right about one thing. Visits to the Surrogate's Court in Manhattan and Brooklyn confirmed that there was no record of Jakob. Jakob had died believing that he had nothing of value to leave to his widow. The U.S. District Court disclosed that he had been naturalized, but that was irrelevant. Death records were the next place to look, but he could have died anywhere, and the lawyer had said that no records existed in New York. This time he was wrong. The lines at the Manhattan vital records office were long, but I eventually paid my fee and was permitted to look at the book indexes of death records. But for which year? I was lucky and found it on the third try; Jakob had died on October 15, 1959. I filled out an application for the death certificate and thought that my quest was over. As the weeks passed with no reply, I realized that more needed to be done. (Curiously, I never did receive a reply.)

Jakob had been a resident of what became West Berlin, and I speculated that he might have applied for some sort of pension from the West German government. A letter to the *Landesverwaltungsamt Berlin Entschaedigungsbehoerde* (State Administrative Office Berlin, Restitutions) brought the reply that, indeed, there was a record. Not only that, but they had a copy of his New York death certificate, submitted by Jakob's widow. I had fulfilled my mission; Jakob was officially dead.

Did this sad story have a happy ending? Yes, but that would require another article describing how I found the properties (street names and numbers had been changed) and the intricacies of German inheritance and restitution laws. Moreover, Mrs. X could now place a stone on her grandfather's grave in New Jersey.

Peter Landé was born in Germany of German parents, but came to the United States as a young child. He joined the Department of State as a Foreign Service Officer in 1956. Since his retirement, Landé has been active in genealogy research and has contributed greatly as a volunteer at the United States Holocaust Memorial Museum. There he has been in-

volved in a major project to identify and collect in a single computerized database the names of all Holocaust victims and survivors, whether Jewish or non-Jewish, as well as to develop a "list of lists", i.e. an inventory of thousands of sources of information which include the names of Holocaust victims and survivors. He was active in the ultimately successful international effort to open for public access the records of the International Tracing Service, the largest collection of Holocaust records. In 2001, he received a Lifetime Achievement Award from the International Association of Jewish Genealogical Societies for his work in identifying sources of information on Holocaust victims and survivors.

.

False Leads, False Hope: A Cautionary Tale
by Ann Gleich Harris

Winter 2005

U sually when people are moved to write about a personal research experience, it is one that contains an accidental find that changes everything, or some success after an exhaustive search down formerly blind alleys. My most compelling research experience to date does not have a happy ending, but it does provide the details of a real life encounter on the path to family history enlightenment.

When I could not sleep one night last spring, I turned to research to pass the time, searching Google for Ulanów, a town in Poland where some of my relatives had lived, including the only one we knew from Europe who had survived the Holocaust.

My cousin Sabina's story is compelling. She and her husband Bernard survived in Poland during the war (and until 1957) on false German papers and by living as practicing Catholics, despite being from religious Jewish families. In 1957, they were able to immigrate to Israel and later to Brooklyn. Sabina is the niece of my grandmother's brother, Schullem Fass, and her first cousin also married another Fass brother, who had survived by immigrating to Israel in 1935.

My great-uncle Schullem, who came to dinner every *Shabbos* during my childhood and high school years, had come to America and worked to bring over his family. World War II began before he could send for them, and, as a result, his wife and three children perished.

In my search for Ulanów, I found a reference to a PowerPoint presentation on a public file server at the University of Pennsylvania. I was startled to open it and see the story of Schullem's son, Marcus Fass, who was killed in the war as a partisan. The information about him was reported to have come from his journal, which was excerpted in the presentation. I was stunned and emotional as I read through these pages and thought that something remained of this young man and of my family that had perished.

I called my 85-year-old mother in Israel and read her the excerpts from the journal as we both wept significantly. Ironically, I had called on Holocaust Remembrance Day, and my mother had just listened to *Kaddish* (prayer for the dead) being recited.

Next, I spent hours trying to find the author of the presentation in order to locate this journal. The University of Pennsylvania web master, who I learned was herself interested in genealogy, graciously helped me and even sent a personal note. The author of the presentation, a teacher of a unit on the Holocaust for high

Hinda Greenspan Fass and her three children, Rivke, Herschel and Marcus in about 1935. In 1942, the Germans rounded up the Jews of Ulanów. Rivke managed to get false work papers and took a train to Berlin. She sent a letter several months later but was never heard from thereafter. Marcus hid in the woods surrounding Ulanów for more than a year and worked with the partisans. He was captured and killed in a sweep of those woods. Hinda and Herschel's fate is unknown. It is assumed they were murdered along with the other Jews of Ulanów in the roundup or deported to Bełżec.

school students, used this story as an example to inspire and reach high school-age children, because Marcus Fass was a teenager at the time of his death.

When the author of the presentation wrote back to me the next day, I was devastated. To make his presentation more dramatic, he had fabricated the entire journal from details in an information packet he had received from the U.S. Holocaust Memorial Museum in Washington, DC, based on testimony given by Sabina. I felt the teacher's apology to me was hollow for representing the journal as real instead of as fiction based on real events.

But I suppose the chances of a relative finding his presentation and believing its contents, against all odds, were slim, even in our Internet Age.

Ann Gleich Harris has been a family researcher for 20 years. Her corporate experience in competitive analysis and language studies was great training for making progress one tiny clue at a time. Currently, she is creating a database of interconnected families in 19th-century Zborów, including a necrology she translated from its yizkor book.

Making a Mother Appear Out of Thin Air
by Steve Stein

Winter 2006

My brother-in-law Harry never knew his mother or any of her family. Born in 1943, he grew up believing that the parents he knew were his natural parents. He learned differently when he was a teenager, after someone remarked that he looked like his mother. When he disagreed, the person responded, "No, like your real mother." It was only then that he discovered, by questioning his father, that his birth mother had died, his father had remarried, and his younger sister was in fact a half-sister. Harry has no full siblings.

His father told him that he had been in a foster home for some time after his mother died—but Harry remembered nothing of that period. He had never seen a picture of his mother, or of himself as a baby, and had suppressed her first name and her maiden name told to him by his father when he was an adolescent. Harry's father died in the 1970s; with him went all memories and artifacts of Harry's mother. Now that our wives' parents, with whom he was very close, have died, and with my brother-in-law's stepmother quite ill, my sister-in-law reopened the issue of my brother-in-law's birth mother.

My sister-in-law asked me to find my brother-in-law's mother's name and something about her. Because she didn't want him to know I was doing this, so as not to raise his expectations, and since she didn't have ready access to his birth certificate, the search began with no documents and no family lore, no oral history, no childhood memories.

We knew just these fragments: his father's name and the fact that Harry had grown up in Connecticut; my sister-in-law believed his mother was born in New York. The family name is unusual. (For privacy reasons it is not given.) First, I searched the 1910 census for his father and determined that he had been born about 1908. Next, I requested a death certificate for anyone with his surname in the early 1940s in Connecticut; none were found. I sent away for his parents' marriage record in Connecticut, but received the record of his father's second marriage rather than the first.

At this point, I realized that I had no idea when my brother-in-law's parents were married. His father was about 35 years old when my brother-in-law was born, so it could have been any time in the 1930s or early 1940s. I decided to pursue a different route. I checked New York City death indexes (in the New York Public Library) for 1943, since my sister-in-law believed that his mother had died in New York as a result of complications from childbirth. Because the surname is so uncommon (fewer than 20 distinct citations on www.switchboard.com in the entire United States), a single entry might provide the clue that would lead to Harry's mother's identity.

No one with that name died in 1943, but there was a listing in early 1944 for a woman in her early thirties. Because this entry looked promising, I went to the New York City Municipal Archives to find the death certificate. It showed that this woman was indeed married to my brother-in-law's father and, therefore, was my brother-in-law's mother. The death certificate also gave her maiden name and her parents' names, and it noted that she was buried in Beth David Cemetery in Elmont, New York. My brother-in-law was 11 months old when his mother died. Cause of death was given only as "natural causes."

Next came a visit to Beth David Cemetery to locate his mother's grave. I found several burials in a family plot, as well as another nearby plot for a family with the same surname, but I could not, by virtue of the Hebrew names, identify a relationship to Harry's mother. Buried next to his mother were two adult males, as well as a male child. I could tell from the Hebrew inscriptions that one of the men was her brother who had died within a year of her, also at a young age. I could not read the inscription on the photo I had taken of the tombstone of the other adult male, so it was not possible to determine kinship. The boy, age three, was her nephew, her brother's son.

The family was listed in each of the 1910, 1920 and 1930 censuses. The censuses allowed me to verify that she and both the men with whom she was buried were siblings. I told my sister-in-law as much history as I could reconstruct from the death certificate and censuses—places of birth, dates of immigration, marriage, places where the family lived and professions. In turn, she told my brother-in-law, who was delighted with the find. I figured I had completed the research.

A few months later, however, my sister-in-law came back to me and asked if I might be able to find a picture of the mother. We discussed possible sources—perhaps a distant relative, a passport application, a high school yearbook photo. Since I had no reason to believe that the mother had ever traveled outside the U.S.—for which she would have applied for a passport—I started looking for high schools in the area where she lived in 1930 at age 21, Richmond Hill in Queens. I wrote to two different individuals at Richmond Hill High School, but received no answer.

Regrouping and checking out the most obvious possibility, I accessed the JewishGen Family Finder for others researching the mother's maiden surname. One researcher was looking in the Łomża area of Poland for someone with that name, another relatively uncommon name. I had a reasonable expectation that this lone researcher was a relative, and I sent an e-mail message.

I quickly received a positive response. The responder, indeed, knew of the three siblings; his grandfather was their first cousin. He also could identify the people buried in the other plot in Beth David. He had a photograph of one of the brothers but not the mother, and he had oral histories he had taken from other family members who remembered the siblings' father, my brother-in-law's grandfather, and his grocery store in Queens.

Their recollection was that after the grandfather had died, and subsequently the mother and her brother and three-year-old nephew died, the remaining brother moved to Florida and fell out of touch with the rest of the family. The remaining brother's family was my most likely opportunity to secure a photo and learn more information. I decided to go back to the basics, use standard methods and work towards additional information.

Harry, sitting on his mother's lap, with his grandmother and a cousin.

My next break came while searching the ProQuest *New York Times* archive at the Rutgers University Alexander Library nearby. Searching for references to Harry's mother's maiden surname, I found obituaries for the mother, the brother buried near her, and a man with the second brother's name, as well as other relatives. I also found a birth announcement for the (later) deceased three-year-old. I wasn't completely sure that the last obituary was for the second brother, but the obituary mentioned a son, whose name was very similar to that of the mother's father and clearly could have been derived from it (my brother-in-law's middle name, though different still, was also clearly derived from it). It would make sense for my brother-in-law, the first brother's son, and the second brother's son all to have been named for the grandfather, who had died only a couple of years before they all were born. I concluded that the last obituary was indeed for the second brother.

Suspecting that the second brother's son might still be living, I Googled his name, used switchboard.com and found the following:

• A single hit in the United States on switchboard.com for his name, someone living in the St. Louis, Missouri, area.

• A reference to that name on a high school alumni website in Florida in the same town mentioned in the second brother's obituary. His current address was the same as the one on switchboard.com in Missouri. The class year means that the person is very close in age to my brother-in-law.

• A mention of the name on a website of a synagogue in the St. Louis area.

All this led me to believe strongly that I had found a first cousin of my brother-in-law. Since the synagogue's website supplied an e-mail address for this man, I composed a message and attached the *New York Times* obituaries and other pertinent facts. Having received no response after three days, I assumed that either the e-mail address was obsolete or the attachments had caused my e-mail to get caught in his spam filter. I sent a letter enclosing the *Times* obituaries. The following Tuesday evening, I received an e-mail message:

I am [cousin] son of [second brother] and grandson of [grandfather] and [grandmother]. It is exciting to be hearing that some research is being done about the family. We have pictures of [mother], [first brother], [grandfather] and [grandmother] among other pictures that we have kept from my mother. We will need some time go through them. I can scan and send some to you or Harry via e-mail. Also I would like to get Harry's phone number and talk to him.

We were very close to our goal, but my brother-in-law was preparing for surgery. I consulted with my sister-in-law and brother-in-law and we agreed to hold this newly found cousin off for a week or so until after the surgery. The day after the surgery, I received an e-mail from the cousin eagerly delivering several photos, among them:

• A photograph of the mother holding my brother-in-law as a baby, with the grandmother holding the original first cousin as a toddler
• A photograph of the mother on her wedding day
• A photo of the grandparents

I was trying to imagine never having seen a photo of my mother, or a baby photo of myself, and suddenly seeing a photo of her holding me.

A few days later, my brother-in-law felt well enough to talk to his first cousin. They exchanged much information about family. My brother-in-law learned about the family's medical history and that his children were very close in age to his cousin's children. As well as we can determine, the deaths of the three individuals so close together in 1944 caused a veil of fear and secrecy to descend over the members of the family from which they are only now emerging. Since it is doubtful that my brother-in-law ever spoke full sentences before his mother died, and because he was separated from his birth family, in all his 63 years, the newly found first cousin was the first maternal relative with whom my brother-in-law had ever had a conversation.

Steve Stein is a project manager living in Highland Park, New Jersey. He has been researching his and his wife's families for nearly 30 years, following the path into seven Eastern European countries. He has been a volunteer for the JewishGen Jewish Online Worldwide Burial Registry (JOWBR), Hungarian-SIG and the Nesvizh (Belarus) Study Group.

How I Found Out I Was
Not Related to Jan Murray
by Varda Epstein

Winter 2004

Four years ago, the birth of my 12th child, added to the loss of my job because of budget cuts, left me feeling as though I was wading through mud. I had a nasty case of the "baby-blues." Around this time, my mother-in-law bought my eldest daughter a PC to aid in her computer science courses. In the mornings, when all were gone from the house except for my small baby and me, I would quickly attend to my household duties. After having been a working mom for so many years, I had a system and the house practically ran itself. Bored and unhappy, I turned to the PC as a source of entertainment and diversion.

I mastered the use of the mouse and then solitaire. I exhausted entering words as URLs, such as www.chocolate.com, and I made dozens of virtual friends with instant messaging. I even managed to persuade two online friends to get married—he was dragging his feet, and she was losing patience. I wrote him an e-mail and, to make a long story short, they now have a beautiful little girl. This was all well and good, but I needed something for me. I wanted something more long-term and intriguing. What was left?

I happened on the site www.jewishgen.org and started following the links. This was interesting stuff! I found a search engine for the JewishGen General Discussion Group archives and entered my mother's uncommon maiden surname, Kopelman, not expecting any hits. Bingo! Lots of hits. I started reading the entries, fascinated. This I liked.

I began by subscribing to the Discussion Group and interviewing family members. I found I had a knack for finding relatives and filling in the story of my family. It was like detective work, following hunches and making discoveries. Learning about my roots lifted the depression and made me proud of who I am. At some point, I had managed to accumulate seven generations on each of my mother's paternal grandparents' trees. Then it occurred to me to follow some of the more esoteric leads I had accumulated.

As a baby-boomer, TV was an important part of my culture. My mother played endless hands of solitaire at the table in our family room, while I was ensconced on the couch watching Hollywood Squares. The slap-slap of the cards as counterpoint to the game show would lull me into a drowsy state. Today, they call it being a couch potato. Pleasantly dazed, I still managed always to hear my mother comment, "I bet anything that comedian, Jan Murray, is related to us. His real name was Murray Janofsky, you know."

It was time to find out if mother was right. The maiden name of my mother's paternal grandmother (my "mpggm" in genealogy-speak) was Janofsky. When I began researching the Janofsky line, I was sure this was an uncommon surname. I was disabused of this notion quite fast. The suffix -sky, connotes a place name, and more than 50 towns in Eastern Europe are named Janow/Janov.

I also learned about the Daitch-Mokotoff Soundex at www.avotaynu.com/soundex.htm, a system that indexes words by how they sound rather than how they are spelled. In spite of a surfeit of Janofskys, Yanovskys and Yanowskis (by now I knew that Y is the same as J and I; F, V and W can be interchangeable), I managed to construct a tree of this branch of my mother's family. At this point, I decided to write to the Discussion Group (www.jewishgen.org/JewishGen/DiscussionGroup.htm) to see what I could learn about Jan Murray's genealogy.

Jan Murray

I had been posting to this group for almost four years and, by now, to several SIGs (Special Interest Groups) as well, and I have never, before or since, generated so much attention with a posting. I had to create a file called "Jan Murray." It seems that if one cannot be famous, the next best thing is being related to someone famous. It started a bit slowly. I received one response the first day and another the next. On the third day, I received no fewer than 18 messages. Over a period of three months, 61 responses came to me.

At first, I received tips about contacting actors' guilds and the like. Then I had what seemed to be a true lead. Someone was sure his grandmother had come over on the same boat as Murray's father. They were certain that his original surname was Jankowsky, and it was family legend that this guy's grandmother and Murray's father became fast friends on the ship to America.

Then someone sent me Murray's address. I was penning a snail-mail letter to the famous man when I heard from a man who had gone to school with Murray's son, Warren. He looked up Warren's address on the web, included this in his response, and asked me to give Warren Murray his regards when I contacted him. I responded that since I now had Murray's address, I didn't know if I should go straight to the top, where I might not have easy access, or go through Warren. In response, I got a rundown on Warren's adolescent spats with his dad. This was becoming interesting. Of course, this correspondent continued, and they have long since patched things up. If it were his call, he would contact both of them. If you throw enough mud, something is bound to stick.

Next, I heard from someone who said he was Warren's "best friend" in the old days, when both were schoolboys in Brooklyn. I had originally posted that I thought there might be a family resemblance to Murray, and he commented: "Don't let a resemblance mean too much, as both father and son have had plastic surgery on their noses." This man had kept in touch with Warren sporadically. He offered to write to him for me. Cool! I was on a roll—and it got better.

I next heard from an old friend of Jan's, who, by happy coincidence, was a genealogist. He out and out gave me Murray's telephone number! He knew Jan wouldn't be angry with him. I was thinking that Jan must be a really nice guy. I told him I'd say, "Hi, from Milton" and pass on his e-mail address.

The topper was when I received an e-mail from Ian Murray, the eldest grandchild of the famous comedian. I was blown away. Someone had actually printed out and given Ian a copy of my posting, and he contacted me on day four of mail overload. It was a lovely chatty note, filled with family details. Unfortunately, it looked like my quest might be over. Ian was quite certain the family name had been something else before it was Janofsky. Still, he asked me to send on my family details, and he would check it out with his grandfather. Not very hopeful, I sent off what I had on the family history to Ian and waited.

Responses from my posting were still overloading my inbox. I heard from college pals of sons, daughter and grandsons of Murray. Lots of people wrote in with Murray's address, easily obtainable on the web. Some simply wanted me to tell them what I learned.

Then a family story with the ring of truth was brought to my attention. A man named Arthur Menton[1] wrote:

> *I assure you that his family name was originally Jablonowsky. Jan Murray's father was Chaim (Hyman) (Hymie) Janofsky. The name was shortened from Jablonowsky. Hymie was married to Ceil and they lived in the Bronx on Harrison Avenue. In the 1920s, they moved to Brooklyn and rented an apartment from Yetta Mintz in a two-family house on Chester Avenue, down the street from Greenwood Cemetery. Yetta Mintz's maiden name was Bersson, but that was an American adaptation. In Europe it was Jablonowsky. Yetta was my grandmother and I was always told that my father, Alexander Mintz (Menton), was a cousin of Jan Murray. At the time Hymie moved the family to Chester Avenue, Jan was an infant. My father used to babysit for him. Ceil missed the Bronx and Hymie moved his family back there after a little while. Ceil was said to have a large, twisted nose. Jan Murray had a large hooked nose but had plastic surgery after moving into show business. Hymie had a brother named Barney, and they had an embroidery business on 7th Avenue in Manhattan that catered to the garment industry. Breine was the mother of Hyman and Barney.*

I knew this was real. I forwarded Arthur's note to Ian and received a note from

---

[1] Arthur Menton is the author of *The Book of Destiny: Toledot Charlap*, King David Press (1996).

Arthur thanking me for my prompt reply. Arthur wrote:

A few years ago I tried contacting Jan Murray by sending him letters via the William Morris Agency, his theatrical agent. The letters were never answered. I have no contact with him or his family at present.

I forgot to mention that my first cousin, Suzanne Levitt, has also heard the same story that I told you. Suzanne was very close to our grandmother, Yetta Mintz. The Jablonowsky name, in Yetta's family, was changed to Bersson upon the arrival in America of Jacob Jablonowsky. He was Yaacov ben Ber (son of Ber), hence, Bersson. I have a tree of the Jablonowskys dating back to the 1600s.

None of this had anything to do with my mother's family history, yet I felt it to be true. I was finished, definitely not related to Jan, but still intrigued. I awaited Ian's reply. When I received his response, I realized he had been miffed on reading the description of his great-grandmother's nose. He wrote:

My grandfather and grandmother are away on a cruise for the next two weeks. I will send them your and Arthur's e-mail messages. I will ask my dad and my aunts and uncle if they have heard of Arthur, Alexander or any Mintz. Arthur was right about the first name of my great-grandmother. It was Celia. However, I have seen pictures of her, and her nose was not big and twisted. Also, I don't believe the family name was originally Jablonowsky. One more thing, I don't believe the family ever moved back to the Bronx.

I had nothing to do but wait. Responses continued to flow in, but I was waiting for Ian. Finally, it came. Ian wrote:

Good news. My grandfather returned from his cruise and sat down and read all of your correspondence. He said that Arthur's e-mail rang true to him and brought tears to his eyes. He believes that he is related to Arthur. Sorry to say, not you. He wants to speak with Arthur. So, I will e-mail him and ask for his phone number.

I was floating on cloud nine. Just picturing Jan with tears in his eyes filled me with intense gratification. The responses to my posting on the end of this story were warm, sympathetic and complimentary as well. The discussion group members were, by now, my online community. They shared my red-letter day as well as my concomitant disappointment in disabusing a long-held notion. Most of all, they understood the lovely feeling of bringing happiness to Jan Murray, who through the years had brought so much joy to his audiences.

Varda Epstein, a former resident of Pittsburgh, Pennsylvania, made aliyah (immigration to Israel) at age 18 and now lives in Efrat. In addition to her genealogical research and volunteer work for JewishGen, she is the mother of 12 and a grandmother who enjoys singing contralto in the Shir A Cappella women's choir.

Sometimes You Have To Be Told To Ask
by Alan Steinfeld

Winter 2005

Questions are the fuel that drives the machinery of genealogy. If who, what, when and where supply the limbs of our family tree, it is "why" that clothes those bare branches with the leaves that make a family history. A search for the answer to one of my why questions led me to the Office of the Chief Medical Examiner of New York in the spring of 1998.

Thirty years of research had uncovered stories similar to most families who trace their ancestry back to Poland and Russia in the mid- to late-1800s. We have tales of coming to America to avoid an arranged marriage, marriages that never really took place and assorted other instances reflecting the complexity of life.

I took the trip to the medical examiner's office to investigate one of these stories. A death was involved—a suicide. I had learned the story only as an adult, and it would be still more years before I had the chance to learn the intriguing details.

My parents and their siblings grew up during the Great Depression of the 1930s and experienced all of the hardships associated with it. One of the great pressures of these times was the residential crowding necessitated by the need to save money on rent. As a consequence, parents often lived with married children, even as grandchildren increased the size of the household. This resulted in halls and living rooms becoming part-time bedrooms and children sleeping in parents' bedrooms for many years.

The story that came down to me was of just such a situation. My father's sister, the eldest of the children and first to marry, moved in with her new husband and his father. The one-bedroom apartment in the Bronx was adequate with her father-in-law sleeping in the parlor. Upon the birth of their child, my eldest first cousin, another bed was needed. I would hear years later that the rest of the family expected that the four of them now would move into a two-bedroom apartment. But years passed, and my cousin continued to sleep in his parents' bedroom.

The weather in New York in July 1946 was hot and sticky. As did many families living in the city, my aunt, uncle and cousin went to the mountains for the weekend, leaving Grandpa in the apartment. On Sunday morning, a call came to the bungalow colony telling my uncle that his father had been found dead. He had committed suicide. Why?

As told to me, it was because the grandfather felt that the house was too crowded and saw no other way to assure that his grandson would no longer have to sleep in his parents' bedroom. Was that really why it happened?

New York's medical examiner's office is a squat building located in the middle of the eleven-block stretch of hospitals that extends from 23rd to 34th Street. The interior has the grim, bureaucratic look that one would imagine as the chief morgue for New York City. Because I am on the staff of one of those hospitals, I had easy entrée to the facility and soon was in the office of the medical examiner's spokeswoman. I told her the story and asked if any of the records might be available. I was reassured when she told me that if the death were an "ME case," the records would not have been destroyed, but they were in the archives, and it would take some time to retrieve them.

Weeks went by, then a month. Finding myself in front of the building while en route from one hospital to another, I stopped in to check on progress. "What a coincidence," the spokeswoman said. "The records came in today." We moved to her office where she picked up a slim manila folder containing half a dozen sheets that had been faxed that day from the Municipal Archives. The first document was the certificate of death. In addition to confirming facts of his identity, it gave his month and year of birth and the number of years the grandfather had lived in New York City. A report from Consolidated Edison (the gas utility) was completed on a pre-printed "Fatal Illuminating Gas Asphyxiation Report." It indicated that the gas burner had been turned on full, and the gas was directed to the "patient's" mouth via a paper funnel. An intriguing entry on the form said, "Note left with police." The death notice from the office of the chief medical examiner confirmed the information on the death certificate. Under remarks was the entry, "Police say suicidal. Left note."

The Police Department's death report offered the most detailed report of the events. It said that the deceased had been found by a neighbor (presumably alerted by the smell of gas), who had in turn called police. It gave the names of all individuals involved and again made reference to a suicide note.

"Hmm," I said aloud, "I wonder if the police still have the suicide note. I have some friends on the force and may be able to locate it." Upon hearing my musings, the spokeswoman said to me, "Are you asking me for the suicide note?" Perplexed, I said, "Okay, I'm asking for the note." Upon hearing this, she reached into the folder and produced one last sheet. The suicide note!

My Dear Children and grandchildren,

You will excuse me for what I have done. I couldn't stand any longer the terrific pain I have suffered lately. Please give a contribution of $25 to the United Jewish Community of the Bronx and $25 for the relief of the Jewish people in concentration camps.

Dear _____,

I wish I could have seen you before I died to tell you how deeply I loved you.

I kiss you all.

Your father

What had been the cause of the "terrific pain" that had driven this old man to take his life? Was it physical or emotional? I went back to the documents and read the handwritten, two-page report of the medical examiner. It repeated the information about how he was found and gave a description of the body. At the bottom of the page was written:

> *Deceased had been complaining of severe pain in rectum. Received injections & (indecipherable). Was treated by Dr. _____ .... Was very nervous."*

The story of my relative's death was now much clearer. Rather than being due to any concerns about overcrowding, it appears as if he had a disease of the rectum, possibly cancer. The pain referred to in his suicide note was due to a physical illness.

One mystery remained. Why did I have to ask for the suicide note? I put this question to the woman in the ME's office who had helped me in my search. She told me that suicide notes are always kept by the ME's office, but given to family only if they ask for it. This rule was apparently put in place to give families the chance to protect themselves from unpleasant information.

Had I not been told to ask, I would have missed learning the true end to this story.

Alan Steinfeld, MD, is a retired professor of Radiation Oncology who lives with his wife, Rena, in Scarsdale, New York. His genealogy research began in the 1970s and resulted in publication of The Pasenkers of Smolensk in 1991. He regularly teaches and lectures on genealogical subjects.

Preponderance of Evidence:
The Curious Case of Jakob Mokotowicz
by Gary Mokotoff

Winter 2006

My American genealogy experts tell me that genealogical evidence does not operate under the theory of preponderance of evidence. Genealogy requires a higher standard of proof than the fact that the number of pieces of evidence that prove a point greatly exceeds the number to the contrary. Someone once told me—I do not know if it is true—that in the case of genealogical evidence, if five items confirm a fact and one item contradicts the fact, then you cannot state that the fact is accurate until you can explain the one contradictory piece of evidence. As Elizabeth Shown Mills states in her book *Evidence!*,[1] "When we find contrary evidence, we will adequately and logically rebut it—or else delay our decision until clearer support can be assembled." I considered this rule unusual until I came across the strange case of Jakob Mokotowicz.

Jakob Mokotowicz was a Holocaust survivor. There is a case file for him in the archives of the Hebrew Immigrant Aid Society (HIAS) in New York. It reads like a melodrama. He first appears on HIAS doorsteps in 1947. He arrived on a ship bound for Australia. Jakob wanted to stay in the U.S. and claimed to the HIAS officials that he was destitute and did not have the money to continue on to Australia. In opening his case file, Jakob stated his birth date was November 9, 1912. HIAS gave him money and sent him on his way to Australia.

We next find Jakob at HIAS' door in 1950. He did go to Australia, but now he was returning to the U.S. with an American wife. He planned to stay in the U.S. Again, in the application he filled out in 1950, he gave his birth date as November 9, 1912.

The HIAS case file continued. In 1967, Jakob applied for Social Security benefits. He said he was born on November 9, 1902, had reached the ripe old age of 65 and, therefore, was entitled to government old-age benefits. He stated he could not prove his age because he was born in Warsaw and his birth record was destroyed during World War II, but he had a lot of people that were willing to testify to his age.

The HIAS case file was the first time I ever heard of Jacob, so I searched the microfilm copy of the International Tracing Service records located at Yad Vashem, and Jakob appeared a few times. In every case, he gave his birth date as

---

[1] Mills, Elizabeth Shown, *Evidence!: Citation & Analysis for the Family Historian*, Baltimore: Genealogical Publishing Company, 1997.

Date	7.4.49		
Name	MOKOTOWICZ, Jakub	File P	18-108
3D	1912	BP	Nat Polish Jew
Next of Kin	parents; Mieczysław & Teofila	Book M.P.185	
Source of Information	Central Jew.Committee in Poland, Warsaw		
Last kn. Location	Warszawa, Zaokopowa 4/55	Dat	caft.war-Jan.47
CC/Prison		Arr.	lib.
Transf. on		to	
Died on		in	
Cause of death			
Buried on		in	
Grave		D.C.No.	
Remarks	addr.in 1939; W-wa		

(left) In 1949, Jakob Moko-towicz told the Central Jewish Committee in Poland he was born in 1912.

(right) He appears on a list of Polish refugees that fled to Russia showing his correct year of birth (Data urodzenia) as 1902.

Nazwisko: Mokotowicz

Imię: Jakub

Imię ojca: Mojżesz

Data urodzenia: 1902

LP	Rodzaj represji	Początek represji			Koniec represji			Kraj	Woj/Obłast	Pow.	Miej.
		r	m	d	r	m	d				
1.	Areszt	1940						Białoruś	Brzeska		

November 9, 1912.

So here we have a case of the "preponderance of evidence" demonstrating Jakob was born in 1912. The one exception is the claim he was born in 1902 when he applied for Social Security benefits. Clearly he was lying about his age so he could collect old-age benefits from the government.

Which year was correct? It turns out that the 1902 date was correct. Many years later, I located his son, or I should say his son found me, and he related the following story to me. After World War II ended, Jakob was one of hundreds of thousands of Jewish refugees trying to flee Europe. Jakob was 44 years old in 1946, and he was afraid that no country would take him because he was too old, so he lied to the authorities and made himself ten years younger. He was, indeed, born on November 9, 1902.

I related this story to my friend, Christine Rose, CG, CGL, FASG, who lectures regularly on the subject of genealogy evidence, and she found it such an interesting example of why preponderance of evidence does not necessarily work that she included the example in her lecture.

Gary Mokotoff is publisher of AVOTAYNU.

Who Rests in the Philadelphia Cemetery?
A HIAS/INS Case Study
by Valery Bazarov and Marian L. Smith

Winter 2003

Genealogists begin their research with what they know. Leizer Orchow's granddaughter knew her grandfather emmigrated from Russia to Philadelphia in 1911 and lived his entire life in that city. Orchow lived with his children, then with his grandchildren, until he peacefully passed away and was buried in one of the Jewish cemeteries in the City of Brotherly Love. No one suspected anything wrong until recently, when the aforementioned granddaughter decided to build a family tree.

She sat for endless hours before the microfilm machine looking for Grandfather Orchow on a passenger list. Finally, she found him aboard the Uranium Line's *Campanello*, arriving in New York on February 10, 1911. He was listed as a 45-year-old Russian-Hebrew tailor. Her celebration would have been complete were it not for the small, stamped word "DEPORTED" to the left of Orchow's name. Deported? But, if Leizer Orchow was deported, who rests in the family plot in the cemetery? This was the question the granddaughter put to the HIAS Family History Service.

Valery Bazarov Comments

I found Leizer Orchow among the Arrival Index Cards at HIAS Headquarters archive in New York (see "Records Used" at end of article). His card was not standard. Rather, it appeared on a form reserved for more complicated, problematic or protracted cases and can be identified by the words "Record of Special Inquiry Case" appearing in the printed card title. The form itself indicated that Orchow was held for a hearing before the Board of Special Inquiry at Ellis Island. Such forms typically indicate the presence of a case file among the HIAS Ellis Island Records, 1905–23, housed at YIVO Institute for Jewish Research (see "Records Used" at end of article). Unfortunately, or fortunately, there was no case file for Orchow.

The absence of any additional paperwork regarding Orchow's case suggested the DEPORTED stamp was in error. As indicated on the card, it seemed that Leizer Orchow arrived on the *Campanello* and appeared before the Board of Special In-

Ellis Island manifest for the Campanello *states that Leizer Orchow was deported.*

quiry as a Likely Public Charge (LPC) case due to a medical certificate for "hernia left inguinal." The back of the card listed "action and steps taken by office," most of which could be read between scratches on the microfilm. The chronology of Orchow's case showed he appeared before the Board on February 14, 1911, and his cousin called the same day to promise financial assistance. The Board apparently denied Orchow admission, for the next day, February 15, a HIAS representative helped the immigrant file an appeal to the Board's decision.

Given the fact that Orchow lived the rest of his life in the United States, it seemed obvious that he won his appeal and was admitted into the country. Of course, I must tell you, I was making that assumption. It was an interpretation that explained the facts of his arrival, detention, appeal and subsequent presence in the United States. Still, I remembered one of the main commandments of genealogy: You shall not assume! So I sent the case to Marian Smith for her opinion.

Marian Smith Comments

Valery came to me with this record, and while I could not say who rested in the Philadelphia cemetery, I knew that if the stamp said DEPORTED, Orchow was deported. The question was how long he stayed deported, and when, where and how he returned to the United States.

In addition to the DEPORTED stamp on the left page of the passenger list, the right page was annotated regarding the cause of Orchow's detention and deportation. It reads, "Med ct Hernia left inguinal which affects," meaning a Public Health Service physician issued a medical certificate alleging Orchow had a left inguinal hernia that would affect his ability to earn a living in the United States, thus making it likely he would become a public charge in this country. Most importantly, the List of Aliens Held for Special Inquiry found at the end of the passenger list makes it clear that Leizer Orchow was deported on February 15, 1911.

Valery insisted the man lived and died in Philadelphia, so I made my own assumption. I reasoned there must be a second arrival record for Orchow. Furthermore, I expected Valery to find that record dated some two to six weeks after February 15, 1911, and suggested he first search the index to Philadelphia arrivals. My advice to search Philadelphia was not based simply on the fact that Philadelphia was Orchow's destination. I recommended Philadelphia because, in the early years of the 20th century, Philadelphia seems to be the favorite port of entry for immigrants recently excluded at New York.

It was not long before Valery reported success. He found Lazer Orchow arriving in Philadelphia aboard the Haverford on March 28, 1911. Previously deported to Rotterdam, Orchow traveled from there to Liverpool, where he boarded the

Entry for Leiser (Leizer) Orchow arriving at the port of Philadelphia on March 24, 1911, just 45 days after he was deported back to Europe from Ellis Island. The "verified" date demonstrates that in 1924 he applied for citizenship and the authorities went to this ship's manifest to prove that he arrived in the United States legally.

Haverford for Philadelphia. Orchow may have gone to Liverpool upon his own initiative or at the direction of the steamship company. Steamship agents knew immigration authorities in Philadelphia were not as strict as those in New York, and they were in the practice of turning rejected immigrants around by re-booking them for Philadelphia. I see many similar cases of immigrants initially excluded at Ellis Island. They appear weeks later at Philadelphia, Boston, Baltimore or via the Canadian Border.

Conclusion

While researchers must always form hypotheses and test those theories by searching a variety of records, our assumptions often hinder our success. The fact of Leizer Orchow's presence in the United States since 1911 caused at least one researcher to dismiss the DEPORTED stamp on a passenger list. They assumed the stamp was in error, because it contradicted the known facts. If Leizer Orchow's granddaughter had not been curious about the stamp, she might still assume her grandfather immigrated to America on February 10, 1911, aboard the *Campanello.*

Records Used

Passenger and Crew Lists of Vessels Arriving at New York, NY, 1897–1957. National Archives microfilm publication T715.

Passenger Lists of Vessels Arriving at Philadelphia, PA, 1883–1945. National Archives microfilm publication T840.

HIAS Arrival Index Cards (microfilms) from 1909 arranged by year of arrival, port of entry, then alphabetically by surname. Ports of entry include (for different years) New York, Boston, Baltimore, Galveston, Philadelphia, Providence, San Francisco and Seattle. For 1940–64, they include Bradley Airfield (CT), Charleston, Gulfport, Laredo (TX), Miami, Mobile, New Orleans, Niagara Falls, Norfolk, Oswego, Portland, Rouses Point, Savannah and Wilmington, DE. Information includes: date of arrival, conveyance, names of all passengers traveling together, age, country of birth, sex, marital status, country of last residence, sponsor and sponsor's address. Some cards are illegible. Location: HIAS Headquarters, 333 7th Avenue, New York, NY 10001 and the YIVO Institute for Jewish Research, 15

W 16th Street, New York, NY 10011.

Valery Bazarov is the Director of the Location and Family History Service at the Hebrew Immigrant Aid Society (HIAS) in New York City. Marian L. Smith is the Historian for Citizenship and Immigration Services (CIS), part of the Department of Homeland Security, in Washington, DC. Her writings do not necessarily represent the views of Citizenship and Immigration Services or of any other agency of the United States government.

Epilogue (by Valery Bazarov)

There is an epilogue to this story. When in 2004, Marian and I made a presentation at the meeting of the Jewish Genealogical Society of Greater Philadelphia, I realized that something pertaining to this story (after all it originated in Philadelphia) could be found in the society's wonderful archives. I was right, as I was able to find a record of the money transaction from Orchow's cousin, Sam Goldenberg; the very same cousin that was waiting unsuccessfully for him in Ellis Island and 45 days later met him in Philadelphia. The transaction was made in the name of Leib Orchow to the *S.S. Haverford* as a payment for his passage from Rotterdam to Philadelphia. This finding closed the circle.

Finding Tevel Leibowitz
by Ira Leibowitz

Winter 1993

I n researching family history, I sometimes feel that two immutable Laws are at work. The First Law assures that when I expect to locate a document, I won't. The Second Law, essentially the converse of the First, guarantees that I will unearth an important nugget when it is least expected. These operated perfectly in my hunt for my paternal grandfather's uncle, Tevel Leibowitz.

It seemed like a simple matter to obtain the record of Tevel's arrival in the U.S. Married, but alone according to family lore, he had docked in New York City in 1902. The story sounded reliable; it was consistent with Tevel's wife's known 1906 emigration and the birth dates of their children. I had good reason to be confident of obtaining the information without much fuss.

A search of the U. S. National Archives name index for immigrant arrivals at the port of New York revealed no Tevel Leibowitz. I tried other port cities— Baltimore, Philadelphia and the Canadian entry points. No Tevel. I substituted the name David, although he used that name (or occasionally, Davis) only later. I used imaginative spellings of the family name. Nothing. The First Law of family research was at work.

I was especially eager to have Tevel's manifest. He was the closest link in America to my great-grandfather Chaim, his older brother, who had remained in Russia. Some said that Chaim had once visited the U.S., but I doubted the story since my father had never heard it, and we had no evidence to suggest it. In any event, Chaim had never emigrated. It seemed that obtaining a record of Tevel's arrival was as close as I could get to Chaim. While my failure to do so was frustrating, I knew that Tevel's naturalization papers would document his port and date of arrival as well as the name of the ship on which he sailed.

Some information had already been given to me. Tevel's youngest daughter— the only one of his five children still living—remembered seeing tattered naturalization papers belonging to her father some 40 years earlier and thought that they included the names of her three oldest siblings. That would place the date of Tevel's naturalization at about 1908–09. He had settled in New York City, but did she know where her father had applied for citizenship? In 1991, his daughter couldn't say.

Obtaining documents from the U.S. Immigration and Naturalization Service (INS) takes a long time—from eight to fourteen months—so I tried to short-circuit that process. The National Archives have microfilmed name cards of individuals naturalized before 1958 in the federal courts of New York's Eastern and Southern Districts. These cards often include dates of naturalization, certificate numbers and other valuable information. After finding several cards in the name of David Leibowitz (or a variation), I wrote to the Northeast Region branch of the U.S. National Archives in New York City. This office is the repository of all federal District Court records, as well as naturalization petitions filed between 1906 and 1911 in the now-defunct U.S. Circuit Court for the Southern District of New York. I provided identifying data and requested a search of all three courts. Again, my quest produced nothing.

Tevel must have filed naturalization papers in a state court, I thought. That option was available until 1924 in the two counties in which he had lived, New York (Manhattan) and Kings (Brooklyn). I wrote to the appropriate State Supreme Courts, always listing every spelling variant of his name that I could imagine. I still came up empty-handed.

Weary of the search, I decided to go through the INS process and wait. One year later, in June 1992, the now-predictable response arrived—no files. Maybe Tevel hadn't become a citizen after all, I thought. I would never find his ship manifest now.

The 1920 federal census, released while I awaited the INS results, held promise as a further source. Unlike the situation with the 1910 census, names from New York (and every other state) had been soundexed in the 1920 census. That permits a researcher to retrieve information with no more than a name. Tevel, I found, had told the enumerator that he had arrived in 1904 and had obtained citizenship in 1908. So, he had become a citizen after all, but the dates had to be incorrect; a minimum wait of five years is necessary before an immigrant can apply for citizenship. Either the arrival date or the naturalization date was at least one year off. Most importantly, though, I now had a 1920 address for Tevel.

Manhattan's Board of Elections maintains voter registration records dating back to 1916. Records often include the voter's exact date of naturalization and the name of the court in which the action occurred. I hoped that Tevel had voted in November 1920—which seemed reasonable since it was a presidential election year—and that he was still living at the East Side address reported by the census taker the previous January. Again a letter was sent, this time to the Manhattan Board of Elections.

A reply came scarcely two weeks after I wrote. The Eighth Election District of the First Assembly District—taken from the 1917, not the 1920 rolls, showed a Davis Leibowitz at the address I had supplied. It indicated that he had been naturalized September 15, 1908, in the Circuit Court of the Southern District of New York. I had broken through.

Now I needed to backtrack. I wrote again to the Northeast Regional office of the U.S. National Archives, this time with precise information. This time, I received Tevel's naturalization papers. They had been made out in the name of

PETITION FOR NATURALIZATION

Petition for Naturalization of Dawis Leibowitz

"Dawis" Leibowitz, just a slight variance to be sure, but enough to have stumped archival researchers the first time I wrote. The papers said that Tevel had sailed from Rotterdam on the *Ryndam* and had docked in New York City on March 17, 1903. Splitting the available recollections, he had arrived between the year attested to by the family (1902) and Tevel's own census account (1904).

At long last, I was successful in retrieving the ship arrival record. In fact, I succeeded in a way I had not imagined. The manifest showed that "Tewel Leibowitz" was going to New York's East Side to join his brother, Chaim. So my great-grandfather really had come to the United States! The Second Law of family history research—uncovering a significant fact at an unexpected moment—had also taken effect, to my surprise and delight.

Ira Leibowitz lives in Bethesda, Maryland. He is a member of the Jewish Genealogical Society of Greater Washington.

Seven Guiding Principles for Family Research
by Judith Saul Stix

Winter 1994

A Gentile friend who is an insomniac turned on his television one morning before dawn and listened intently to a rabbi giving advice on bringing up children. This is the gist of what the rabbi said: Pray for luck.

That is also the first of my principles for researching family history—*Pray For Luck*. Looking into the past and tracing one's ancestors is an adventure into the unknown. There is no way to know what documents, what stories, even what artifacts may appear along the sometimes straight, sometimes twisting path. But this is exactly why the journey may become a joy.

My second principle is *Be Persistent*. Write a second letter; make a second call. My research began with an attempt to find the family of my grandmother. Connections with them had lapsed more than 50 years earlier. After a long search, I received the name of someone to write to, but he did not reply. Months later, when I wrote again, he had returned from a long season away and promptly called me, putting me in touch with every member of the Schloss clan in three of its five branches.

Third, *Don't Think You Are Alone*. One member of the Schloss family had meticulously compiled a family tree. Another cousin had done the same for the family of my paternal grandmother, the Prices. A pen pal put a big chunk of my genealogy on a computer for me—something I couldn't do. At various times, three people I didn't know at all sent me photographs of family graves in Baltimore, Cincinnati and New York. The last had to clear the stones in an overgrown, neglected, vandalized Bayside Cemetery on Long Island.

Fourth, *Be Skeptical*. My mother had meticulously kept a baby book for me, and in it she had written down my family tree—getting almost all of it wrong. For example, she had the name of her own grandfather as Isaac Lipka. I now know for certain that his name was Nathan. I have found him documented in 16 different permutations of his last name.

It has been said that there is an almost 20 percent error rate in census data. Information should always be scrutinized carefully and corroborated whenever possible. Nathan Lipka appeared in the 1880 census as Emil Lipker, the extra *r* throwing off the Soundex code by which his record was accessed. I found him, nevertheless, by being skeptical, not believing he wasn't there, and persisting. From his address in the city, I was able to recover the census record.

Even carefully made family trees should be rechecked. I knew from letters that I was related to the Schloss family, but my great-grandmother Carolina Schloss Lipka did not appear on the family tree. How I fitted into it was a conundrum.

Eventually, documents from Germany enabled me to prove that she was one of five siblings, only four of whom appeared on the genealogy. She had made the mistake of dying young. Another great-grandmother, Sarah Baylson Price, also died young, and she had been omitted from a Baylson family tree.

Fifth, *Be Patient*. There may be long waits to obtain documents for which you have written or microfilms that you have ordered. Some individuals are slow to reply or never reply. The documents for which you have waited are not the ones you need. Patience and persistence must go hand in hand.

Even after you have done a great deal of work and sent out many queries, you may lack a sense of what to do next or simply feel burned out. It may be time to sit still and let things come to you. In one month, after a dry period, four things came to me. An Atlanta cousin found a descendant of our great-grandfather Price's brother, and a cousin in Oregon received five documents of the Bass family from Pusalot, Lithuania. Also, the Mormons came through with the left-hand pages of Nathan Lipka's town synagogue records—only the right-hand ones were available five years earlier.

Also in that month, a letter came from a woman who mistakenly believed that I had done a great deal of work researching my husband's family. Though inquiring, she also gave us interesting new information.

Sixth, *Organize*. At some point, you will want to distill everything you have garnered into a single family tree or set of trees or into a book or album. No one else can go easily through your material and make it coherent. An organized product or several of them make it possible to share what you have found—the eventual goal of almost all collectors. But do not wait for perfect completeness to give form to your gatherings.

Also, do not wait until you are ready for some final result. Organize on a computer, in looseleaf binders, or in files, but sort as you go along. Pattern bits of data as you get them, which helps both to find them again and to study them. For example, from my file on the Saul family in census and directory, I have a page on which I charted family members and a family business with addresses in Washington, DC, in the 1890s. This enabled me to see a neighborhood pattern. It also enabled me—and it came as a complete surprise—to discover that the original name they used in America was not Saul, but Sholsky. This change came not at Ellis Island or Castle Garden, but after the family had lived in America for more than 15 years.

My seventh and last principle is *Visit the Sites*. I like to say that what I do is family history, not genealogy, though making family trees and timelines is always useful. I want to enrich my story with data on where they lived, what they worked at, how they looked, the way that they are a part of everyone's story. In Cincinnati, for instance, I learned that my husband's family lived across the street from

William Howard Taft, later President of the United States.

I can't explain why I wanted to go to Germany to visit Lindenschied, the tiny town in the Hunsrück where my great-grandmother, Carolina Schloss, was born. I already had a description from a cousin and many documents. Nevertheless, the urge was irresistible. And was it just luck that while there, I was put into contact with two amateur historians who lived in nearby towns? One was the unofficial historian of Lindenschied, who possessed old maps that showed exactly where my family had lived in 1860. The other, a young man interested in Jewish history, had in his collection the actual documents—not just copies—of the declarations in which my family adopted the names Stiefel and Schloss in 1808. This happened under Napoleon, and the documents are in French. They are not official German records, and I never dreamed of finding and seeing them.

I come back to my first principle: *Pray for luck.*

Judith Saul Stix is a poet and author of biographical and other non-fiction articles. A number of her works have appeared in previous issues of AVOTAYNU. She lives in St. Louis.

The Virtue of Persistence:
A Story of Discovery and Some Rules Learned Along the Way
by Sam Schleman

Winter 2004

About two years ago, not long after I was seduced by the siren call of genealogy, I decided it was time to research my maternal side, having spent my initial six months of genealogical endeavor in pursuit of my paternal connections. My maternal grandmother was born in New York in 1881, the first-born child of Joseph Schwartz and Hannah Spitz, both of whom had come from Hungary in 1880.

I easily learned my great-grandparent's dates of death and wrote requesting their death certificates. The documents duly arrived and revealed their place of burial as Mt. Zion Cemetery in the Maspeth, Queens, section of New York City. At Mt. Zion, I discovered that my great-grandparents had a small plot of their own. In the middle of this "family plot" was the grave of an Esther Bleich (1839–1919). Who was Esther Bleich?!? What was she doing in my great-grandparent's burial plot?

Being logical, frequently a fatal flaw in genealogical research, I theorized that she was an unknown aunt. Since I knew her date of death from her gravestone, I sent for her death certificate, fully expecting it to indicate that her maiden name was Schwartz. I should have known better. The death certificate gave her maiden name as Kramer.

Next, I called my sister and my Schwartz cousins, all of whom are older than I, and asked if they knew the name Bleich or Kramer. Of course the answer was negative; no one had a clue who Esther was. To make it even worse, I had a piece of "genealogical gold"—my mother's address book from 1928. There, on the page with other members of the Schwartz clan, were a "Mr. and Mrs. Bleich" and a "Mr. and Mrs. Kramer," apparently living next door to one another in the Bronx. Clearly the names Bleich and Kramer were known to the prior generation, but they had been lost with the passage of time. Unfortunately, the names in my mother's address book provided no answers, but merely intensified the mystery.

A year passed, during which time I continually obsessed over the question "Who was Esther Bleich?" I tried to find her in the 1900 and 1910 censuses and in the Ellis Island database, but to no avail. I then turned to JewishGen's Family Finder (JGFF), a database listing researchers and the surnames, towns and countries they are researching. I sent out about 40 e-mails to persons researching the names "Spitz" and "Ehrenreich" (Joseph Schwartz's mother's maiden name) in

The seven Kramer siblings: (seated) Hermina, Ben, Shamu, Anne; (standing) Edwin, Zelma and

Hungary and added, "I also am looking for descendants of an Esther Bleich." Nothing happened.

Six months later, I tried again. Two weeks later, I received an e-mail that announced, "Esther Bleich is my great-great-grandmother."

Rule Number 1: *The JGFF is a powerful tool for finding connections. Use it.*

Amy, the newfound cousin who had responded to my inquiry, explained that my great-great-grandfather, Joseph Schwartz, had an older sister, Theresa, who married Esther's brother, Moritz Kramer. (So that's why my grandmother named one of her twins Theresa!) In other words, my great-great-grandfather buried his sister's sister-in-law in the family plot.

Barraging Amy and another newfound cousin, Helen, with a volley of questions, I soon filled in the genealogies of Theresa Kramer's seven children: Hermina, Ben, Shamu, Anne, Edwin, Zelma and Armin. All but Shamu had immigrated to the United States.

I am related to the descendants of Moritz Kramer and Theresa Schwartz. Since

Theresa was my great-grandfather's sister, I am not related to the descendants of Esther Kramer and Ignatz Bleich, except for the group of Bleiches descended from the marriage of Esther's son, William, to his first cousin, Hermina, Theresa's daughter.

I was off and running, researching and documenting like a crazy man. One of the branches was that of Zelma Kramer, who married a Henry Stern and who had lived in Atlanta. I found Zelma and Henry in the census and learned the names of their children. After fruitlessly checking telephone directories and the U.S. Social Security Death Index, I ran out of leads. I succeeded only in finding a trace of one son, Samuel, and the informant on his wife's death certificate was a daughter, not listed in the Atlanta telephone book. Probably her name changed as a result of marriage.

About this time, one of the Bleich cousins whom I contacted asked if I had spoken to the Atlanta Bleiches. "What Atlanta Bleiches?" I contacted my cousin Helen with this new development. She explained that there was another branch in Atlanta, not related to me, but she did not know them. They were descendants of Esther rather than Theresa.

About a year ago, I had volunteered to proofread a database of forced laborers from a town to which I had no connection, in a country from which none of my relatives came—but it was an opportunity to "give back." The project manager was from Atlanta, so I wrote to her explaining my brick wall. A few weeks later an e-mail arrived from a member of the "Atlanta Bleich branch."

Rule Number 2: *Volunteer! You'll feel good, you will "give back" and you will make friends who may be able to help you some day.*

I wanted to document the Atlanta Bleiches, even though I am not related to them, because I reasoned that by getting to know them, they might help me find the descendants of Zelma and Henry Stern. And sho' nuff, as they might say in Atlanta, that is exactly what happened. In fact, they also led me to another Kramer branch in Florida that I had been unable to access.

Rule Number 3: *What goes around, comes around. One good deed begets another.*

Now I had information on five of the six Kramer branches; only one continued to elude me. Edwin Kramer had three children: Theresa, Bernice and George. Theresa and her husband had died childless. Bernice never married, was in her late 80s and, according to the doorman at her former residence, "had been whisked away to a senior citizen home by her relatives" some years earlier, with no forwarding address. I tried to find George, but the number of George Kramers in New York City was intimidating.

At this point, I was completing my work on the Atlanta Sterns, and the last person I spoke to said, "You know I have a sister?"

"What sister?" Of course, I knew nothing about her. I called the sister, who now lives in Kansas City. After collecting the information I needed from sister Julia, I promised to send her a copy of the family descendants chart and a photograph of the seven Kramer siblings.

A few hours later a telephone call came from a woman named Robin, also from Kansas City, who said that she was Julia's best friend. Julia had shown her the photograph I had e-mailed and Robin thought that one of the people in the photograph was her grandfather.

I thought for a minute and then said, "If your grandfather is in that picture, your father's name is George, and you have an Aunt Bernice." There was a stunned silence at the other end of the line.

"How could you possibly know that?"

"Easy," I replied. "If your grandfather is in the picture, that is the only possibility, because I know all the descendants of everyone else."

Robin and Julia had been best friends for eight years. Their children were good friends as well. Only now did Robin and Julia discover that they were second cousins. Imagine what it must be like to discover that your best friend is your second cousin!

Rule Number 4: *Serendipity is what happens when you least expect it.*

Sam Schleman is a retired management consultant who has been researching his Lithuanian and Hungarian roots for almost three years and has found 1,600 cousins so far. He and his wife, Margo, live in the Philadelphia area and were excited to recently add their first grandchild, Zachary, to the family tree.

Genealogical Research by Telephone
by Bonia Shur

Winter 1993

I knew from reading my father's autobiography, which he wrote in 1976 at the age of 84, that Anatoli, the eldest son of his older brother, Moisei Shur, might still be alive and residing in St. Petersburg, Russia.

I asked a cousin in Haifa, Israel, if she knew Anatoli's address. She replied that she did not know his address, but did remember the address of his father's apartment: The Island of Vasilii, Eighth Line Street 59 #14, St. Petersburg, Russia. She added that our uncle Moisei's wife, Mira, had died in Russia in 1942 and that Moisei had remarried a relative of hers. This fresh and solid information encouraged me to start a search for my mysterious cousin in Russia.

After returning home from my trip, I decided to attempt to find Anatoli Shur in St. Petersburg with the assistance of the telephone operator. I had an address, which is essential to finding a telephone number in Russia.

At the beginning of August [1993], I called the AT&T international operator for information in St. Petersburg. The operator asked me to spell the name of my party. I replied that the English spelling of my cousin's name was irrelevant since the Russian operator at the other end of the line would write it down in Cyrillic letters. I suggested that she allow me to communicate directly with the Russian operator since I speak Russian fluently. She agreed. She rang and immediately had a connection—a miracle in itself.

The AT&T operator made the initial connection and then let me take over and speak to her Russian counterpart while she remained on the line. I asked for the telephone number of Anatoli Shur. There was a long pause. Our waiting was accompanied by the continuous hum of radio waves beamed to earth from a satellite somewhere in space. About five minutes passed. Finally, the Russian operator returned and said to me in Russian:

"There is no Anatoli Shur in Petersburg. Do you know any other initials with your family name?" "No," I replied, "but I have the old address of his father, my uncle Moisei Shur. Perhaps the son is still living in his father's apartment?" (This is a common phenomenon in Russia.)

The operator asked me to wait and stay on the line. Suddenly, I became fearful that my AT&T operator might refuse to wait any longer. I had to do something to keep her occupied! So I did what I have always done in the past while waiting for AT&T operators to get an open line to Russia; I made a personal acquaintance with the operator.

"Do you always work the morning shift?" I asked her. "Yes," she answered. "For the last six years I have been working this shift." "You are lucky," I replied. "Do you happen to know Rhoda who got married a year or two ago?" I asked. "Yes, I know her," came the response. I was glad that she knew Rhoda out of the 700 to 800 operators who work in a huge building in Pittsburgh, Pennsylvania, where all AT&T international calls are processed.

"I talked to her," I said, "before her wedding. I asked her when she is going to make love to her husband since she worked the midnight shift." We both laughed. Time began to move faster. My fear of being cut off began to subside. "Are you married?" I began. Suddenly, the Russian operator returned.

"I called the apartment you gave me. It is a communal apartment complex where there is only one telephone for many residents. I already phoned the number I found, but there is no answer. Maybe in the evening after work somebody will answer the phone. If you wish to call there later, here is the number."

I thanked the operator and replied that, unfortunately, according to my cousin's information, my uncle moved out from that apartment and lived somewhere else. There was a pause. My AT&T operator asked me in English what was going on. I told her that the operator in St. Petersburg was still searching.

"Do you have any other initials with your surname? You have plenty of relatives in this city with the name of Shur." I thought for a moment. "Try M.K. Shur—Moisei Kusielevitch Shur," (my uncle and his patronymic name). Again, a pause. I resumed talking with the AT&T operator.

"My name is Bonia. What's your name?" "My name is Anita." "Are you married?" "No, I have been divorced for the past six years." "Really? Was it a painful separation?" "Yes, I broke up with my husband when my youngest child was only six months old." "This must have been hard."

Again, the voice of the Russian operator interrupted our chat. "There is nobody with such initials." At that moment, I thought that my attempt to find my cousin was a total fiasco. "Do you have a minute?" the Russian operator asked. "Yes," I answered. "I will call the Bureau of Addresses and ask for a Shur whose father's name is Moisei." "O.K.," I said, "I will be waiting." "By the way, what is your name, Operator? You are so nice to me." "My name is Tina." "I am glad to meet you."

I thought that this operator must be a genius. Knowing that Russians address each other by adding the father's name to the first name—Anatoli Moisei'yevitch—the son of Moisei, she was trying to locate my cousin. I looked at my watch; for more than 22 minutes the AT&T operator had been with me on the telephone!

"Do you have other children?" I asked Anita. "Yes, I have two daughters; one is 16, the other is 12. They are both with me. They cannot stand their father, who admitted to them that he doesn't know how to be a dad." "Do you have somebody you date?" This was a delicate question, but she was open with me and told me that she dated somebody and... We kept talking and I kept praying in my heart that a miracle would happen and that Tina, the Russian operator in St. Petersburg, would find my cousin, Anatoli. I looked at my watch again; 27 minutes had passed! Unexpectedly, Tina came back on the line.

"I have found only one person in St. Petersburg whose father's name is Moisei—Vladimir Moisei'yevitch Shur. Born in 1921. He resides on Seashore Street 17, #276, St. Petersburg. Telephone: 355-6545." Success, almost. The date of his birth was right, but the name Vladimir was unfamiliar. Never did my father mention such a name. I thanked both operators for their patience. The cost of the whole search—$3.00!

After I hung up, I immediately telephoned Ela Markuze in Haifa. I knew it was late—midnight in Israel, but the urge in me to confirm the information I had just received couldn't wait. I woke up Ela and, after apologizing for being so rude, I asked her if she recalled the name of Moisei Shur's son. She said that she did not. "If I mention a certain name, will it help you to recall?" I asked her. "Yes." "Vladimir." "Yes!" she exclaimed. "Volodia (a derivative of Vladimir). Now I remember."

Her confirmation lifted my spirit. Volodia in Yiddish is Vulf (Wolf), and Vulf Shur was my great-great-grandfather on my father's side. I called 011-7-812-355-6545. No answer. For the next three weeks, I kept calling every day, but there was no answer. I began to worry. Maybe he was on vacation, or perhaps he had been hospitalized, or maybe...he died.

The day I returned from Los Angeles after visiting my son, Ophir, I decided to try again to reach Vladimir Shur. I dialed. I waited. One ring. Two rings. Three. A voice said "*Dah*?" (meaning "yes" in Russian). I answered, "I am calling from America. I tried to reach you for the last three weeks." The voice on the other end replied, "During the summer months I stay in a village. I have come to town just for one day."

"Are you Vladimir Shur?" He answered, "*Dah*." "Was your father Moisei Shur, born in Griva, Latvia?" "*Dah*." "Was your mother, Mira, also born in Griva?" "*Dah*." "Then you are my cousin!" "How?" "I am Bonia Shur, the son of Yasha Shur." "You are the son of Yasha Shur!"

We talked for about 10 minutes; calling Russia is very expensive. As it turned out, he was the younger brother. His older brother, Anatoli, had been killed in the war in 1942 near the city of Stara'ya Rus, where I, too, was wounded during an offensive against the German army. His father, Moisei, had died in 1975. He was a retired radio engineer. I told him that while constructing my family tree, I had discovered him. He answered that he had made a family tree of his own, and he would send it to me. I promised to mail him my biography, photographs and letters, because he had not even known that I existed.

Two weeks later, I decided to check to see if my letters had reached my cousin. I again called St. Petersburg. A woman answered. She was Masha, my cousin's younger daughter from a second marriage. She is 34; her mother was Russian. I learned from her that Vladimir also had a 47-year-old daughter, Valeri, from his first marriage. She said that my registered mail had not yet arrived and that I should expect my letters to be delivered to them in a month or two. This was disappointing news.

Among the Rosh Hashanah greetings this year was a card from a friend, Beverly Gural, in Silver Spring, Maryland. For years, she has been singing in the Arts Chorale in Washington, DC. At the end of September, this group, with the National Orchestra, under the direction of Mstislav Rostropovitch, would be going to Russia to present concerts in commemoration of Tchaikovsky's 100th birthday. They would be in Moscow and St. Petersburg.

I suddenly had an idea. Why not speed up the process of getting acquainted with Vladimir and his family by asking Beverly to be a messenger of good will. Again, I telephoned my cousin's daughter. I asked what I could send with someone, something that doesn't take up much space. Does anyone in her family need medicine that is hard to find in Russia? Masha answered that her mother suffers from glaucoma. On the black market they pay $2.00 for a medicine called Pilocarpine, an enormous amount for them. I promised to see if it was available in the U.S. As it turned out, this medication needs a prescription from a doctor; in addition, it comes in different doses. Again, I called Masha, explained that considering the fact that I would need to have a prescription for the medicine, I had decided to send her money to purchase it in Russia. I said that my friend, Beverly Gural, would be coming to St. Petersburg at the end of September. She should meet her. She would have money for her and would also tell her about me, my family and my work.

When I began researching the roots of my family, I could not foresee that my family tree would bring me closer to my relatives and allow me to become a source of support and inspiration for them. Now I look forward to receiving Vladimir's family tree, pictures and information about the rest of my relatives in St. Petersburg. And who knows, maybe one day soon I may meet them.

Bonia Shur is a composer and director of liturgical arts at Hebrew Union College Jewish Institute of Religion in Cincinnati, Ohio. He was born in Latvia. During World War II, he fought with the Russian army against the Germans. After the war he immigrated to Israel and subsequently to the U.S.

Beware of Both
Documented and Oral Histories
by Manny Hillman

Summer 2004

AVOTAYNU readers probably have been told some family legends (oral history) that have turned out to be not entirely true or just plain wrong. The most dramatically erroneous legend I can recall was someone's belief that a grandfather was an only child—and it turned out that he had 17 siblings!

From stories like the one above, AVOTAYNU readers have learned to be wary of oral history, as have historians generally. However, as I shall show below, genealogists should adopt healthy skepticism not only for oral history in all of its phases, but toward all history. During my travels in eight countries along the Danube, Main and Rhine Rivers, I was left feeling that the people of many of these countries believe that the histories told or written by their neighboring countries are simply myths. Whom should one believe?

Oral History

My personal favorite is a story told by a cousin that (according to her mother and grandmother) her grandfather, Meyer, immigrated to Canada as a rabbi. He didn't like being a rabbi, so he shaved off his beard and never worked again. But documented history in the form of passenger lists and naturalization papers told quite a different story. After leaving Jerusalem in 1902, Meyer first went to Sheffield, England, where he lived for 18 months before emigrating directly from Liverpool to the United States. I found no evidence of an intermediate stop in Canada. Meyer arrived in Philadelphia, applied for citizenship in Pittsburgh and moved to New York City in time for the arrival there of the rest of his family in 1907.

Meyer

What about the beard, the rabbinate and never working? His nieces (my aunts) recall that he was the least religious of all of his brothers and sister, and they could not conceive of his being a rabbi at any time. They also reported emphatically that they worked for him in his factory where he manufactured ribbons for hats. He even invented the machine for that purpose.

Another family story is somewhat more complicated, and I have no documents to verify any part of this story. This one concerns another great-uncle, Chaim, a brother of Meyer. The first story I was told about Chaim was that he had left Jerusalem at age 19, leaving behind a wife and son, and went to Germany. There, starving, he was helped by priests and converted to Catholicism, later becoming a priest himself. Little by little, other parts of the story were disclosed to me. (Families ordinarily don't speak about skeletons in the closet.) Reportedly, Chaim later became a bishop in England. Even later, he left the church and went to visit his brother, Shlomo, who lived in Argentina.

The most religious members of the family didn't tell the story in this way. For them, Chaim had become irreligious and was disowned by his father who sat *shiva* (seven-day mourning period) for him. His mother, however, still read his letters. Finally, I was told about Chaim by Chasha Leah Feinberg Moron who actually knew him. Chasha Leah was the daughter of Chaim's brother, Shlomo, who lived in Montevideo, Uruguay (not Argentina). As a young bride, Chasha Leah went to visit her father, whom she had never met, although he had seen her when she was an infant. Her Uncle Chaim, the putative priest/bishop, also was living in Montevideo at the time of her visit. Her father would have nothing to do with his Christian brother, but when Chasha Leah learned of Chaim's existence, she went to see him and continued to do so. He had a German wife (which makes one wonder about his supposed Catholic priesthood), and his son from his former Israeli wife was

Chaim

living with them. Chaim was a pharmacist and taught English. Later, he left Montevideo and went back to England to be a journalist.

I have not managed yet to find any documents about Chaim in England or about his son who lived in New Jersey in the 1930s and was an artist. By coincidence, the cousin who had related to me my first story had met the artist when she was a child. [Since this article was first published, I encountered some relevant documents. One was a passenger list for Chaim and his wife, Anna, leaving England for Buenos Aires as missionaries. Another contained information that Shlomo died in Buenos Aires. Perhaps his death in Argentina was what led the family to believe that he lived there. It seems that new information always arises that either confirms previous knowledge or complicates matters.]

A Gray Area

Between oral history and documented history is a gray area that develops when someone puts oral history in written form. Books are written about family legends, and the books then are viewed as "documents." The problem of assessing validity becomes especially acute when genealogists rely on older manuscripts of this type, but no corroborating documents are available. It was largely on the basis of such sources, for example, that Rabbi Stuart Steinberg based a recent article about the Hillman family.[1] Rather than comment directly on Steinberg's arguments, I use my own research to illustrate some important problems inherent in such sources.

My ancestor, Yitzhak Michaslavitz (or Itzele Chaslavitzer), a member of the *Perushim* (disciples of the Vilna Gaon), settled in Safed, Israel, in 1809. Contemporaneous documents cited by Yaari[2] substantiate this event, but the earliest mention I can find of Yitzhak's family is in the 1839 Montefiore census which was compiled after Yitzhak had died. A book published in 1954 by Yishayahu Cheshin, entitled *Divrei Yishayahu* (The works of Yishayahu), includes a family history. According to Cheshin, Yitzhak Michaslavitz had two sons—Moshe, the progenitor of the Cheshin clan, and Yaakov, progenitor of the Soffer clan from whom I descend. (Actually, I know of three sons.)

Apparently the author of *Divrei Yishayahu* was unaware that his grandfather, Yitzhak Cheshin, had two wives. Cheshin writes extensively about his grandmother, the second wife, but never mentions the first wife, the mother of some of his uncles and aunts.

One way to understand the omission is to conclude that Yishayahu Cheshin did not know of the first wife's existence, because, if he had known, surely he would have written about her. Another argument could be that if a first wife had existed, Cheshin certainly must have heard about her. After all, he does mention one of her sons and one of her sons-in-law. Consequently, the argument goes, if he did not write about her, this must mean that she did not exist. The 1849 Montefiore census of the Jews of Palestine lists Ada Leah as the wife of Yitzhak Cheshin; the 1856 Montefiore census shows that his wife was Rachel Leah. I know that the Montefiore censuses incorporate many errors and initially concluded that Ada Leah must be an error in the 1849 census since *Divrei Yishayahu* does not mention her existence.

Some time later, while perusing every gravestone inscription in the book *Chelkat Michokek*, by Asher Leib Brisk, I came upon a gravestone for an Ada Leah, wife of Yitzhak Cheshin, who died in childbirth at age 24. Her child was buried with her. By that time, Ada Leah had four children.

What is the moral of this story? Just because we have not found evidence of a person or an event is not proof that such never existed.

Documented History

Many assume that written documents are more reliable than oral history. This

[1] AVOTAYNU Vol. XIX, No. 4 (Winter 2003): 27.

[2] Yaari, Avraham. *Zichronot Eretz Yisra'el*, Jerusalem, 1947.

is not my personal experience. I was always told that my father, Morris Hillman, was born in Graz, Austria. The family story holds that his mother, who was ill when pregnant with him, went to Graz for medical help and he was born there. This is the story that I grew up with, and I never questioned it, even though the rest of my Hillman family and my Moinester family came to the Americas from Jerusalem.

When I began to research the family history, I obtained copies of my father's documents and discovered that he had immigrated to the United States from Jerusalem in 1923 with an Italian passport rather than an Austrian one, because the Italian government took care of Austrian affairs in Palestine at that time. His name then was Moses Hillman. His father's name was given as Moses and his mother's name as Reizel. Strangely, her maiden name was listed as "Chescen" (rather than Soffer) which would be an Italian spelling of Cheshin. On the passport, his birthplace was given as Graz and his date of birth as January 18, 1901.

Morris Hillman

My father also carried two documents from the American consulate in Jerusalem. One repeated some of the information on the Italian passport, adding that the purpose of his trip was to work and gave the name of his sister, Annie Reises, as a reference. The other American document was a visa that contained only one piece of information about his background: that he was born in Austria.

My father left Haifa on July 2, 1923, aboard the *SS Madonna*, an Italian ship, and traveling in the first class section of the ship arrived in New York on August 1, 1923. According to my sister, the purpose of incurring the extra expense was to avoid a visit to Ellis Island. However, my cousin Goldie Shechter also arrived as a first class passenger and was sent to Ellis Island, because she had no money.

Passenger lists can be inaccurate sources of information. For example, my father was listed as an Italian national of the Hungarian "race or people" who resided in "Jerusalem, Palestine." Clearly, that was wrong—or so I thought at the time.

In June 1966, I made my first visit to Israel. In the course of conversation with an Israeli cousin, I mentioned that my father had been born in Graz. She thought that I must be either stupid or insane. She knew that my father had been born in Jerusalem four months after his father had died. Since my widowed grandmother was too poor to keep him at home, my father grew up in the Diskin Orphan Home, staying there until he was 16, visiting his mother on weekends. I also learned from my cousin that the forger of his passport later was caught.

When I returned home, I confronted my father with what I had learned, and he acknowledged all of it. I had always wondered why he was insistent on avoiding authorities like police and firemen; now the reasons for this characteristic and for his secrecy concerning his origins became clear. An intriguing part of this story was that some very close relatives did not know that my father had listed Graz as his birthplace on his American visa. When my father died, I listed his birthplace as Graz on his death certificate as a tribute to that part of his life that obviously had troubled him.

I knew one other person who had come to the United States on false papers. To the end of her life, this person insisted to her own children that she had been born in Germany even when her children knew that she had been born in Jerusalem. There are others about whom I have heard strong suspicions and, of course, there were all of the Chinese immigrants who were known as "paper sons."[3] These were Chinese immigrants who had purchased documents in China to establish that they were sons of American citizens of Chinese descent. What do their documents tell of their true genealogies?

The moral of these stories? Never believe any single family legend or any single document without reservations.

Manny Hillman was born in St. Louis and raised in Brooklyn. He has a BA in mathematics and a PhD in chemistry. Now retired, he is an incessant traveler (58 countries visited). He is married and has two sons.

---

[3] Chin, Tung Pok. *Paper Son: One Man's Story*. Philadelphia: Temple University Press, 2000.

Jewish Caricatures in Polish Vital Statistics Records

Spring 1990

Harold Perloff of New York submitted to AVOTAYNU the birth records below from the 1844 vital statistics register of Siedlice, Poland. Apparently a creative registrar sketched in the corner of the document the profile of the man recording the birth.

A Spoof on Jewish Surnames

Winter 2003

The following was written by an Austrian writer, Karl Emil Franzos, during the second half of the 19th century. It appears in Alexander Beider's forthcoming book, A Dictionary of Jewish Surnames from Galicia. *Dr. Beider notes that Franzos' spoof of the assignment of derogatory surnames to Jews was exaggerated.*

At a ball in Tarnopol in East Galicia where numerous Jewish dignitaries of the city were gathered, a young, unknown student was introduced to a lovely young woman, but he missed her name. During a quadrille, he allowed himself to ask about it. The pretty child looked at him sorrowfully and whispered blushingly: "Küsse mich!" (literally: Kiss me!) "You... You mean?" stuttered the young man. "Küsse mich!" she repeated somewhat louder. "Shh!" he whispered confused. "I... gladly... but..." "Nannette Küssemich," she repeated for the third time laughing. "I am the daughter of the businessman Abraham Küssemich."

The student took a deep breath, turned bright red and stole back to the quadrille. Not far from him sat a young Jewish girl, not of the educated class, but so pretty and round that he asked her to dance the next waltz. He stepped in front of her and, with a deep bow, introduced himself.

She sat up, flushed red and said clearly "Grober Klotz!" (literally: Rough block of wood)

"What?" he stuttered, confused.

"Grober Klotz!" she repeated, and aware of his amazement added, "Since you told me your name, I must introduce myself, too. My name is Sarah Groberklotz, and I am a daughter of the glazier, Ruben Groberklotz."

At the end of the second quadrille, the young man asked another young woman to dance—but because of his previous experiences, he did not did not wish to know her name. The woman was so spiritual and well educated, however, that he stayed at her side after the dance and eventually told her of his two previous experiences.

He was astounded that her laughing personality changed, and she said sharply, "That is cheap entertainment to interrogate people about their names. No person should actually do that. I would have taken you, sir, for a man with more tact."

As he began to apologize, she turned her back to him. He hurried over to the friend who had brought him to the ball and told him what happened. "Yes," the friend laughed. "After all, in a house where someone was hanged, you don't talk about a rope. The woman's name is Auguste Mist (dung or manure), born Wohlgeruch (good smell). She is a daughter of the rich landowner Adolph Wohlgeruch from Podolia."

People from Tarnopol told stories of this kind to visitors to their town. Whether or not all these stories are true, the four names that figure in this tale are not invented. The families Küssemich, Groberklotz, Mist and Wohlgeruch actually flourished in Austria and/or Podolia.

Holocaust

End of the Search
by Steven Byars

Winter 2006

After considerable genealogical success with my father's (Baptist) family, I tried to focus seriously on my mother's (Jewish) family. I did considerable work, with little success. Thinking that I needed to refine my techniques for doing Jewish genealogy, I bought several books to study and attended several of Gary Mokotoff's and Eileen Polakoff's week-long genealogy classes in Salt Lake City. I learned an awesome amount, but the results on my family were poor.

One day I was at a local Reno, Nevada, synagogue studying in its library. For some odd reason, I began to look through the books used by the synagogue's school kids. I found a history book and looked up my ancestral hometown of Turka, Ukraine. In two short paragraphs, the book related how the local Ukrainians helped the Nazis march all the town's Jews into the woods, murder them and then bury them in a common trench. Afterward, all the records about the Jews were collected—and burned.

The librarian later told me that she watched me sit there, staring at that book without moving for more than two hours. She was just getting ready to call for help when I laid the book down and walked out, leaving my notebooks, backpack and all it contained laying there. I never went back to get them. I knew all I was ever going to know about my mother's family.

Steven Byars has been working on his family's history since 1974. He has added new births and such to his Jewish line, but Europe is still lost to him.

A Note from a Train to Auschwitz
by Bernard I. Kouchel

Winter 1992

Some 80,000 Jews were deported from France to Auschwitz during the Holocaust. The letter, a portion of which is shown, was written by 54-year-old Lisa Kouchelevitz Rosenblum whose train left Drancy, outside Paris, on October 28, 1943.

It reads:

Wednesday

My Dearest: The day before yesterday I received your letter. I have no more strength to cry. Tomorrow, Thursday at 3 o'clock after midnight, they will finish us up. We are here 1000 people. Among us are many old people and small children. Where they are going to take us, we do not know.

My dearest Henri, Paulette, son, and my elderly mother. I clasp you to my heart. All of you should pray to G-d for me. I would like to live to see all my children. I am kissing all my family and all our good friends. I plead with you, do not go out any place, because every day new prisoners arrive. I do clasp you to my heart.

Do not forget Bernard Zalman and Esther and their son are also on the same train.

/s/ Lisa

According to the *Memorial to the Jews Deported from France*, by Serge Klarsfeld, Convoy #61 departed Drancy on October 28, 1943, and arrived at Auschwitz on October 30, 1943. Upon arrival, of the 1000 persons, 284 men and 103 women survived the selection. The remaining 613 were immediately gassed to death. One of them was Lisa Rosenblum.

Bernard Israelite Kouchel is founder of the Jewish Genealogical Society of Broward County (Florida), Kouchel has been associated with JewishGen for many years and was instrumental in initiating a number of JewishGen components including Tools, SIGs, InfoFiles, Sefard Forum and ViewMate. He was their Special Projects Manager and on the Board of Directors from 1989–2001. Holocaust victim Lisa Rosenblum is Kouchel's aunt. The letter was obtained from her son.

My Father Was Not an Orphan After All:
Building a Family Tree After the Holocaust
by Sara Wenger

Winter 2004

In 1988–89, I spent my junior year of college studying at the Hebrew University in Jerusalem. My "History of Eastern European Jewry" professor assigned, as a final paper, a family tree written within the historical context of what we had learned during the class. I found myself severely limited because I knew only the names of my grandparents and my father's birthplace (supposedly Łódź, Poland). I knew that my father had grown up in Hungary, after having moved there at a young age, and that he had survived Auschwitz as the sole remnant of his family.

Seeking more information, I called my father for additional details. Although he was always eager to answer my questions, I found a different voice on the other end.

"Why are you prying into my life?" he asked. "Stop asking me so many questions," was how the conversation ended.

I do not remember exactly what I wrote. All I remember is feeling deeply disturbed at not knowing the most basic facts of my family history.

The end of the course marked the end of my year abroad and concluded with a class trip to Poland and Hungary. During a break in our tour of Auschwitz, I took the opportunity, together with my twin sister, who had also spent the year at Hebrew University, to visit the camp archives. Knowing my father's tattoo number by heart, I submitted it to the clerk at the Auschwitz archives with the hope of obtaining some documented evidence that my father had, indeed, survived this G-d forsaken place.

The clerk produced several cards of data on my father. All the information confirmed what Dad had always told us—the city from which he was deported, the trade he made up and told the guards when he entered, and more. Much to our surprise, however, the name listed was completely and utterly different from the family name with which we had grown up and the first name by which we knew our father. The cards said Sandor Schweiger. We knew our father as Murray Kenig, which he had adapted from Moniac Koenig.

When we returned to Canada after this trip and approached our father, it immediately became clear that we had dug up a deep, dark, long-buried secret. The story he told us now was so matter-of-fact that we were sure he must be withholding information. According to our father, he had ended up in a displaced person's camp in Germany after the war. He tried to enter British-mandated Palestine, but was refused. Desperate to leave Europe, he heard that Canada was accepting a limited number of war orphans. The guidelines stipulated that the orphan be no older than 18. Dad was already 20, but he managed to obtain illegal papers providing him with the identity of a younger survivor from Poland, which enabled him to apply to enter Canada. Early in 1948, he arrived in Canada—to a new home and a new language—with a new identity. He never told anyone his real background.

Upon our inadvertent discovery, my sister and I were sworn to secrecy. Our father implored us, "You can tell whomever you want after I die, but as long as I am alive, please don't tell anyone!"

We could not understand the need for such secrecy. After all, the actions he had taken were entirely understandable. Nonetheless, we respected his request and kept his secret.

When my father died seven years ago [1998], genealogical research seemed beyond my grasp. I told myself that one day I would have the time to go to Hungary and research my father's life and the lives of his family members. I thought that research could only be done there. The opportunity arose in an unexpected fashion—via the Internet and e-mail.

A year ago [2003], I started to poke haphazardly around the Internet, armed with the most basic information on the Schweiger family (my father's true surname) from Kiskunfelegyhaza, Hungary. I quickly found the Internet sites that became the pillars of my

CANADIAN CITIZENSHIP is a cherished possession of Murray Kenig, 20, who will participate in "I Am a Canadian Day" ceremonies, Sunday. A DP, death missed him by inches in several German concentration camps during the war. On his arm is tattooed his camp number.

Photo (1950) of author's father taken from a Canadian newspaper.

research. The Nevek-Klarsfeld database on Hungarian Jewry (www.neveklarsfeld .org) held a deportation record for my grandfather that revealed the maiden name of his mother!

I subscribed to the JewishGen Digest, and a fellow researcher in Salt Lake City spent much time and effort voluntarily researching for me the vital records of my family's town in Hungary. In the span of a few weeks, I had started to build a family tree and had names of uncles, aunts and great-grandparents, none of whom previously were known to me.

With few expectations, I e-mailed a request to Yad Vashem's Hall of Names—the repository for Pages of Testimony on Holocaust victims submitted by surviving family or friends. While I waited for the museum to mail me any Pages that may have been entered for the Schweiger family from Hungary, several family members and friends asked what I hoped to achieve by this research. One person even suggested that all I would find would be "dead people." My answer was that I knew my father's entire family had been murdered, but we didn't know who they were. The least we could do as their surviving descendants, I reasoned, would be to know their names.

I was totally unprepared for what came next—an envelope from Yad Vashem with 30 Pages of Testimony. Five of these pages fit the details of my family. My grandfather and grandmother were among those persons memorialized. I scanned to the bottom of the page and saw that a nephew named Moshe Fisher living in Haifa had submitted the information. I quickly calculated that he was my father's first cousin. Having grown up with the belief that my father was the only one of his family who had survived, I was in total and utter shock.

I frantically tried to find this individual. Having no success, I turned to a professional. Within hours she gave me the unfortunate news that Moshe Fisher was no longer alive, but she also supplied contact information for his widow. After an emotion-filled discussion with his wife, I also connected with his two daughters, my second cousins.

My research had reached a point that I never had expected in my wildest dreams, and I clearly realized the potential of the Yad Vashem database as a genealogical tool. I went to Yad Vashem several times in person in order to find more Pages. Through the Pages that I found, I directly and indirectly located cousins in Australia, Canada, Hungary, Israel, Romania and the United States. I found two women in Israel who remembered my father from grade school in their small town. One of these women even sent me a picture of their first grade class. Another woman had shared an apartment with my grandmother in the ghetto and remembered clearly her climbing into the cattle cars upon their deportation to Auschwitz.

I was on a mission, and the obsession was all-consuming, always hoping that I would find just one more piece of information. My dream was to locate a relative who actually had known my father before the war. All of the cousins I had found so far were children of the previous generation and had very little first-hand knowledge. I became overwhelmed with the intensity of the research. Every phase was filled with yet another once-in-a-lifetime finding.

I began a dialogue by e-mail with Robbie, my newly found cousin in Romania. Having only one picture of my grandfather and another of my grandmother, I asked cousin Robbie to send me any pictures he had, and I was fascinated to receive numerous scanned photos by e-mail. I froze as I scrolled down to one of the last pictures. The woman in the picture whom I was staring at on my computer screen was the same woman in the only picture that my father had of his mother. I had recently been pondering what was written on the back of that original photo. I just had it translated, and the inscription implied that it was not actually his mother. Though cousin Robbie also didn't know who she was, the name on the back of his picture, together with my research from the LDS (Mormon) Family History Library, allowed me to identify her as an aunt. The fact that my cousin and I both had a picture of the same person in our possession and lived halfway around the world from each other dispelled any doubts as to our true relationship.

After a couple of months of researching the Schweiger family, I wanted to switch efforts to my grandmother's side—but I did not know her maiden name. I commissioned a professional researcher in Budapest who dug through the Kiskunfelegyhaza newspapers from the few years before my father's birth. In the June 1926 edition, he found an engagement announcement for my grandparents. Ferenc Schweiger was to be married to Rozalia Katz in Kecskemet, February 1926.

With two months of genealogical experience behind me, it didn't take long to put my grandmother's family together. Always having identified with my father as an orphan and an only child even before the war, it was hard to grasp the magnitude of the facts unfolding before me. My grandmother was one of nine children with between 20 and 30 aunts and uncles. Theirs had been a huge and prominent family.

I returned to Yad Vashem to find yet more Pages of Testimony of cousins. This time, however, the results were closer to what I had wanted. Alive in Budapest, Hungary, I found Istvan Katai (née Katz), my father's first cousin. Dad apparently had spent summers with Istvan when they were children. After the deportations and the war, they never saw each other again. Istvan had assumed that his cousin did not return from Auschwitz. It was at this point that the realization hit hard. My father had died an orphan at the age of 70, never having reconnected with any of the family members I was currently locating.

As fate would have it, Istvan turned out to be an avid genealogist! On the beautiful handwritten family tree he sent me, our branch ended with my father. After corresponding with me, he was pleased to continue my father's branch and add 15 new leaves. In addition to the tree, Istvan also sent a priceless family photograph, one that illustrates the greatness of this huge family. At the head of the table sat Uncle Aharon Katz, Chief Rabbi of Budapest, 1935.

When I was growing up, a search to find surviving relatives of my father was never discussed. Dad apparently had applied to the Red Cross after the war and came up empty-handed. It was an accepted fact that no one but him had survived. Perhaps Dad didn't want to continue looking, for psychological reasons, or perhaps, because of his new identity, he was afraid of being sent back if his real name were discovered. It is impossible to know his reasons. What is obvious, however, is that modern technology allowed me to do in six months what my father would not have been able to achieve in 60 years. Online databases, e-mail and the Internet in general were my main tools for putting together a family about which I previously had known absolutely nothing.

Looking back on my research, the printed words of Avotaynu's *Getting Started in Jewish Genealogy* ring loud in my ears:

> Two major events shaped Jewish life of the past two hundred years: migration and the Holocaust. Few Jews today live where their ancestors lived a century or two ago. As a result many Jews believe they cannot trace their family roots because:
> · My family name was changed
> · No one in my family knows about the past
> · No one is left alive to tell me about my family's past
> · All the records were destroyed in the Holocaust
> · My town was wiped off the face of the map

Every one of the myths above applied to me until just over a year ago [2003]. Having started my search with the wrong family name and country, and having no one alive to give me any direction, I succeeded in building a family tree with the names of hundreds of individuals and in making contact with new/old relatives all over the globe. The fulfillment in discovering who my descendants were, as far back as 200 years, has been an experience unparalleled in my lifetime.

Sara Wenger has been actively researching her family history since October 2003. She became interested in genealogy when she discovered that her father, a Holocaust survivor, had changed his name and identity to gain entry to Canada after the war. Her research has led her to information resources and family in Hungary, Canada, Israel, Australia, Romania and America. Her most recent research resulted in tracing her mother's family back almost 300 years through England and originally Holland. She is Director of Administration of ATZUM Justice Works in Jerusalem and lives in Beit Shemesh, Israel, with her husband and four children.

Closing the Circle:
A Personal Encounter with the Holocaust
by Randy Daitch

Winter 1995

O n a June day this year in the nation's capital, I visited the U.S. Holocaust Memorial Museum for the first time and closed a circle whose starting point had been a June day in Jerusalem 14 years earlier. I had traveled then to Israel on the assumption that I could find there some surviving remnant of the European branch of my father's family, which had been torn so savagely from the tree of life.

I did not grow up with a personal connection to the Holocaust. My grandfather and his six siblings had arrived in the United States before World War I. We con-sidered ourselves a family untouched by that terrible destruction. We mourned for the six million, but from a distance. Still, I knew there were names, inseparable links to the shared destiny of our family, wait-ing to be found.

On frequent visits to Southfield, Michi-gan, I would badger relentlessly my great-uncle, Max, the last surviving link to the "world of our fathers." Occasionally, his memory would yield a diamond.

"Where did Cousin Charlie come from?" I once asked. "Bildzhuis," came the unex-pected reply. I looked at a map of Russia and saw for the first time the tiniest speck of a village, Bildyugi, where Charlie Deitch had lived.

Just before I left for Israel, I nudged my great-uncle one more time. "Grandpa had an uncle," I declared, without really know-ing. "What was his name?" Max's memory took the bait. "Chaim Noson," he replied. "He lived in Bildzhuis."

Sonya and Lozer Daitch

My arrival in Israel was followed by a series of fortuitous contacts that led me to Henya, a Brooklyn woman on vacation in Jerusalem, who had grown up in Bildzhuis. I told her I was looking for relatives from her village, descendants of Chaim Noson Daitch. She listened with interest but had no specific information.

A short while later, I spoke again to Henya by telephone. This time she had news for me. Our conversation had reminded her of Ettel, a Jerusalem resident, whose father had been a family friend in Bildzhuis. Ettel had immigrated to Palestine as a teenager in 1939, but the rest of her family had remained in Byelorussia.

Suddenly, Henya remembered that Ettel's maiden name had been Daitch! Quickly telephoning her friend, she asked a simple question and received a heart-stopping reply: "My grandfather's name was Chaim Noson." She was my father's second cousin.

On greeting me, Ettel declared that I had the face of her grandfather. During the coming months, we had several opportunities to visit, and she shared with me the names of my father's cousins who had been slaughtered near her village. Her father, Berl, and mother, Chai-Tsirl; her brother, Lozer, and his wife, Sonya; and her nephews and niece, Chaim Noson, Eizyk, Hirshela and Nisa Beila.

On June 29, 1995, at the close of the 1995 Summer Seminar on Jewish Genealogy in Washington, DC, I entered the archive room of the U.S. Holocaust Memorial Museum to look at microfilmed records of the Extraordinary Soviet Commission of Inquiry. This was organized after World War II to document—town by town, village by village—the names of Soviet citizens who had died at the hands of the Nazis.

I located the reel that included the region where my grandfather had lived. Among the many documents on that reel was a list in Cyrillic script, several pages long, headed by the words: "Village: Bildyugi; Township: Sharkovshchina; Province: Polotsk."

On page 3 of that list, I found the names that pulled at my heart, echoing the words of my late cousin 14 years before:

Daitch, Lozer Berkovich, 1895
Daitch, Sonya Chaimovna, 1900
Daitch, Chaim Leizerovich, 1922
Daitch, Eizyk Leizerovich, 1925
Daitch, Girsha Leizerovich, 1929
Daitch, Beila Leizerovna, 1935
Daitch, Gorka Chaimovich, 1875
Daitch, Chaya Simonovna, 1875

Absorbing the names with my eyes, I could feel the circle closing. A family, at last, had been buried.

Randy Daitch, has been an "Ask the Experts" columnist for AVOTAYNU since 1985. A co-creator of the Daitch-Mokotoff Soundex System, he worked from 1996–2003 as historical geography researcher for Steven Spielberg's Shoah Foundation in Los Angeles. He made aliyah to Israel in 2004, where he continues to do genealogical research.

The Lady in the Vienna Telephone Book
by Arye Barkai
Winter 1987

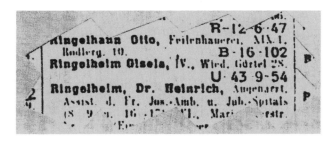

I have always been fascinated by my great-grandmother's maiden name: Ringelheim. If a surname does not pertain to an occupation (Schwartz, Schneider), to an ancestor (Levi, Cohen), or a place name (Kalish, Wilner), there is a good chance everyone with that surname may have a genealogical connection.

Such is the case with the name Ringelheim. Everyone with that surname I have located has roots within an area 50 kilometers from Rzeszów in Galicia.

Unlike family names adopted from larger towns, Ringelheim is named after a very small town in northern Germany—a town so small it was incorporated into Salzgitter. For some reason, no other family, Jewish or Gentile, now uses this place name. (The Counts of Ringelheim died out in the Middle Ages.) As a consequence, I have used every possible source of surnames to locate Ringelheims: census indexes, birth, marriage and death indexes and telephone books.

The New York Public Library annex has, on microfilm, pre-World War II telephone books from many major cities in Europe.

I found her name in the 1937 telephone book of Vienna: Gisela Ringelheim, IV Bezirk-Weidgurtel 25. Who was she? Was she the Gitel Rachel Ringelheim I found in the Tarnów birth records at the Mormon library (born 6 September 1867)? My own great-grandmother was born Gitel Ringelheim.

I asked Dr. Henry (Hoenig) Ringelheim, an opthamologist born in Jarosław, Galicia, who lived in Vienna from the early 1900s until the *Anschluss*, if he knew of this Gisela Ringelheim. Despite his curiosity about his surname, he was never curious about the Ringelheim listed next to his name in the telephone book.

At the Library of Congress in Washington, DC, I went through the Viennese telephone books of the 1930s. She lived at the same address during this period. The 1939 edition had a swastika on its cover. I imagined the terror Gisela may have felt during this time.

I wrote to the *Stadtarchiv* of Vienna hoping to get information about a woman who almost certainly was one of my genealogical cousins. I also sent a letter to the Jewish community of Vienna. Both addresses are listed in Dan Rottenberg's *Finding Our Fathers.*

At about that time, I planned a trip to Galicia to do more on-site genealogical research. Since I also planned to make a stop in Czechoslovakia, my travel agent gave me what is called an "open jaw" itinerary; New York to Warsaw to Vienna and back to New York.

For me, the lure of Vienna was not its pastries but more information on Gisela Ringelheim. When I arrived, I tried to locate Gisela's home but became lost in an area of factories and canals. Any attempt to find information about her was unsuccessful.

When I returned to New York, I found a response to my letter to the *Stadtarchiv*. They had no information about Gisela Ringelheim. Sometime later, I received a reply from the Jewish community in Vienna. They told me Gisela was born 27 January 1877, birthplace unknown. She was deported from Vienna on 5 June 1942.

The neighbor who translated the letter for me cried as she read it. Her own mother was deported three days earlier. I imagined the horror of the Viennese Jews, forced from their homes where they lived in comfort for many years into the crowded, windowless cattle cars.

To this day, I still do not know how Gisela Ringelheim is related to me. This story is written so that others will know that once there lived at IV Bezirk-Weidgurtel in Vienna a lady named Gisela Ringelheim.

Arye Barkai, a retired caseworker worked for the New York City Department of Social Services. By interviewing his grandmother when he was a teenager as well as later interviewing many European-born relatives before they passed on, he assembled his Ringelheim family tree from just a few names to a tree containing a 35-page closely printed genealogy.

How (and Why) I Wrote a Yizkor Book
by Michael Nevins

Winter 1990

$\mathbf{M}$y first efforts at exploring family origins were conventional, but atypically evolved eventually into a self-published booklet commemorating the *shtetl* my grandparents had emigrated from nearly a century ago.

My father's parents had died several years before I became interested in genealogy. When I began my research in 1979, I was appalled at how little I knew about their lives. In due course, I discovered an elderly relative living in Miami who, although in frail health, had a scholarly and retentive mind. He served as a primary source of information about my grandparents, as well as of the Polish-Russian *shtetl*, Dąbrowa Białystocka, (Dubrowa, in Yiddish) from which he too had emigrated.

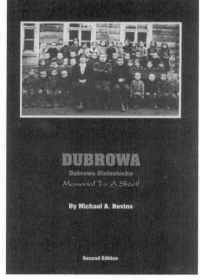

As a result of our correspondence and telephone discussions, my perspective gradually shifted from my own family to that of their community. I reasoned that if I concentrated exclusively upon our family, I was unlikely to gather much more material. I might learn far more about our background by widening my scope.

Early on, I was envious of what appeared to be the good fortune of others, who, in exploring their roots, had made startling discoveries with apparent ease. It became clear, however, that one makes one's own luck through perseverance. The search began with the usual sources familiar to Jewish genealogists: encyclopedias; LDS Family History Library records; and YIVO, the institute for Jewish research in New York, but Dąbrowa was elusive, and, except for its presence on detailed maps, it seemed almost as if, like Brigadoon, it had never really existed.

After World War II, hundreds of *landsmanshaftn* (town societies) had written *yizkor* (memorial) books to record their communities' histories, but no such document had ever been written for our *shtetl*. The Chevra Bnei Rabbi Menachem Mendel Anshei Dąbrowa had been formed in New York in 1892 and flourished for decades, but as its members aged, the organization lost its vitality. Now, only a few elderly survivors and their children continue to meet sporadically and supervise the *chevra's* (society's) burial plots in Brooklyn and Queens cemeteries.

The thought of writing a memorial began to take shape. Obviously, any attempt by me to write a *yizkor* book would lack the authenticity of a native's account. On the other hand, by virtue of my general history reading, I might be able to provide a more objective perspective. Also, since I would be writing in English, my effort would be more accessible for general readers, since most *yizkor* books are in Yiddish or Hebrew.

This became my self-appointed task. If the project began tentatively, I gradually felt an increasing sense of obligation, indeed urgency, knowing that if I did not complete the job, very likely it would not be done at all. To provide a detailed account of all the minor tragedies and triumphs involved in compiling Dąbrowa's story would require as much space as the final 38-page booklet itself.

Two factors critical to the project's modest success should be mentioned. First, after several frustrating years, I obtained several general articles about the town from both the Public Library in Warsaw and from the U.S. Library of Congress. When translated from Polish, these provided details of Dąbrowa's early history, as well as something of its post-World War II fate.

Secondly, the substance of the book was derived from detailed oral or written histories of seven émigrés whom I tracked down through the *chevra kadisha* (burial society). Their combined experience spanned the period from about 1900 through the Holocaust. Through extreme good fortune, during a trip to Israel, I located the town's only survivor of the German occupation, Sonia Grabinsky Lefkowitz, whose personal story was extraordinary and deeply moving. Along with a few hundred Jews from Dąbrowa, she was transported to Treblinka in 1942. There she worked in a laundry, but escaped to the forest in 1943 and was one of only about 40 survivors of the more than 800,000 Jews brought to Treblinka. After the war, she was among a handful of Jews who returned to Dąbrowa. One was killed by Polish townspeople; she and the others escaped to Israel.

The manuscript was published in 1982 by a friend who specializes in small projects such as this (Alvin Schultzberg, Town House Press, 552 Farrington Post, Pittsboro, NC 27312). Only one day after publication, a woman noticed a copy of the new booklet while attending my publisher's Passover seder. She expressed amazement. For years, she had been trying unsuccessfully to get details about the town since her husband's grandfather had come from the same Dąbrowa Białystocka. On page 32, she found the only English-language list available of the community's Holocaust martyrs included the name of her relative!

My own elderly relative, who had been the original inspiration for the project and to whom it is dedicated, died shortly before publication. When his family entered his apartment to gather his belongings, they found that he must have been reviewing the manuscript shortly before his death.

The booklet was distributed to many Jewish libraries and archives, and, in due time, letters of acknowledgement arrived promising that Dąbrowa's story would be preserved along with those of hundreds of other *shtetls* and, therefore, would not be lost to history.

Three years ago, the Schlachter sisters, Rena Holstein and Lillian Gritz, both of whom had escaped before the war and now live in Silver Spring, Maryland, revisited Dąbrowa. They found no recognizable houses. Upon their return to the United States, they vowed to raise money to restore Dąbrowa's despoiled Jewish cemetery and to erect a suitable monument. To date, they have been able to raise only about half of the $20,000 needed to complete the task. Anyone interested in contributing, please write: Mrs. Rena Holstein, 403 Irwin Street, Silver Spring, MD 20901.

Poignant experiences, such as those described here, are among the special rewards that await other Jewish genealogists who may be seeking fresh avenues along which to channel their research. I found the memorial book project so gratifying that it inspired me to embark on other historical studies concerning the origins of Jewish painting and the early practice of medicine in Eastern Europe. No, I have not yet visited Dąbrowa, but hope to do so someday, particularly if plans for a monument are realized.

Inspired by his experience in writing the Dąbrowa memorial book, Dr. Michael Nevins went on to study, write and lecture about shtetl medical care. He then expanded his research further to encompass Jewish medical history at other times and places. Eventually, he published four books on various aspects of this subject, the last, Jewish Medicine: What It Is and Why It Matters, *in 2006. Currently, Dr. Nevins serves as Medical Director at Bergen Regional Medical Center, Paramus, New Jersey. He lives in Rivervale, New Jersey, and has three married children and seven grandchildren.*

Epilogue

The sisters Rena Holstein and Lilly Gritz single-mindedly raised money and overcame bureaucratic obstacles until their mission to restore Dąbrowa's Jewish cemetery was accomplished. Construction of an enclosing wall, entrance gate and memorial stone was supervised by Lilly and Rena's high school friend Jan Jarjecki, a Righteous Gentile. In the summer of 1995, a small group from the United States, Israel and Poland participated in a moving rededication of the cemetery. This was described in a second edition of my *yizkor* book which was published in November 2000.

Peretz Amsel (1898–1942):
One Man's Holocaust
by Melody Amsel-Arieli

Winter 1998

M y grandfather and two of his brothers emigrated to America from Strop-kov, Slovakia, in the early 1900s. They left behind a widowed father, three sisters and their youngest brother, Peretz. In time, the girls married, moved out of the house and raised families of their own. When Peretz married Mirl Schwartz, however, the couple remained in his father's home, taking over the farm work and running the family tavern. Peretz raised wheat for their bread, vegetables for their table and hay for the cows. He sold liquor to Gentiles who passed through on their way to the Stropkov weekly market. By 1942, the family included four children—Ruzenka, Sara, Samuel and the youngest, Izidor.

In March 1942, the German deportations from Slovakia began. The family was torn apart. At the Yad Vashem Archives in Jerusalem, I found lists showing that Ruzenka, age 18, was taken to Auschwitz on March 24, 1942, part of a girls' transport from Stropkov.[1] Her mother, Mirl, the three other children, and her 80-year-old grandfather were taken together on Shabbat, the second day of Shavuot, May 23, 1942.[2] No Stropkov list, however, showed the name of Ruzenka's father, Peretz Amsel.

Hoping to learn more, I sent what little information I had—Peretz Amsel, born in Strop-kov on November 23, 1898—to the Interna-

Mirl and Peretz Amsel

tional Tracing Service in Bad Arolsen, Germany. Peretz appeared in two entries:

> *AMSEL, Pavel (a variant of Peretz), born in 1898, last place of residence: Stropkov, Jew, was evacuated with the II Transport from Zilina to an unknown destination on March 31, 1942*

Zilina, on the Polish border some 150 kilometers east of Stropkov, was a way

---

[1] File M5/117, Transport 24.3.1942, Yad Vashem Archives, Jerusalem, Israel.
[2] File M5/117, I Transport, 23.5.1942, Yad Vashem Archives.

station for thousands of Slovakian Jews on their journey north. Arriving by cart, truck or bus, Jews were often concentrated here for several days until the optimal number of "pieces"—1,000 Jews—filled the cattle cars to capacity. Perhaps Peretz had arrived here on a transport from Stropkov that had fewer than 1,000 people. Survivors from Stropkov confirmed this for me. A week after the girls' transport left on March 24, 1942, a second transport of young men was taken.

At the Yad Vashem Archives, the transport list from Zilina, dated March 30, 1942, showed the name Peretz Amsel among the very first entries.[3] From the birth dates beside the names, I saw that the men ranged in age from 16 to 40-plus. Peretz, the farmer, must have been lean and healthy. He was among the oldest taken that day, 41 years old.

The second entry sent by the International Tracing Service shows:

AMSEL, Paul (another variant of Peretz) born in Stropkov on 23.11.1898, occupation: farmer, was committed to Concentration Camp Auschwitz on 30th June, 1942, Prisoner's No: 43888

According to Danuta Czech,[4] a transport with 400 Jews did indeed arrive at Auschwitz from Majdanek on June 30, 1942, and the prisoners were given numbers 43833 through 44232. So Peretz, whose number was 43888, must have been one of them. I understood that if Peretz was given a number, if he were not gassed immediately, he arrived healthy enough to work. But Czech notes that of the 400 men who arrived in that transport, only 208 were still alive six weeks later.

Ruzenka Amsel, Peretz's 18-year-old daughter and the only survivor of the family, had been in Auschwitz for three months when her father arrived. Somehow he learned where she was, and he managed to smuggle her a note, writing that he was sitting, cutting logs. Ruzenka knew that only men with swollen legs, only men unable to work much longer, sat in that place cutting logs. I wrote to the Auschwitz Museum (which is actually an archives) asking for confirmation of all the facts relating to Peretz. I received confirmation and more. I received the date of Peretz' *yahrzeit*, the date of his

Sura, Shia, and Ruzenka as young children. Only Ruzenka survived.

[3] File M5/110, Zilina II Transport, 1105-2217, 30.3.1942, Yad Vashem Archives.
[4] Czech, Danuta, *Auschwitz Chronicle 1939–1945* (London: Tauris, 1990), 189.

death.

I was unbelievably lucky in my research. While millions perished nameless and forgotten, unaccountably, the last tortuous months of Peretz's life had been documented—from Stropkov to Zilina to Majdanek to Auschwitz. Peretz Amsel died in Auschwitz on August 27, 1942.

Still, even with the documentation, I did not have a sense of Uncle Peretz, the man. So I traveled to Stropkov, walked the streets of his town, stood where his house and farm had been, and spoke with the people who had been his neighbors. "Ah, Peretz," each said, smiling, "a wonderful man, so calm, so good, so fair... a man of gold." Although nearly 60 years had passed since they had last visited with him, spoken with him and worked with him, his neighbors remembered him with love.

Then my research took a completely unexpected turn. A JewishGen friend who also is researching eastern Slovakia mentioned the book *I Cannot Forgive*,[5] noting that it is an autobiography of a Slovakian Jew who had been in Auschwitz, like my uncle. Rudolf Vrba, the author, was one of two men who succeeded in escaping from Auschwitz, traveling back to Slovakia through Zilina, and first alerting the world to the ultimate fate of the Jews in that camp.

While reading the book, I noticed many similarities between Vrba's experiences and those of Uncle Peretz. Both Vrba and Peretz were from Slovakia, both were transported through Zilina, both were interned in Majdanek. According to Vrba, at Majdanek a request was made for farmers to step forward. On June 30, 1942, those men who identified themselves as farmers were transported to Auschwitz. Rudolf Vrba was among them. So was Peretz.

Not long after reading the book, I was startled to find a letter written by Rudolf Vrba himself on the H-Holocaust Mailing list on the Internet, complete with his e-mail address! I e-mailed him:

> Dear Dr. Vrba,
>
> I am very excited to find your letter in my mailbox via the H-Holocaust Mailing List! I have read your book I Cannot Forgive. Do you remember my uncle Peretz (Paul, Pavel) Amsel of Stropkov, Slovakia? He was incarcerated at Majdanek sometime after March 31, 1942. Then on June 30, 1942, he was moved to Auschwitz, where he was given the number 43888—and stated that his profession was "farmer."
>
> I remember in your book that the Nazis were looking for farmers then and there. He died in Auschwitz on August 27, 1942, according to the records. Peretz was approximately forty years old, with a wife and four children, a simple, good man.
>
> Perhaps he was with you?

Vrba answered immediately:

---

[5] Vrba, Rudolf, *I Cannot Forgive* New York: Bantam Books (by arrangement with Grove Press), 1964.

Dear Ms. Amsel,

Many thanks for your kind message. My number in Auschwitz was 44070, which is quite close (to) his number 43888 and so we certainly were in the same group during the Auschwitz registration. That group which came from Maidanek on June 30, 1942, consisted of 400 men including me and I think perhaps half a dozen survived; those I remember. The dead were so many not even an encyclopedic mind could remember them all. I am sure I must have seen your uncle at that time, and as he is not with us I share with you the loss.... B'acharet Hayamim (the end of days, when the Messiah arrives)..... In any way we all promised to one another that whoever survives will transfer the greetings and blessings from their dear dead. Thank you for giving me an opportunity to do so!

Rudolf Vrba

The words seemed to echo through the years. Peretz spoke once more.

Melody Amsel-Arieli, who lives in Maaleh Adumim, Israel, is a professional flutist, teacher, avid genealogist and freelance writer. She is the author of Between Galicia and Hungary: The Jews of Stropkov *(Avotaynu, 2002).*

How Far Should a Genealogist Go?
by Karen Roekard
Summer 2007

To get to the memorial for the Jews in Rawa Ruska, Ukraine, you have to leave the town center by the road that goes past what used to be the old stucco school, walk alongside the railroad tracks that took the Jews to their deaths at Belzec, double back over the potholed dirt road past the farmers' barns and then go through the empty field.

"There," my guide and I were told, "you will find it."

What we ended up finding were random pieces of Hebrew-lettered gravestones, the clearest of which had only one word on it—*niftar*—the Hebrew for "died." Truly, I thought, it has all died, gone, not even reminders of dead Jews here.

The second time we searched, we went all the way through the field, right up to the edge of the forest. In the distance, through the trees and across the river, was a glinting object, a small Jewish star atop a ten-foot high pole, the standard bearer for about 30 gravestones. Some were standing, most lay piled face down; some were whole, most broken—the memorial. The stones cover a mound which covers the pit into which Jews fell after they were shot. "A mass grave," my guide said, translating the farmer's words. I lit a candle and recited prayers for the dead, among them my namesake grandmother and aunts who probably died there.

Adjacent to this burial mound are the remains of the new Jewish cemetery, a place to which these ancestors would go before Yom Kippur to light candles of remembrance for some of their ancestors (now our ancestors). On the third trip, I tread carefully through the cemetery/field. The ground was lumpy and pockmarked with strange, human-sized, under-

Local residents still dig holes in the abandoned Jewish cemetery looking for gold among the graves.

ground, gopher-highway-like ridges. One even had a foot-wide cave's hole opening, which yawed its way into the earth on the diagonal.

"They still dig for Jews' gold," my guide told me when I asked her what it was, "and the locals are stealing stones from the memorial."

We met with an official of the town. I told her that I wanted to lift the gravestones at the memorial and collect the information chiseled on them, so that the names of these last few Jews will not be lost to history. Back and forth my guide and the official had words; back and forth with an intensity that was almost like native Yiddish speakers.

Finally the translation: She said, "Lifting the stones at the memorial might be possible, but the street in front of this building is paved with gravestones from the Old Jewish Cemetery, under a thin layer of dirt. The town wants to repave but not over the Jewish stones." After a pause, my guide added, "She said that it is the Jews' responsibility to take away the gravestones. The Jews should want to do this. And you will have to pay to repave the road."

I felt an instant urge to say, "The Jews' responsibility? What Jews?" I wanted to insist that we go speak with the town's non-existent Jewish community and tell the members about their responsibility that now, 65 years after being forced to be the slave labor that dragged these stones to this street, before being murdered, now it is their responsibility to remove them, or my responsibility as their descendant.

Young boys turning over a Jewish tombstone used to pave a road in Rawa Ruska.

"Why don't you tell it like it is?" I thought. "Don't imply that it's about being respectful. You just see an opportunity: if we take out the gravestones, you can properly grade your road or maybe even get us to build it for you!" I numbly allowed her to take me downstairs to the street where some boys turned over a piece of gravestone upon which the writing was still in good condition.

"The Nazi in charge lived there," she said, pointing to a very fancy house for a fairly poor town. "He paved with the gravestones to make it easier to get home."

We were all being polite. The rational, multi-cultural, Berkeley voice in my brain insisted that I must have misunderstood her suggestion, and it was likely just some cultural difference. My inner-genealogist shouted, "Stones from the Old Cemetery; the Old Cemetery! Maybe you'll find the 18th-century gravestone of Reb Sholom, your ancestor who 'loaned' money to the Kaiser and was given a one-generation title of 'Baron' in repayment! Maybe you'll find it intact?"

I asked, "If I figure out a way to get funding to lift the stones, where would they go?"

Now she was silent

"I can't take them back to California." The guide didn't translate my inner cynic's words.

"To the memorial with the other stones," she replied.

"Not there," I said. "That's too hard to get to, and gravestones are being stolen. If you find another place, I'll work to get funding."

We shook hands. I left them and could not stop pondering: During World War II, the muddy streets of Ukrainian towns often were paved with Jewish gravestones. If some of these roads are still only dirt-covered and the stones accessible, do we have a spiritual responsibility to collect them? Our ancient cemeteries are often overgrown, the few remaining gravestones crumbling and the Hebrew writing becoming illegible. The *shtetls* are gone, and at least some of the locals still hate us. Should we be attempting to reclaim cemeteries we may not be able to keep up, in places we no longer live? Even for our descendants' sake?

How far should a genealogist go?

Recently, I told the official, by telephone, that for me to seek financing, the gravestones must be used to create a historically informative monument that honors the memory of the centuries-old lost Jewish community of Rawa Ruska, in the main park, site of the old Jewish cemetery. She promised to bring it up to the city council. I am still trying to figure it all out.

Karen (Gitl Chaye Eta) Rosenfeld Roekard, MBA, combines a Yeshiva of Flatbush up-bringing with a professional specialization in strategic market analysis to nurture her genealogical passions: working to identify as-yet-unnamed Holocaust victims; recreating destroyed Eastern European shtetls; using genealogical information as a basis for healing old enmities; and rebuilding family trees when few vital records exist. This article was a 2007 First Prize award winner in the Excellence-in-Writing Competition sponsored by the International Society of Family History Writers and Editors.

Epilogue

February 2008: Within the past few months, the authorities of Rawa Ruska lifted a large number of complete, or broken-in-half, gravestones from the road in Rawa Ruska. Removal of the stones was made possible by the intercession of Father Patrick Desbois (the French Catholic priest scouring Ukraine for Jewish mass graves), in the course of his work in the town. Roekard plans to inventory the information on these stones after which they will be used to create a monument to the town's lost Jewish community, which is currently in an early stage of planning.

When Good Men Did Nothing
by Olga Zabludoff

Winter 2004

As I stumbled over rocks in the old Jewish cemetery and unraveled vines that clung to my clothes, I thought I was seeing only the remnants of a cemetery. The weeds and brush were waist-high in many sections, and there were too few headstones for a burial ground that had to be at least a few centuries old. How many people die in 200 years? I tried to calculate.

In 1992, I made my first trip to Lithuania. I had been doing family research for four years. It was time to see the *shtetlach* (villages) where my parents had been born and lived until their marriage.

First I went to my mother's *shtetl*, Butrimonys, which she had always called Baltrimantz. In addition to the old Jewish cemetery, there are two mass graves in Butrimonys. The larger one, where more than 1,200 Jews were massacred in September 1941, is located in the woods just beyond the town. The second mass grave, where 265 elders and children were murdered, is virtually inaccessible. Located on what today is farmland with no access road, one must walk a long distance through marshland—and then encounter the cows and bulls that graze on the land. On the day that I tried to reach the site, the bulls behaved fiercely, blocking my route. I turned around.

I returned to Butrimonys six years later, in 1998. The cemetery had deteriorated further. Many headstones were leaning; others were flat on the ground, some fragmented. The cemetery was enclosed by a chain-link fence. Sizable sections of the fence were now missing; the double drive-in gate was broken. Horses were roaming and defecating on the grounds. The atmosphere of abandonment recalled to me a letter written in 1927 by Rabbi Avraham Moshe Vitkind of Butrimonys to Dr. Henry Hurwitz of New York City. History was repeating itself.

Yizkor Book Project

When I returned home to Washington, DC, I spoke to Stephen Grafman, another Baltrimantz descendant, whom I knew had been dreaming of restoring the old Jewish cemetery where his ancestors were buried. Steve and I were in the process of working on the production and publication of an English-language *yizkor* book of Butrimantz (the official Yiddish name of Baltrimantz and its Lithuanian equivalent, Butrimonys).[1] Although our work had been voluntary, we de-

---

[1] *If I Forget Thee...The Destruction of the Shtetl Butrimantz: Testimony by Riva Lozansky and Other Witnesses.* Translated from the Russian by Eva Tversky; edited by Lily Poritz Miller and Olga Zabludoff. Washington, DC: Remembrance Books, 1998.

cided to try to raise funds for the printing of the book. Results exceeded our expectations; we raised considerably more than our printing costs. Subsequently, all the donors approved of our idea to establish a fund with the surplus money—a fund for the restoration of the old Jewish cemetery and the mass graves.

The *yizkor* book exceeded our expectations too. While we had initially planned a small press run to distribute free copies to universities with Holocaust education programs, libraries, Holocaust museums and institutions, and individuals with a connection to Butrimonys, we soon realized there was also a market for the book. In the next few years, we sold more than 200 copies to booksellers and individuals around the globe.

All of the sales proceeds went into the fund—and the fund kept growing. Meanwhile, Marcia Pailet Jaffe of Dayton, Ohio, another member of our small Butrimonys group, had made a trip to the *shtetl* with her husband. They photographed, videotaped and documented hundreds of tombstones, often excavating buried stones. The grass had been cut prior to their arrival, exposing dozens of stones that had not been visible before the overgrowth was cleared. In 1999, they made a second trip to Butrimonys, concluding their documentation.

The Jaffe database includes photos of 534 tombstones (with inscriptions translated into English) plus more than 150 large rocks that are markers for graves (with illegible or no visible inscriptions). The oldest tombstone documented is dated Adar 5508 (February 1748); the newest stone, December 1939.

Planning to Restore the Cemetery

For the next several years, our group tried to devise ways to trigger our restoration project into action. We connected with the leadership of the Jewish community in Vilnius (the capital of Lithuania), the Chabad Lubavich organization in Vilnius and the U.S. Commission for the Preservation of America's Heritage Abroad. Somehow, things just didn't gel. Communication was frustratingly slow; language barriers led to misinterpretations of our proposal; and cost estimates, when they finally arrived, were too high and exceeded our budget.

Our aspirations were realistic and modest. We did not want elaborate makeovers of the sacred Jewish sites. We did not want chemical cleaning of stones or costly walls built. We simply wanted to restore the cemetery and mass graves—after 60 years of neglect—to a condition reflecting the simple lifestyle of our ancestors. We wanted to preserve the only Jewish legacy of our *shtetl*. And we wanted the local Lithuanians to understand our respect for these memorials.

A dream gave birth to an idea, and an idea grew into a conviction. There was only one way to accomplish this.

I wrote to the grandson of an old Lithuanian woman I had met in Butrimonys in 1992, a woman who had known my grandmother, uncles, aunts and cousins before the war. She had directed me to their mass graves. Domicele Kurlaviciene, who was illiterate in all languages, spoke Yiddish fluently. Since the age of ten she had worked as a maid in the homes of Baltrimantz Jews.

For almost a whole day during my first visit, she had walked with me through the *shtetl*, showing me where my grandmother's house had stood, where the *shul* (synagogue) had stood, where the rabbi had lived. We conversed in Yiddish, although she kept apologizing that she hadn't spoken the language for more than 50 years. She sang Yiddish songs with such soul that I started to contemplate whether she might have been a Yiddishe mama in another life—or even in this life, unknowingly. She invited me to come back and said she would make *kreplach* (dumplings) and *gefilte* fish (poached fish patties) and *imberlach* (honey nut candy) and *taiglach* (fried dough dredged in honey). By the end of my second day with her, she had become the *bobba*

Domicele

(grandmother) I had lost. I had asked her how she had felt when all the Jews were killed.

"Like I lost my own people," she answered. Then she told how she had watched from her window as the Jews were led to their death. "They passed my house like sheep going to their slaughter. Their heads were lowered. Their hands were tied behind their backs with wire." Domicele was 24 years old when it happened.

Now, 11 years after I had met Domicele, I was writing to her grandson, Audrius. A teacher who lives in Klaipeda, Audrius knows English well. I told him what our group wanted to accomplish in Butrimonys, asked whether we should consult the mayor of the town and invited any suggestions he had. I was fairly sure that the cemetery and mass graves now were the property of the municipality. Thus, I wanted to secure as much cooperation as possible from the locals. Audrius responded with warmth:

> *Your letter has been a pleasant surprise to me. Though we have never met, I somehow feel close to you. Also, I admire your ambition to value and cherish the past, knowing how difficult it can be to change something from so far.*
>
> *Domicele was very happy to hear from you again. Your letter brought her many happy moments to remember. She lives with her son Vaclovas now as she is in poor health—[but] she is still bright though she is 86 now.*
>
> *If you are thinking about fixing up the cemetery, you should contact the elder first [elder=mayor]. I think you can write a letter, send it to me for translation [into Lithuanian], and then I will send it to Butrimonys. Domicele's son Vaclovas has*

promised to take it to the elder and to talk to him.

I think for better and quicker correspondence, you can write to me at my e-mail address. I am looking forward to your letter and am ready to help with everything.

I wrote to the elder on March 1, 2003, e-mailing the letter to Audrius:

I would like to consult you regarding my desire to restore the Jewish cemetery and the mass graves in Butrimonys. As I am sure you realize, these are the only Jewish sites left in the town. In order to preserve these sites and to honor the memory of all those who had once lived in Butrimonys, I feel it is necessary to do some work. The fence around the cemetery is in poor condition. The gate is broken. Many of the headstones have fallen over or have sunk into the ground. At the mass graves, the railings/fence need repair and painting and the stone monument has some badly chipped areas.

We need your support and the cooperation of the local population of Butrimonys to achieve real success. I would like to add that if we are successful, this would be the first or one of the first such projects in Lithuania.

Less than two weeks later, I received an e-mail from Audrius. The elder, Mr. Jusas, was supportive of our project. He was not sure that all of the skilled labor we might need would be available in Butrimonys, but it would be better to discuss such details in person. He was looking forward to meeting with us.

Trip to Butrimonys

I wanted to be in place by May 1 and allow three weeks to accomplish the project. My husband, Sid, had decided to come along, as well as another member of

Audrius

the Butrimonys group, Lisabeth Kaplan of Carmel Valley, California. Lisabeth wondered if I could arrange for her to stay with a family in Butrimonys since she did not want to commute daily from Vilnius, and she was willing to "rough it." (Butrimonys is about 90 minutes from Vilnius by car. Most of the homes do not have plumbing. Some of the newer homes have hot water and a small tub in the kitchen for bathing. There are no toilets—only outhouses.)

Again, Audrius came to the rescue. His uncle and aunt, Henrikas and Ceslova, would accommodate Lisabeth, though they were desperately worried about the "limited luxuries" in their home. (Henrikas is the eldest of Domicele's three sons.)

On April 28, we flew to Vilnius. I was full of apprehension. The responsibility I had taken on seemed overwhelming. During the planning stage of the project, when it wasn't yet a reality, nothing had seemed unattainable. Now that the day had dawned, my head pounded with anxiety.

May 1, we drove to Butrimonys. Sid and I had decided to go directly to the cemetery and mass graves to survey their condition and to compile a list of the work that was necessary. After that we would go to the little market in the center of town and pick up bread, cheese, drinks and pastry. And then to Domicele's house. The first thing she would say would be, "*Ier moost zayn hoongerick!*" (You must be hungry!)

I had prearranged the visit to Domicele via e-mail to Audrius. But how would he communicate with Domicele, I wondered, since Klaipeda (where Audrius lives) is 165 miles from Butrimonys. I knew there was no telephone in Domicele's house. Wired phones are virtually nonexistent in Butrimonys. I was to learn later, however, that Domicele's son has a cell phone! Primitive and poverty-stricken as is Butrimonys, many people there now own cell phones.

We were pleasantly surprised—if not astonished—when we arrived at the cemetery. Most of the leaning tombstones were now erect. The missing sections of fence had been replaced with factory pre-painted green chain-link fencing, including a double drive-in gate. The new fencing, of course, made the original fence appear rusty and dull. We decided that if we could find green metal paint that matched the color of the new fencing, we would paint the entire fence. The cemetery also needed a good clean-up after the severe winter. Large branches had fallen everywhere, and the grounds were full of debris and litter.

Vaclovas

Our list of work for the mass graves was much longer, but these sites are so small compared to the size of the cemetery that we felt undaunted and greatly relieved to find that our job would be quite manageable after all.

Before we could even knock, Domicele's door flew open, and her son Vaclovas was announcing in a loud voice, "Vel-kom, Vel- kom!" Then Domicele appeared at the door with a slightly dazed look, almost as though she didn't know whether to laugh or cry. She did both as we hugged. She looked weaker and moved more slowly than the strong, sturdy peasant of 11 years ago.

"You look the same," I half lied.

She stepped slightly back to get a better angle, looked at me intently, and said, "And you have gotten so much older." She shook her head sadly, as though commiserating over the difficult years she believed I must have had. "*Ier moost zayn hoongerick!*" she said with urgency as she led the way into the main room. The Yiddishe mama was back.

Ceslova and Henrikas

Reprimanding us for bringing food, she coaxed us to eat what was already on her table—fish, goat cheese, hard-boiled eggs and bread. Domicele and I conversed in Yiddish. She spoke rapidly, as though afraid she would run out of time. Sid and Vaclovas struggled in conversation with the help of a Lithuanian-English dictionary. It wasn't long before she started to sing her Yiddish songs. This was very intimate for her. As she had done 11 years ago, she pulled her chair directly opposite mine, our knees touching, her eyes gripping mine like magnets as she sang. When she finished a song, she would say with a wistful smile mingled with self-satisfaction: "Nu?" as if she had succeeded in bringing back the past.

Henrikas and his wife, Ceslova, came by. I had never met Domicele's sons before. Now, looking at both Vaclovas and Henrikas, I was astonished at their dignified faces and bearing. Their mother was a poor, illiterate peasant who had worked with her hands all her life, yet her sons looked like gentility. Audrius's father, Domicele's third son, had even earned a university degree. I wondered about their father, but neither Domicele nor her sons ever seemed to want to speak about him. All efforts on my part were terminated with, "He died 20 years ago."

Ceslova chose to hang out with the men after she heard Domicele and me speaking a strange language. But Henrikas sat down near us, listening with fixed concentration to every word we uttered. In the following weeks I was to discover his fascination with Yiddish.

"*Es, es!*" (Eat, eat!) he would joke whenever we sat down to a meal.

"*Geray, geray!*" (Okay, okay!) I would answer with the only Lithuanian I had learned.

Henrikas knew many Yiddish words, and I suspected he also understood the language. I once asked him how he knew so many words, and he told me that sometimes his mother would speak to him and his brothers in Yiddish when they were children, and she often sang Yiddish lullabies to them at bedtime. If there were ever a Gentile who grieved over the loss of Jewish traditions in her life, it was Domicele.

It was getting late, time for us to drive back to Vilnius, but Ceslova pleaded that we come to her house to see if it was adequate for Lisabeth who was to arrive in a few days. She led us through the little cottage, anxiously watching our reactions. It was an immaculate, orderly little house, with white lace curtains on the windows. I gestured my approval and compliments, and in an unexpected, unrestrained moment, Ceslova embraced me and discharged a huge sigh of relief.

Ceslova slept well that night. So did I.

Meeting the Mayor

Arnas is a 15-year-old high school basketball star. He is Ceslova's grandson. She had imported him from Pren (Prienai) the night before to serve as interpreter for our meeting with the elder. Arnas stands at 6 ft. 5 in. and has a shy, angelic face, large blue eyes, blonde hair and pink cheeks. His English is excellent. While most Lithuanian high school students know some English, few are as fluent as Arnas. He understood everything we said, no matter how complicated, and translated between English and Lithuanian with great poise.

"What about school today?" I had chided him gently as we walked to the elder's office in Vytaugo Square.

He smiled impishly, "It is okay. I'll go tomorrow."

Six of us filed into the elder's office at the appointed time. Shaking hands, I said to Mr. Jusas, the elder of Butrimonys, "B-I-G delegation." He broke into laughter, obviously understanding these words. I introduced Sid, Lisabeth and Arnas. The elder already was acquainted with Henrikas and Ceslova. Elder Algirdas Jusas is a soft-spoken, gracious man about 45 years old. He looks at people very intently when they speak. He sat at the head of a long table; I sat to his right, and Arnas sat across from me, waiting for a sign to start the meeting. I nodded to Arnas and said, "Please tell Mr. Jusas that we wish to thank him very much for all the work that has already been done at the cemetery." After Arnas delivered the message in Lithuanian, the elder waved off our thanks, signaling that it wasn't necessary to thank him.

I then told him we wanted to paint the fence green to match the new sections. He responded that he liked this plan very much and was sure the proper kind of paint was available. He offered us technical advice. When I told him we intended to do a major clean-up of the grounds, he said he would dispatch a truck and a crew to haul away the mountains of debris. This was a big relief to us because even Henrikas had worried over how we would dispose of the huge branches and other debris that littered the cemetery. When I discussed the condition of the mass graves and what we proposed to do, Mr. Jusas said that he already had lined up cement workers to redo the crumbling monuments. They were to start their work in two days. We were overwhelmed. This was another major item we were worrying about because Henrikas did not know of any skilled cement workers in Butrimonys.

Census of the Jews of Butrimonys

As we were winding down our business, Mr. Jusas addressed Arnas, who in turn asked me, "What was the family name of your relatives in Butrimonys?"

"Shapiro," I answered, taken aback by this unexpected question.

The elder began leafing through a stack of pages on the table, resting his finger when he found the right spot. "Shapiro, Etel, 68; Shloma, 39. . ." He was reading the names and ages of my grandmother, uncle, aunt and two girl cousins, all of whom were now in the mass graves I had come to restore.

Arnas explained that Mr. Jusas was reading from a 1937 list of Jewish residents of Butrimonys. This census had been made by the parish priest four years before the inhabitants of the *shtetl* had been annihilated. The original document had remained in the church archives for 66 years. In May 2002, it was "resurrected" by the current priest, Stasys Ciupala.

"Would you like to have a copy of this list?" the elder said. I asked if I could take the original to the larger town of Alytus and have it duplicated there. I truly was afraid of the results of a Butrimonys copy machine, if one even existed. (I visualized a purple mimeographed copy, 1940s vintage.) I knew from experience that old handwritten documents needed the best technology that money could buy if we were to end up with a decent copy. Mr. Jusas explained that the original could not be removed from the church archives, and his copy was not suitable for duplication because it was "messed up" and out of sequence. He would ask the priest to have the church secretary make a copy for me. I think he recognized my anxiety because he exchanged a compassionate, reassuring look. Perhaps he understood that, for me, seeing the names of my family in their own *shtetl*—the grandmother, the cousins I had known only through photos—evoked feelings that could not be translated into words.

In a few days, the copy of the list was delivered, bound in a protective plastic covering and quite legible. It wasn't until a few months later, after I had translit-erated the 848 names, 215 families, that I made a stunning discovery: Rabbi Avraham Moshe Vitkind and Dr. Abel Gabay, two of the most distinguished Jews in the community, were not included on the list; neither were their families. Why not?

Could it be that Juozapas Andrikonis, the priest who had made the census in 1937, had a feeling or a vision of what was to come? And by eliminating the names of his colleague, the rabbi, and his friend, the doctor, could he have been trying to save these families from the Nazis?

Andrikonis was described by survivors of Butrimantz as "an honest man and a true believer in God, who liked people of all kinds." Standing at the mass graves after the war, he had said, "When I look at all this destruction, I feel ashamed that I am a Lithuanian."

Getting Supplies

We were all jovial when we left the elder's office. The meeting had been short, but we had learned a lot, gained a lot and now felt ready to proceed. The elder had been cordial and supportive. We were on a high. There were still several hours left to the afternoon, so we decided to drive to Alytus and to buy all our supplies. Alytus is a fairly large town about 30 minutes' drive from Butrimonys. As we drove, I made a list.

Henrikas directed us to the Lithuanian counterpart of Home Depot. While the store did not offer quite the same selection, we purchased everything we needed, down to details such as work gloves, masks and mineral spirits. Our assembly-line communication system worked well. I would show Arnas a word on my list; he would tell Henrikas the Lithuanian equivalent, and Henrikas would negotiate the purchase with the sales clerk. I had planned to buy supplies for seven workers since we would be hiring a crew, but Henrikas was shocked by my spending spree and tried to curtail my numbers. Compared to U.S. prices for the same merchan-dise, everything was so inexpensive, and though we knew we would be returning for more supplies at some point, we didn't want to run out too quickly. Our next worry was whether everything could fit into the trunk of our small car.

On the drive back to Butrimonys, I told Henrikas that we would need four workers in addition to Sid, Lisabeth and myself. As Arnas was relaying this in-formation, I saw Ceslova perk up and speak to Henrikas.

"Ceslova wants to work," Arnas announced. I was very pleased because I had already witnessed what a quick, efficient and organized worker she was, one mo-ment preparing a beautiful meal, the next, tilling the soil in her vegetable garden, and doing everything well. She was definitely a perfectionist.

Dainos undercoats fence to Jewish cemetery.

I asked Henrikas if he wanted to be the manager because I didn't have the *chutzpah* (nerve) to suggest he be a common laborer. He could pass for a banker. He blushed a bit and squirmed uncomfortably, and Arnas advised me that Henrikas would rather work than supervise. Ceslova and Henrikas then spoke between

Vilia

themselves, and I learned through Arnas that they had two other workers in mind. Vilia, a woman who worked part-time as a secretary at the Butrimonys secondary school, and her 18-year-old son Dainos, a student in a technical school, joined our team eagerly. Vilia kept up with her job at the school, working with us before and after her regular job and on weekends, often until the last rays of light faded. Dainos traded in school for work because he needed the money. All our crew skipped church for the next two Sundays.

Butrimonys is a poverty-stricken town, not unlike most of the small towns and villages in Lithuania. A chicken-production factory had employed almost the entire working population, but it was so inefficient and poorly run that it had gone bankrupt five years earlier. Since then, most of the town has remained unemployed. The people receive very small pensions from the government. They grow their own vegetables and get eggs from their chickens. Some have goats and cows for milk and cheese, and they trade with one another. When students graduate from high school, they look for jobs in the larger cities.

Working at Restoring the Cemetery

For the next two weeks, we arose each morning at 6 a.m. By 7 o'clock we were driving out of Vilnius, entangled in the morning rush-hour traffic. But once we were out of the city, the drive to Butrimonys was idyllic: lush green pastures, rolling hills, dense forests, little towns and villages inhabited by people who looked much like their predecessors of a hundred years ago.

We would drive through Trakai, a medieval town situated on a large lake surrounded by forests. Its fortresses had Gothic towers rising out of the mist. We would always stop in Aukstadvaris, 13 miles outside of Butrimonys, to buy gas in the town's modern gas station. The attendant was consistently dressed in a suit and tie, polite and formal, but he never made eye contact with us. People in the small towns of Lithuania tend to be very reserved with strangers.

As we drove, we watched the sky for signs of the weather. One moment the sun would shine, and we would celebrate that the day was going to be good for outdoor work. But the next moment the skies would darken with the threat of rain. They said it was the rainiest May they could remember—and the rain was our only adversary over the next 14 days.

I would plan the work for the day and pray that the rain would not sabotage the project. I would always calculate how many days were left and whether our overall goal could be achieved in that time period.

We spent the first few days cleaning the cemetery grounds and excavating stones that had sunk into the soggy earth or were obscured by layers of dried leaves and dirt. As the elder had promised, a truck and crew arrived to haul away the huge piles of debris.

Seven of us worked for about two days scraping the chain-link fence with metal brushes to remove the rust and dirt. The circumference of the fence is equal to the length of five football fields—about 1,500 meters. (The cemetery is about four acres.) After the fence was smooth and rust-free, we applied a coat of rust repellent. On the day we had planned to start the first coat of green paint on the fence, it rained. Even though it cleared up in the afternoon, both the fence and the cemetery grounds were just too wet. So we went to work on the bridge at the first mass grave, the larger of the two graves.

Restoring the Mass Graves

This bridge has always been for me the most haunting symbol of the Holocaust in Baltrimantz. It marks the end of the life of the *shtetl*—a one-way bridge for the Jews. A concrete walkway with metal railings, the bridge crosses a

Bridge over which the Jews of Butrimonys were marched to their deaths.

narrow ravine with a stream running through it. The mass grave is about 30 feet from the ravine.

The metal railings on the bridge, which had been painted previously, were now down to the bare metal and coated with rust. We treated the railings as we had treated the cemetery fence, first scraping them with metal brushes and then undercoating them with rust repellent. Finally we applied two coats of brown metal paint. We carried out this work over a three-day period in order to allow drying time between applications. Sometimes we would work at one site in the morning and another in the afternoon since the work frequently needed to be done in stages.

As we approached the bridge one afternoon, we were taken aback to see a wheelbarrow and tools at the end of the bridge. Then came the sound of rhythmic metal tapping. In that solitary place, it is unusual to hear any sound other than the faint, plaintive call of a cuckoo. We crossed the bridge and walked to the mass grave, which is shrouded by a circle of pine trees.

Two men, one old, the other young, were standing on the elevated section of the stone monument, methodically chipping away at the cracked concrete. Strongly silhouetted by the sun behind them, they looked like a part of the monument—a sculpture in black. To me the image of Lithuanians rebuilding a memorial to the people destroyed by Nazi-inspired Lithuanians was so poignant that I videotaped the scene for a long time. Neither of the men acknowledged me nor took his eyes off the work. They stripped the monument to its brick foundation and re-cemented the entire surface. The elder had kept his word.

The days passed quickly, and our work stopped only for rain, quick lunches and nightfall. The women worked harder than the men, with the exception of Dainos. Sid and I usually got back to Vilnius after 8 p.m., but we had the reward of a hot shower. The rest of our team envied us.

One Saturday around noon, as we were breaking for lunch, I saw a shadowy figure moving among the headstones in the cemetery.

"Who's that?" I asked.

The figure was a tall, slender man wearing a trench coat and a black beret. Ceslova followed my eyes, clasped her hands in a prayer-like gesture and looked to the heavens. It was the priest, Stasys Ciupala, paying us a visit.

"And why are you working on the Sabbath?" he asked. It was more a jest than an accusation.

"Because we are doing holy work," I answered.

"Aha," he said, satisfied with the answer.

When we worked at the cemetery, the atmosphere was jovial. The Lithuanians among us joked and laughed. And even we, the three Jews, seemed to forget where we were. But a heavy gloom settled over everyone when we worked at the mass graves. Nobody spoke except when necessary—and then in whispers. Only the distant call of a cuckoo or the mooing of a nearby cow broke the silence. The second mass grave, where the elderly and the children were murdered, had been a sand pit in 1941. When sand was needed for construction or road work, it was dug out of that pit. They did not even have to dig a hole for the grave; it was already there.

After the war, when the few survivors of Baltrimantz went to the site, they were advised by the priest, Andrikonis, to rebury the bodies in another area because the grave would sink further into the ground as sand continued to be dug from the pit. When the survivors attempted to move the bodies, they began to disintegrate. Thus, they left them there.

Today grass grows over the grave and the area is farmland. Despite this, you feel like you are in a pit when you're standing there. You cannot see the monument and the fence surrounding the site until you are right there because they are well below ground level. It is a steep descent.

I told Henrikas that my grandmother and two little girl cousins are there. He stood and stared at the ground for a long time. When they died in 1941, my cousins were eight and ten years old—the same ages my grandchildren are today. I knew them only from one photograph taken in 1940: two little girls, Rochele and Bertale, in matching dresses and white knee socks.

I am sure Dainos had never been to this mass grave, or knew it existed. This piece of the history of his hometown had been omitted from his education. He looked around perplexed, uncomfortable. Then he and Henrikas walked over to

A small fence surrounds the mass grave where 965 Jews were shot and buried.

the monument and read the inscription, which is in both Yiddish and Lithuanian: "265 Jewish elders and children, murdered on this spot by the Nazis and their helpers on September 9, 1941."

After a few hours of work, Dainos returned to the monument to read the inscription again. He stood there for a long while lost in thought. The rest of the day he seemed unusually sober and withdrawn. Perhaps he was feeling the burden of guilt.

"You're working with the children and grandchildren of the murderers," a survivor in Vilnius had said to me.

I defended myself with the standard remark: "But you can't hold them responsible for what their parents and grandparents may have done."

It is hard to argue with either of these statements. Both are true. Yet truth alone does not always appease the soul or resolve the conflict in the mind.

Plans for Exhibit in Vilnius

I didn't keep a diary. The days were too long and exhausting. By the time we got back to Vilnius, showered and ate, no time was left for anything other than sleep. Thus, I cannot recreate each day. During the two weeks of work, there was one day we did not go to Butrimonys. The skies in Vilnius were dark gray. The rain poured down mercilessly, and the forecast was that this would last all day. I

A smaller mass grave contains the burial site of 265 Jewish elders and children.

called Henrikas in Butrimonys to learn that the weather scenario was the same there. We canceled our work plan for the day.

Since I had been working with Rachel Kostanian, director of the Vilna Gaon Jewish State Museum, on her planned exhibition on the *shtetl* Butrimantz, it was a good day to meet with her about the project. I had told Rachel about Domicele and how forthcoming she was with her memories of the Holocaust in Butrimantz. Rachel wanted to mount a multi-media exhibit and thought a videotaped interview with Domicele would make a compelling presentation. She asked if I would be willing to interview Domicele. (I had been videotaping our project as it moved along.)

I told Rachel the only language in which I could interview Domicele was Yiddish. She said the interview had to be in Lithuanian since the majority of the people who would be coming to the exhibit would be Lithuanians. We decided that if Domicele agreed to be interviewed, Rachel would send one of her museum staff members to do the interview, and I would do the filming.

Ruta Puisyte was selected as the interviewer. She would drive with us to Butrimonys on the appointed day. Ruta is a young, highly educated Lithuanian woman who had discovered the Holocaust accidentally when she was already in high school. She asked her father some questions, and "he gave me the right answers," she says. She has been a scholar of the Holocaust ever since.

The following day in Butrimonys I spoke to Domicele during our lunch break. She said, "I will tell them everything I know; everything as I remember it. I've always told only the truth."

We were nearing the end of our work. The cemetery was clean. Only the last coat of green paint had yet to be applied to the fence. The bridge to the first mass grave looked new. Both the metal railings and the white concrete posts encircling the monument had been repainted. The monument had been completely resurfaced, and we had cleaned and polished the metal plaque with the inscription until it transformed from black to bronze. The second mass grave, so remote and solitary, looked like a sinister secret as one suddenly came upon it, a hidden pit among rolling green pastures. Its freshly painted railings and posts were almost a mockery. I think we do these restoration projects to make ourselves feel better. One could argue that they are out of character.

We ran out of green paint. The store in Alytus had to back-order since we had depleted its stock. We calculated that about one-eighth of the fence remained without a second coat. The paint would not be available until our last day in Butrimonys, but we would get it and leave the completion of the job to our crew.

Interviewing a Witness to the Butrimonys Holocaust

We are sitting in Domicele's small bedroom. Only a curtain separates the room from the main room of the house. Vaclovas has brought in two chairs for the interviewer and me. Domicele is sitting on her bed. She prefers the interview to be held in her room—not in the main room. Her hair is pulled back neatly in a bun, and she is wearing the same green sweater she always wears. Vaclovas and Sid are on the other side of the curtain in the main room.

Ruta asks the first question. Domicele answers in a considered way. She speaks slowly, using her hands expressively, never taking her eyes off Ruta. She seems totally unaware of the camcorder pointed at her. In the small dark room, the window behind Domicele backlights her, but the lace curtain helps to filter the sunlight. Still, Domicele is in silhouette.

Ruta told me she has conducted many interviews before, and even though I don't understand the language, I sense that she knows how to relax her subject and how to lead

Ruta

into the substance of the interview. Now they must be getting to the painful part, because Domicele's emotions are taking hold. Her voice is tremulous, her speech no longer calibrated. In profile, her eyes are luminous, almost feverish. Her face, wrinkled like a seaman's and carved in years of living, is like a map of suffering. She is animated, talking as if in a trance, emphasizing certain words, repeating phrases—louder the second time. Like a pressure cooker releasing a gush of steam, the words can't stop. Ruta knows not to interrupt.

"No, Mama, no! No, Mama, no!" Vaclovas has burst through the curtain, shouting with his broadcaster's voice. He lashes out in Lithuanian at his mother.

Ruta reproaches him in Lithuanian, and I ask in English, "What is the problem?"

"He is the problem!" shouts Ruta, pointing an accusing finger at Vaclovas.

Evidently Domicele is telling it like it was, divulging damning information. Vaclovas is fearful that his mother is talking too much; perhaps he is terrified of reprisals against them. Or perhaps, because he is a sensitive man, a dreamer, he cannot bear to hear the truth about what the people in his town did to the Jews. As Vaclovas continues to rant, Domicele looks passively at her son as though they live on different planets. And she goes on. . .

After I had converted the videotape to PAL (the system used in Lithuania) and sent Rachel Kostanian her copy, she wrote, "It is the most incredible film. I have never seen anything like it." Rachel is a survivor. Of a family of about 100 before the Holocaust, she is one of only four who survived.

Final Days in Lithuania

Lisabeth had spent some time preparing a closing ceremony for the end of our mission. We would go first to the cemetery and then to each of the mass graves. The ceremony was held a few hours after Domicele's interview. In a perfect world—or in a movie—the scenario would have gone like this:

The priest and the elder lead the procession into the old Jewish cemetery, followed by Domicele and her family. Then come the townspeople. And then the teachers followed by all the schoolchildren carrying flowers. There are some speeches, a sign of remorse, a pledge of unity. And then the children sing songs, maybe even HaTikvah (national anthem of Israel) to show the Jews who have come back to their shtetl that shadows are still alive of their past.

But it is not a perfect world. Even though all had been invited, nobody came. Actually I shouldn't say "nobody." Henrikas and Ceslova came dressed in their church clothes. They stood at the Jewish sites with solemn faces and bowed heads, like mourners at a funeral.

The ceremony opened with my address to Henrikas and Ceslova. I spoke in English and, without any prompting, Ruta simultaneously started translating for them into Lithuanian. They appeared deeply moved by my words of gratitude. Then Lisabeth chanted selected prayers, after which we recited the 23rd Psalm and said *Kaddish*, the memorial prayer for the dead. At the first mass grave, we again recited prayers, ending with *Kaddish*.

Restored Jewish cemetery of Butrimonys.

I had not expected that our guests would go with us to the second mass grave, but there was no question in their minds. We first drove back to their house where Ceslova found high boots for us and for Ruta to navigate through the marshes on the way to the grave. Afterwards, as we were walking away, I turned around to take one last look. Henrikas had remained behind, standing by himself and staring at the ground.

Our Last Day

It is our last day. We drove from Vilnius directly to the building supplies store in Alytus to pick up the green paint for the crew to finish the job and to have enough left over for touch-ups. Then we drove to Henrikas and Ceslova's house. I had prepared envelopes for each of our four workers with their pay. (They had told me they preferred to be paid at the end of the job, not in installments.) Shortly after we had hired them, I had asked Audrius to determine a fair hourly wage. He consulted with Henrikas and then told me that they would be very pleased if we could afford to pay them three or four litas per hour. (The exchange rate at the time was three litas to the dollar.) I told them we would of course pay four litas.

They had all submitted their "time sheets" the day before. They obviously had minimized their working hours, because I had kept a rough record of my own. I realized they were charging only for the number of hours they had actually worked—not for the time it took to get to the sites, nor the preparation time and the clean-up. With bonuses and additional hours to compensate them more fairly, each envelope contained almost double the sum they had expected.

Ceslova accompanied me to the elder's office. I had written a letter to him that Ruta had translated into Lithuanian and rewritten in her beautiful script. I included a contribution for the town.

Mr. Jusas greeted me warmly, but when I was about to hand him the envelope, he recoiled and exclaimed, "No! No!" I protested that this was a contribution for Butrimonys, not for him personally. But the elder was adamant in refusing to accept the gift, waving his hands to indicate that it was totally out of the question. When I saw his decisiveness, I removed the money and left the letter on the table.

I have often wondered why he refused to accept a $100 (300 litas) contribution. The town is poverty-stricken; the people are equally poor and unemployed. Surely they could have benefited in some way from this modest donation. But it was a matter of principle with Mr. Jusas. Perhaps he believed that we didn't owe anything to the town of Butrimonys. From the first time I had met him, he had struck me as a man of conscience.

The priest was not at home when we knocked on his door. Nor was he at his office. Thus, he could not accept or reject my contribution to the church. Ceslova would deliver my letter and donation later.

We headed to the school. Simply constructed, but light and modern, the building was full of students on their lunch break. They looked and dressed like American kids. In Lithuania there is a sharp divide between the generations. The younger generation looks like a Western society; the older people, especially in small towns and villages, look and dress almost exactly as they did a century ago. But there are exceptions. In upscale areas of Vilnius, you can see chic men and women who could blend in quite well on Fifth Avenue.

Ceslova asked for the English teacher so that I could communicate with her. Mrs. Sigita Miklusiene was a charming, friendly woman who told me that her father had known my grandmother and other members of my Shapiro family. That is always bait for me, especially if it isn't intended to be ingratiating. Because I had never known my own grandmother, others who had—and who can tell me ordinary things about her—hold a special power over me.

I brought along a book for the school library: the English-language *yizkor* book, *If I Forget Thee: the Destruction of the Shtetl Butrimantz*. Sigita started looking at the book with great interest, at times stopping to read sections. By then a group of other teachers had surrounded us. The book was passed around among them, and they studied it wide eyed and solemnly, particularly the photographs since most of the teachers obviously could not read English. They talked among themselves in Lithuanian.

Sigita relayed to me that the teachers were interested in teaching about the Holocaust. She asked if I could provide the school with a few more copies of the book, which would be used as a text in the fall. I asked how many books they would like.

"Can you spare ten books?" she wanted to know.

"One for each student in the class?" I asked.

"No," she answered, "one for each table in the classroom."

Sigita knew that the previous day we had conducted a closing ceremony at the cemetery and mass graves. She asked if I had videotaped the event. I told her I had done so.

"Could you possibly send us a copy of the tape to use in the classroom?"

I told her about the interview with Domicele that I had videotaped and promised to send her both tapes in PAL version. She intermittently communicated with the other teachers, acting as an interpreter between them and me. The group seemed excited about the curriculum materials, which would form the basis of their Holocaust studies program. Happily, I subsequently sent them 20 copies of the book as well as copies of the videotapes.

It didn't sink in until later that this was probably the most meaningful achievement of our mission. The grandchildren of the murderers will now learn what happened in their town 62 years ago—a story that has been omitted from Lithuanian history classes. The script will be enacted by one of their own, Domicele Kurlaviciene, and confirmed by the testimonies of a few Jewish survivors who wrote their story, *If I Forget Thee.*

Ruta Puisyte had told me that before she discovered the Holocaust, she had thought the Jews were a people who lived in Israel. She had never known that Jews were also Lithuanians who had lived on the same streets as her grandparents.

I didn't think it would be that difficult to say good-bye to Ceslova and Henrikas because our relationship had been fairly formal—mainly because of the language barrier. But Ceslova's eyes already were red rimmed, and she kept wiping the tears away. She was half laughing, half crying and talking to Sid and me in Lithuanian between embraces. I had given her a necklace that morning that I had bought in Hong Kong—made of large beads with a Chinese motif. She was overwhelmed and ran into her bedroom to find a necklace to give to me. It was made of amber stones mined in Lithuania.

When Henrikas hugged me for a long time, I felt his body shaking—the eruption of sobs that he couldn't contain. He backed away and turned around, trying to gain control of his weeping. I still can't articulate why this normally reserved man broke down. Perhaps it had something to do with the bond he knew I shared with his mother, or perhaps it was the bond that develops when people work together day after day. Or perhaps he was crying over a past when good men did nothing.

Domicele was looking for us through her window. As we walked into her house she said to me, "You're flying away tomorrow." Her head fell to her chest as though her neck had snapped, and there followed one sob, but she quickly came back with a smile. "I think we'll still see each other again."

It was both a question and a statement. For once she didn't run to the stove, didn't offer food. We were standing by her door looking through the glass pane. The rain was now heavy. It had drizzled and rained most of the day. She points across the street and says, "The *mikvah* (ritual bath) is still there." I look at her and watch her eyes journey back 60 years.

"Do they ever mention his name in America?" she asks. I know she is referring to Hitler. "Yes," I answer.

"Here they never say his name."

After a long silence she looks at me and asks, "How could it have happened?"

Olga Zabludoff worked as an editor for the Macmillan Company in New York City. In Washington, DC, she served as editor-in-chief and staff writer for magazines in the public television and public radio field. In 1998, she founded the Washington-based publishing company Remembrance Books. She has been a member of the LitvakSIG Board of Directors for two years.

Epilogue

Shortly before this book went to press, I received an e-mail from Lithuania saying that Domicele died on February 19, 2008, at the age of 91. Without Domicele there wouldn't have been a story.